= INDEX =

＝目次＝

Beneath
Umbrella
of
Zubaraie LLC.

英語デキン日本人の感じ方

でんぐリングリッシュ

英語出来る人々の考え方

by 之人冗悟

Noto Jaugo

http://zubaraie.com

http://zubaraie.com/denglenglish ←Be sure to check!

— How this book is composed –

This is a book on (and in) English for starters and restarters (especially the latter) to enable them to have a clear-cut image of what they are studying, a reliable set of methodology to guide them to English mastery, and a mental attitude common to all those who succeed in linguistic studies... in conscious contrast to the time-honored (and corpse-ridden) way the Japanese generally fail in mastering English, with the original English sentences on the left and Japanese translation on the right. Hence the title of "ReversENGLISH (でんぐリングリッシュ:DENGLENGLISH)", meaning "ENGLISH UPSIDE DOWN" or "A Copernican revolution in your English studying attitude".

This book is full of quite bookish knowledge about English, or rather, about studying English. It is no workbook full of practice to introduce and inure you to actual English usage, nor is it a kind of "placebo" giving you a sweet (but vain) hope of English mastery through incredibly small numbers of magical formulas

This book alone does not enable you to command English; it enables you to correctly study (and consequently master eventually) English. It shows you a summary of what all Japanese junior high school graduates should have known (at least, should have been taught) but it does not expound such knowledge in detail. It only shows you what to make of those separate pieces of knowledge you have been (or are being) taught at school. It shows you "a big picture" of the world of English, instead of telling you what pigments to use to draw some particular corners of the world.

This book is composed of eighteen(18) sections. The first one is purely introductory, a sort of preface to the book. The following ten(10) sections (2 — 11) will give you a general view of what and how you study at the onset of your English studying career. A complete beginner in English (the 1st grader in a junior high school in Japan) may still find them intangible, while others (especially restarters) will find them confidently familiar, being assured they have not missed much in their past attempts at English mastery... if they have, they have only to read through these 10 sections and try reviewing their old English textbooks to get comfortably reassured.

―本書の構成―

この本は、英語を初めて／改めて学ぼうとする人々(特に後者＝再挑戦組)のために(英語で)書かれた英語に関する本である。自分がいま何を学習しているのかの明確なイメージと、英語修得に至る確実な方法論と、語学で成果を上げる人々に共通する心的態度とを、「大方の日本人が英語の習得に失敗する際の伝統的＆死屍累々(ししるいるい)のやり口」と意識的に対照する形で、英語原文(左頁)／日本語訳(右頁)対訳形式で書いてある・・・という次第で、標題の『ReversENGLISH:でんぐリングリッシュ』の意味するところは「引っ繰り返しの英語」というか「諸君の英語学習態度のコペルニクス的転回」といったところである。

本書は、「英語」というか「英語の学び方」に関するかなり堅苦しい知識満載の本である。英語の実際の用法を紹介して諸君の習熟を促すための練習問題満載の学習帳ではないし、信じられないほどわずかな数の魔法の公式を通して英語をモノにする(虚しい)夢を諸君に与える「見せかけの妙薬」でもない。

この本一冊だけで英語が使いこなせるようになるわけではない;本書は、英語を正しく学ぶことを(その結果として最終的には英語をマスターすることを)可能にするための本である。日本の中学校を卒業した人ならば誰もがみな知っているはずの(少なくとも「教わった」はずの)知識の「総まとめ」は提示してあるが、それらの知識に関する詳細な説明はない。諸君が学校で教わった(あるいは習っている最中の)てんでんバラバラな知識を総括的に解釈するとどうなるか、を示してあるだけである。本書は英語世界の「おおまかな全体像」を諸君に見せる本であって、その世界の特定の一角をどの色の絵の具で塗ったらよいかの個別的指示を与えるための本ではない。

本書は全部で18項より成る。最初の項は純然たるごあいさつ、本書の「序文」みたいなものである。続く10項(第2項から第11項)は、英語学習道中に踏み出したばかりの諸君が「何を」・「どのようにして」学ぶかに関する考え方を概括的にまとめてある。英語学習の全くの初心者(日本の学校で言えば中学一年生)の場合はこれらの項を読んでもまだ何となくつかみ所がない感じかもしれないが、それ以外の読者(とりわけ英語学習の再挑戦者)ならば、馴染みの内容として自信を持って読めるだろうし、英語習得のための過去の自分の努力にさほど大きな穴はなかった、と安堵の胸をなで下ろすことができるだろう・・・できなかった諸君も、これら10項を通して読んだ後で昔の英語の教科書を復習してみれば、かなりの自信がつかめるはずだ。

The next four(4) sections (12 — 15) will lecture you not so much on particular facts and knowledge of English as on desirable attitudes to enable you to master this language. Though rather abstract and partly difficult for beginners, all Japanese students of English would be well-advised to read these instructions first. Most readers may find themselves shockingly averse to most of what the author says in these sections; then, that is where the difference lies between you and me, who have written this book in English language and offered Japanese translation for you to follow me.

The last three(3) sections (16 — 18) will focus on how to make the best use of learning materials — dictionaries, typewriters, and textbooks. Although some Japanese may find section 16 (on the electric dictionary and personal computer) and 17 (on the typewriter or word-processor) irrelevant to themselves, this author strongly recommends you to read them and reconsider your attitudes accordingly. The last section (18) will be found most shocking by most Japanese students and teachers, and will be of the greatest help to those who get the message right.

All in all, this book is more guideposts standing at the most critical points than a constant guide or attendant in your journey to English mastery. Though it will not accompany you all the way, it shows you the right direction in which you should go and the correct methodology for you to follow at the very beginning of your attempt at conquering (or revenging on) English. Take a wrong step, and you are sure to go astray. If you want to reach your desired goal, read through this book and take the right step at the start of your English studying (or re-studying) career. Bon voyage.

October 18, 2012

Jaugo Noto(之人冗悟:のと・じゃうご)

Beneath **U**mbrella of **Z**UBARAIE LLC.

http://zubaraie.com

addition... There is another version of this book consisting entirely of ANATOMICAL INTERPRETATION for each and every sentence of it. See it to gaze into the lucid mind's image of ENGLISH LITERATE intellectuals.

その次の4項(第12項から第15項)は、英語に関する個別的な事実や知識というよりも、英語という言語の習得を可能にするための望ましい態度についての講義である。かなり抽象的な内容で、初心者には難しい部分もあるけれど、英語を学ぼうとする日本人ならば誰もがまずこれらの教訓を最初に読んでおいたほうが賢明だろう。これらの項で筆者が述べる内容の大部分は、多くの読者にとって衝撃的で反感を抱かせるものかもしれない・・・もしそうなら、その感覚の違いこそがまさに、本書を英語で書き上げた(上に、諸君にも理解できるよう&筆者の後に続けるよう、日本語訳もして見せた)この筆者と諸君の違いである。

最後の3項(第16項から第18項)では、「辞書」・「タイプライター」・「教科書」といった学習用教材を最大限に活用する方法に焦点を当ててある。第16項(電子辞書とパーソナルコンピュータ)や第17項(タイプライターまたはワープロ)なんて自分には関係ない、と感じる日本人もいるかもしれないが、筆者としては読者に、これらの項を読んだ上で自らの態度を然るべく再考することを強くお勧めする。最後の第18項は、日本人の学生や教師にとっては最も衝撃的な内容に感じられるだろう;が、その言わんとするところを正しく理解してもらえたならば、本書の中で最も役立つ項となるだろう。

総じて本書は、英語修得に向けての諸君の道中の「いつもそばにいるガイド役・随行員」というよりはむしろ「要所要所に配置された道しるべ」の趣である。道中ずっと諸君と一緒に歩むことはしないが、英語を征服するための(あるいは、英語に復讐戦を挑むための)諸君の試みの出発点に於いて、歩むべき正しい方向と、従うべき正しい方法論を示してくれるのが本書である。間違った一歩を踏み出してしまえば、諸君は確実に道に迷うことになる。望み通りのゴールに至りたければ、本書を最後まで読み、英語学習(あるいは再学習)道中の出発点で、まず正しい方向へと第一歩を踏み出すことだ・・・では、諸君、良い旅を。

2012年10月18日

Noto Jaugo(之人冗悟:のと・じゃうご)

合同会社ズバライエ傘下出版本

http://zubaraie.com

追記・・・本書には、その全文に解剖学的解釈を施した別ヴァージョンもある。英語読み書き自在の知識人の頭の中では英文がどう見えているものか、明瞭に知りたければそちらの解剖版も御覧あれ。

1. School teaching curricula are made exclusively for teachers and schools, not for learners

The first thing for English learners in Japan to consider is the last thing any ordinary teacher would ever teach you: NEVER put easy trust in your teachers' curricula, for they are made for the convenience of teachers or schools, not for the benefit of learners.

A school's basic functions are twofold. First and foremost, it should be a place for learners to acquire knowledge and skill. Secondary to the first learning and teaching function, a school is a place for teachers to give grades to learners. Good grades at schools give social grace to learners. Poor marks in exams encourage idle learners into studying harder. Schools maintain such social interactivity on the strength of their function as grade providers. Therefore, schools must have criteria for deciding what grades to provide to learners. When schools prepare teaching materials, fragmentation, separation and grouping of things to teach are made. They are divided into such small parts just in order for teachers to efficiently judge the performance of learners. If 8 out of 10 things to master are shown in an exam to have been successfully acquired by a particular learner, the grade to be provided should be EXCELLENT; two out of ten should be shamefully branded as FAILURE.

If mastery of English is the real goal, however, anything less than PERFECT — 10 things mastered out of 10 things taught — should not be accepted. In actuality, schools give such benevolent grades as SATISFACTORY or AVERAGE or PASSING to learners who only marked 5 or 6 out of 10. FAILURE of learners brings shame to schools too, so that schools have to brand even BELOW AVERAGE learners as CONDITIONALLY PASSED and let such low achievers get away with it; or should we say, just get rid of such encumbrances.

In the world of English grammar, some things should, logically, be collectively taught and comprehended in one set of knowledge, not in many separate pieces, however tough and daunting they may at first appear. They can't, of course, be mastered at a time. But to offer such essentially collective

1. 学校の教育課程は「学ぶ側」より専ら「教える側」の都合に合わせて作られている

日本で英語を学ぶ人々がまず第一に考えるべき事柄・・・それは、普通の先生ならまず決して教えてくれない事である・・・センセイ方の用意するカリキュラム(教育課程)は決して安直に信頼してはならないということである;何故ならばそれは教師や学校側の便宜のために作られたものであって、学習者のためのものではないのだから。

学校の基本的機能は二通りで、まず何よりも第一にそこは学習者が知識と技能を身に付けるための場であるべきだが、その第一の学習・教育機能に付随する二次的な役割として、学校は、教師が学習者に成績を割り振る場でもある。学校で良い成績を取れば、学習者には社会的に箔(ハク)が付く。試験で悪い成績を取れば、怠け者の学習者はもっと頑張って勉強しようという気になるだろう。このように学校は、成績を割り振ることで、世の中との双方向性の関わりを保っているわけである。なればこそ学校には、学習者に割り振るべき成績を決定するための基準が必要なわけだ。学校が教材を用意する時、教えるべき物事の全体をまず細分化した上で、本来一緒だった物事を切り離したり一まとめにしたりの細工を加える。そうして教育内容を細かく切り刻むのは、学習者の達成度を教師が効率的に判定できるようにするためーただそれだけの目的のためである。修得すべき10の事柄のうち8までを確実に修得済みであることを試験成績で示した学習者ならば、「優秀」の成績を与えるのが妥当であろう;10のうち2しか修得していない学習者に宛がう恥ずべき成績は当然、「落第」である。

しかし、「英語の修得」が真の目的ならば、「完璧=教えられた10のうち10の全てを修得済み」に満たない達成度は、許容すべきではなかろう。ところが現実には、10のうち5か6の点数しか取れていない学習者に対しても、「まずまず」とか「ふつう」とか「合格」とかの寛大な成績を配給するのが「学校」というものである。学習者の「落第」は学校にとっても恥であるから、「ふつう以下」の学習者にだって「条件付きで合格」のハンコを押して、そういう低成績者にも逃げ道を与える(というか、そういうお荷物をさっさと厄介払いする)のが学校というものなのである。

英文法の世界では、まとめて教わって一群の知識として理解するのが(論理的に言って)当然の事柄がある。そうした学び方が一見いかにしんどそうで尻込みしたくなる感じでも、多くの細切れ知識の寄せ集めではなく、一まとめで学ぶのが妥当な事柄があるのである。無論、一度限りの学習で一気にモノにできる知識ではないが、本質的

set of knowledge in too many seemingly unrelated fragments will only make their mastery all the more difficult for the number of separate lessons and the lapse of time between them.

Take, for example, the subject of tense. In English, they have the past tense, present tense, future tense and perfect tense. While the perfect tense is further divided into the present perfect, the past perfect and the future perfect, the past perfect tense is intricately associated with subjunctive mood. These temporal elements of English may seem too complicated to teach and master at a time. But perfect separation of the present tense from future or past and spending several months of lessons solely in the present tense at the total exclusion of the past or future tense makes no sense at all from logical point of view. From practical point of view on the side of teachers and schools, however, such nonsensical separations make perfect sense: they make it easier to judge the performance of learners and give them grades accordingly. If the past, present and future were to be dealt with at a time, just like in the world of actually spoken English, there would be chaos in classrooms for some weeks or months, during which time no exact grades could be awarded to learners according to their respective performance. It is, therefore, logical for teachers to separate the past and future from the present tense, with the result that the future and past tenses in Japanese teaching of English have their presence with considerable time lag after the present tense.

If it is mastery of English that learners and teachers have as their aim, the arrangement and management of things to teach and learn — being actually taught but not exactly learnt — at most Japanese schools are too problematic to be practical. They present learners with jigsaw puzzles with too many missing pieces to imagine what the whole picture looks like. No wonder few Japanese can fully draw realistic pictures in English words.

The actual and practical world-picture of English ought to be treated as a whole, not as fragmented pieces put together after long patient efforts of garbage collection. Perfect comprehension and mastery of the whole picture will take some time anyway, but that time-table should be set by learners' ardency and intellectual capacity, not by teachers and schools cutting a picture into pieces conveniently arranged for judging, not improving, learners' performance.

にまとまって存在するこうした一群の知識を、あまりに多くの(一見無関係な)断片的知識の形で提供するのは、分断されたレッスン数の多さとレッスン間の時間差が長い分だけ、習得困難になるものである。

「時制」というテーマを例に取ると、英語には「過去/現在/未来/完了」という時制がある。「完了時制」は更に「現在完了/過去完了/未来完了」に分岐し、「過去完了」はまた「仮定法」と難解な形で結び付いている。英語の持つこうした「時制」の要素は、いっぺんに教えたり身に付けたりするには複雑すぎるように見えるかもしれない。だからと言って、「現在時制」を「未来時制」や「過去時制」と全く切り離した末に、「過去」も「未来」も全く排除して「現在」時制のレッスンだけに何ヶ月も費やすのは、論理的観点から言って全くのナンセンスである。しかしながら、先生や学校の立場から言えば、こうしたナンセンスなまでの細切れレッスンが、完璧に意味を成すのである。何故ならば、細切れにすることでレッスンごとの学習者の習得度の判定が容易になり、それに応じて成績を付けるのも楽になるからである。「過去」・「現在」・「未来」の時制をまとめて取り扱うような(現実に話されている英語の世界みたいな)マネをすれば、教室内は何週間あるいは何月間もの間混乱に包まれて、その間は学習者各人の達成度に応じて正確な成績を付けることも不可能になるであろう。従って、「過去」や「未来」を「現在」時制から切り離すのは、先生方にとっては極めて合理的な措置なのであり、その結果、日本の英語教育に「未来」や「過去」の時制が現われるのは、「現在」からかなりの時間差を置いてから、ということになるわけである。

もしも、学習者及び教師の目的が「英語の修得」だと仮定すれば、日本の大方の学校に於ける「教えるべき事柄/学ぶべき事柄(=実際教えられてはいるけれど必ずしも学習はされていない事柄)」の並べ方や扱い方は、問題だらけで到底現実的とは言えない。日本の学校の多くは、欠落ピースが多すぎて全体像も思い描けないジグソーパズルを学習者に突き付けているのである。英語の言葉でまともな絵を描き切ることのできる日本人がほとんど存在しないのも、道理というものである。

まともで実用的な英語の世界像は、一つの総合体として取り扱われるべきものであって、細切れの断片的知識へと切り刻まれたものを長くしんどいゴミ拾い作業の末にせっせとツギハギして組み立てるべきものではない。全体像を完璧に理解し我がものとするためには、いずれにせよある程度の時間を要するが、その所要時間の長さは、学習者の熱意と知性の器の大小によって個別的に決すべきものであって、先生や学校が学習者の達成度を判定するのに好都合な形で(学習者の達成度向上を目指して、ではなく)一つの絵画をバラバラの断片へと切り刻んだ結果として出来上がった時間表のごときは、筋違いというものである。

Now, you must have understood: what is important in English learning is not preparation for lessons to come, but reviews of lessons already taught but not quite learnt yet. This book deals with collective knowledge of English in a bulk. They may fly past before you like runaway horses at first: you may feel run over by them once, but going over them twice will get you somewhere; running them over again and again, you will come to know where and how to go. With each additional review, you will get the nearer to the goal. The test of an English textbook is in the re-visiting: a good one gives you the big picture you failed to see at the first reading; a poor guide insists on teaching you how to move your feet but gives you no idea where you are going and how far you have come or how much is left to be conquered. This book is written in conscious opposition to such poor guidebooks of English as tedious contrary teachers to avoid; whether it is a good guide or not is left for you to judge... after several reviews, with the visual assistance of the incredibly meticulous anatomical interpretation guide of this book – Anatomy of reversENGLISH – that is.

さぁ、これでもう諸君は理解できたはずである:英語学習で重要なのは、未習の授業の予習ではなく、既習の(しかし修得済みとは必ずしも言えない)授業の復習の方なのである。この本では、英語の総体としての知識を、一塊の巨大な存在として取り扱う。最初はまるで暴れ馬の如く諸君の眼前を駆け抜けて終わり、の感を催すかもしれないし、まるで暴走車にひき逃げされた気がするかもしれないが、その一塊の知識を後で再びなぞってみれば、それなりの手応えは掴めるものだ;何度も何度も復習を繰り返すうちに、自分が何処を目指しているか、どうすれば目的地に辿り着けるか、次第にわかってくるはずである。復習を繰り返すその度ごとに、ゴールへ一歩一歩近付くことになる。英語の教科書の真価は、再訪に耐える内容を有しているか否かで決まる:良い教科書ならば、最初に読んだ時には見落としていた全体像が、再読時に見えてくるものである;ダメな案内役に引っかかると、足の動かし方ばかりムキになって教えるばかりで、これからどこに向かおうとしているのか、目標達成まであとどれくらい残っているのか、さっぱり教えてくれやしない、という羽目になる。そうした退屈極まる回避すべき反面教師のようなダメな英語のガイドブックとは正反対のものを意識的に目指して、この本は書いてある;それが良いガイドであるか否かの判断は、諸君に委ねよう. . . もっともその判断は、(信じ難いほど事細かに書き記された本書の解剖学的解釈本―「Anatomy of reversENGLISH:でんぐリングリッシュ解剖学的解釈ガイド」―の視覚的助力を頼りに)度重なる復習を経た後に下すべし、と念押ししておく必要があるが。

2. Japanese avoidance of personal pronouns

- Japanese language has no personal pronouns -

As incredible as it may be to native English speakers, Japanese language has no "人称代名詞(NINSHOU-DAIMEISHI:personal pronouns)": Japanese people use so many nouns as substitute personal pronouns that regarding them all as personal pronouns would make no linguistic sense at all. There is no definite rule for nouns to be used as substitutes for personal pronouns: only personal choice of the speaker will decide what substitute personal pronoun to use for any given person or persons in Japanese language.

- No mystique or mistake with English personal/impersonal pronouns -

English personal and impersonal pronouns are definitely fixed. It can be further divided into four forms according to its function in the sentence, namely, "主格:SHUKAKU: the subjective case" (I, we, you, he, she, it, they), "所有格:SHOYUUKAKU: the possessive case" (my, our, your, his, her, its, their), "目的格:MOKUTEKIKAKU: the objective case" (me, us, you, him, her, it, them) and "所有代名詞:SHOYUU-DAIMEISHI: the possessive pronoun" (mine, ours, yours, his, hers, its, theirs).

All English personal/impersonal pronouns can be systematically defined and memorized in the following manner, with which, as a reference, this author will enumerate possible counterparts in Japanese pseudo personal pronouns in the subjective/objective case (should you want to use them in the possessive case/possessive pronoun, simply add "の:NO" at the end):

一人称(ICHI-NINSHOU: the first person) = the person who is speaking along with or on behalf of the person(s) on the side of the speaker:

単数(TANSUU: singular): I - my - me - mine

Japanese substitutes: 私(WATASHI),私(WATAKUSHI),あたし(ATASHI),僕(BOKU),俺(ORE),俺っち(ORECCHI),あっし(ASSHI),あちき(ACHIKI),手前(TEMAE),自分(JIBUN),当方(TOUHOU),小生(SHOUSEI),儂(WASHI),うち(UCHI),こっち(KOCCHI),こちとら(KOCHITORA),etc,etc.

複数(FUKUSUU: plural): we - our - us - ours

2. 日本語は人称代名詞を避けたがる

ー日本語に「人称代名詞」なしー

英語を母国語とする人々には信じられないことだろうが、日本語には人称代名詞というものが存在しない：日本人が人称代名詞の「代替表現」として用いる「名詞」の数はあまりに多すぎるので、それらの代用呼称の全てを「人称代名詞」扱いすれば言語学的に全くのナンセンスを演じることになる。「人称代名詞の代用品」として用いられる「名詞」に関しては、確たる規則など何も存在しない：日本語の中では、任意の人物(たち)を指す人称代名詞の代用品として何を用いるかは、もっぱら話者の選択に委ねられているのである。

ー英語の「人称／非人称代名詞」には謎や間違いの発生余地なしー

英語では、「人称代名詞」・「非人称代名詞」は厳密に決まっている。これらの代名詞は更に、文中で果たすその役割に応じて4つの形態へと区分される。即ち、(1)「主格：the subjective case」(I, we, you, he, she, it, they)、(2)「所有格：the possessive case」(my, our, your, his, her, its, their)、(3)「目的格：the objective case」(me, us, you, him, her, it, them)、(4)「所有代名詞：the possessive pronoun」(mine, ours, yours, his, hers, its, theirs)である。

英語の「人称／非人称代名詞」の全ては、以下に示すような形で体系的に定義して覚え込むことが可能である。ここではそれらに加えて、それぞれの英語の代名詞に相当する日本語版の「擬似的人称代名詞」の数々をも(「主格／目的格」の形で)参考のために列挙しておくことにしよう(これら和風疑似代名詞を「所有格／所有代名詞」の形で使いたいなら、「主格／目的格」の末尾に単純に“の”を付加すれば事足りる)：

一人称(the first person)＝話者当人／話し手側に立つまたはこれを代表する人(々)：
単数(singular): I - my - me - mine
日本語版代替表現: 私(わたし)、私(わたくし)、あたし、僕、俺、俺っち、あっし、あちき、手前(てまえ)、自分、当方、小生(しょうせい)、儂(わし)、うち、こっち、こちとら、その他諸々
複数(plural): we - our - us - ours

Japanese substitutes: 私達/ら(WATASHI TACHI/RA), 私達/ら/ども(WATAKUSHI TACHI/RA/DOMO),あたしたち/ら(ATASHI TACHI/RA),僕たち/ら(BOKU TACHI/RA),俺たち/ら(ORE TACHI/RA),あっしら(ASSHI RA),我々(WAREWARE),我等(WARERA),手前ども(TEMAE DOMO),自分たち/ら(JIBUN TACHI/RA),当方(TOUHOU),儂ら(WASHI RA),うちら(UCHI RA),こっち(KOCCHI),こちとら(KOCHITORA),etc,etc.

二人称(NI-NINSHOU: the second person) = the person or persons whom the speaker is directly talking to
単数/複数(TANSUU/FUKUSUU: whether singular or plural): you - your - you - yours
Japanese substitutes:
単数(TANSUU: singular): あなた(ANATA),あなたさま(ANATA SAMA),あんた(ANTA),君(KIMI),お前(OMAE),貴兄(KIKEI),兄(KEI),貴殿(KIDEN),おたく(OTAKU),汝(NANJI),そっち(SOCCHI),そちらさん(SOCHIRASAN),自分(JIBUN),われ(WARE),うぬ(UNU),おのれ(ONORE),おんどれ(ONDORE),おんどりゃー(ONDORYAA),きさま(KISAMA),こいつ(KOITSU),てめぇ(TEMEE),おめぇ(OMEE),この野郎(KONOYAROU),こんにゃろう(KONNYAROU),なろう(NAROU),こんちくしょう(KONCHIKUSHOU),こなくそ(KONAKUSO),etc,etc.
複数(FUKUSUU: plural): あなたがた/たち/ら(ANATA GATA/TACHI/RA),あんたがた/たち/ら(ANTA GATA/TACHI/RA),君たち/ら(KIMI TACHI/RA),お前たち/ら(OMAE TACHI/RA),貴兄ら(KIKEI RA),兄ら(KEI RA),おたくたち/ら(OTAKU TACHI/RA),汝等(NANJI RA),そっち(SOCCHI),そちらさん(SOCHIRASAN),自分ら(JIBUN RA),われ(WARE),うぬら(UNU RA),おのれら(ONORE RA),おんどれ(ONDORE),おんどりゃー(ONDORYAA),きさまら(KISAMA RA),こいつら(KOITSU RA),てめぇら(TEMEE RA),おめぇら(OMEE RA),この野郎ども(KONOYAROU DOMO),こんにゃろうども(KONNYAROU DOMO),こんちくしょうども(KONCHIKUSHOU DOMO),こなくそ(KONAKUSO),etc,etc.

三人称(SAN-NINSHOU: the third person) = the person(s) or thing(s) the speaker is indirectly referring to, not directly talking to
男性単数(DANSEI TANSUU: masculine singular): he - his - him - his

日本語版代替表現: 私達/ら(わたしたち/ら)、私達/ら/ども(わたくしたち/ら/ども)、あたしたち/ら、僕たち/ら、俺たち/ら、あっしら、我々、我等(われら)、手前ども(てまえども)、自分たち/ら、当方、儂ら(わしら)、うちら、こっち、こちとら、その他諸々

二人称(the second person)=話し手が直接語り掛けている相手の人物(たち)
単数/複数(singular or plural): you - your - you - yours
日本語版代替表現:
単数(singular): あなた、あなたさま、あんた、君、お前、貴兄(きけい)、兄(けい)、貴殿(きでん)、おたく、汝(なんじ)、そっち、そちらさん、自分、われ、うぬ、おのれ、おんどれ、おんどりゃー、きさま、こいつ、てめぇ、おめぇ、この野郎、こんにゃろう、なろう、こんちくしょう、こなくそ、その他諸々
複数(plural): あなたがた/たち/ら、あんたがた/たち/ら、君たち/ら、お前たち/ら、貴兄ら(きけいら)、兄ら(けいら)、おたくたち/ら、汝等(なんじら)、そっち、そちらさん、自分ら、われ、うぬら、おのれら、おんどれ、おんどりゃー、きさまら、こいつら、てめぇら、おめぇら、この野郎ども、こんにゃろうども、こんちくしょうども、こなくそ、その他諸々

三人称(the third person)=話者が間接的に言及しているだけで、直接的に語り掛けているわけではない人物あるいは物事(単数／複数)
男性単数(masculine singular): he - his - him - his

Japanese substitutes: 彼(KARE),あの男(ANO OTOKO),あの人(ANO HITO),あの方(ANO KATA),あのお方(ANO OKATA),氏(SHI),彼氏(KARESHI),あの者(ANO MONO),その者(SONO MONO),あの御仁(ANO GOJIN),あいつ(AITSU),あやつ(AYATSU),やつ(YATSU),きゃつ(KYATSU),そやつ(SOYATSU),やっこさん(YAKKO SAN),あんちくしょう(ANCHIKUSHOU),あんにゃろう(ANNYAROU),あちらさん(ACHIRA SAN),あの子(ANO KO),あの野郎(ANO YAROU),etc,etc.

女性単数(JOSEI TANSUU: feminine singular): she - her - her - hers

Japanese substitutes: 彼女(KANOJO),あの女(ANO ONNA),あの人(ANO HITO),あの方(ANO KATA),あのお方(ANO OKATA),あの者(ANO MONO),その者(SONO MONO),あの御仁(ANO GOJIN),あいつ(AITSU),あやつ(AYATSU),やつ(YATSU),きゃつ(KYATSU),そやつ(SOYATSU),やっこさん(YAKKO SAN),あんちくしょう(ANCHIKUSHOU),あんにゃろう(ANNYAROU),あちら(ACHIRA),あちらさん(ACHIRA SAN),あの娘(ANO KO),あのアマ(ANO AMA),あのスケ(ANO SUKE),etc,etc.

非人称単数(HININSHOU TANSUU: impersonal singular): it - its - it - its

Japanese substitutes: あれ(ARE),それ(SORE),あいつ(AITSU),そいつ(SOITSU),その物(SONO MONO),その何か(SONO NANIKA),etc,etc.

男性・女性・中性または非人称複数(DANSEI・JOSEI・CHUUSEI or HININSHOU FUKUSUU: plural whether masculine, feminine, neuter or impersonal): they - their - them - theirs

Japanese substitutes: 彼ら(KARE RA),それら(SORERA),そういう人たち(SOUIU HITO TACHI),そういう物たち(SOUIU MONO TACHI),あの人たち(ANO HITO TACHI),あの方たち(ANO KATA TACHI),あの男ども(ANO OTOKO DOMO),彼たち(KARE TACHI),あの女ども(ANO ONNNA DOMO),彼女ら/たち(KANOJO TACHI),あの連中(ANO RENCHUU),ああした連中(AASHITA RENCHUU),ああいう者ども(AAIU MONO DOMO),あいつら(AITSURA),あやつら(AYATSURA),やつら(YATSURA),きゃつら(KYATSURA),そいつら(SOITSURA),やっこさんたち(YAKKOSAN TACHI),あんちくしょうども(ANCHIKUSHOU DOMO),あちら(ACHIRA),あちらさん(ACHIRA SAN),あちらさんがた(ACHIRA SAN GATA),あんにゃろうども(ANNYAROU DOMO), etc,etc.

日本語版代替表現: 彼、あの男、あの人、あの方(あのかた)、あのお方(あのおかた)、氏(し)、彼氏(かれし)、あの者、その者、あの御仁(あのごじん)、あいつ、あやつ、やつ、きゃつ、そやつ、やっこさん、あんちくしょう、あんにゃろう、あちらさん、あの子、あの野郎、その他諸々

女性単数(feminine singular): she – her – her – hers

日本語版代替表現: 彼女、あの女、あの人、あの方(あのかた)、あのお方(あのおかた)、あの者、その者、あの御仁(あのごじん)、あいつ、あやつ、やつ、きゃつ、そやつ、やっこさん、あんちくしょう、あんにゃろう、あちら、あちらさん、あの娘(あのこ)、あのアマ、あのスケ、その他諸々

非人称単数(impersonal singular): it – its – it – its

日本語版代替表現: あれ、それ、あいつ、そいつ、その物、その何か、その他諸々

男性・女性・中性または非人称複数(plural whether masculine, famine, neuter or impersonal): they – their – them – theirs

日本語版代替表現: 彼ら、それら、そういう人たち、そういう物たち、あの人たち、あの方たち(あのかたたち)、あの男ども、彼たち、あの女ども、彼女ら/たち、あの連中、ああした連中、ああいう者ども、あいつら、あやつら、やつら、きゃつら、そいつら、やっこさんたち、あんちくしょうども、あちら、あちらさん、あちらさんがた、あんにゃろうども、その他諸々

- The essential reason why the Japanese avoid calling someone by definite names or pronouns -

To English speakers who are at a loss how to make conversation possible with so many possible substitutes without definite personal pronouns, suffice it to say that most Japanese sentences are complete without SHUGO(subjects: I, we, you, he, she, it, they) or MOKUTEKIGO(objects: me, us, you, him, her, it, them) and consist mainly of DOUSHI(verbs) and its accompaniment. Quite incredibly for English natives, "(S)I (V)love (O)you" is almost always "(V)好きです(SUKI DESU)" instead of being expressed in such perfectly formal Japanese as "(S)私は(WATASHI WA) (O)あなたが(ANATA GA) (V)好きです(SUKI DESU)".

While subjective or objective ellipsis is quite rare to find in English sentences, their formal existence is rarer still in Japanese. In essence, Japanese people positively hate to call or be called by definite names. Sounds crazy? Maybe, to Indo-European speakers; but the avoidance of direct name-calling is a time-honored custom of Japanese language which has its root in their spiritual belief called "言霊(KOTODAMA: spirit inherent in each and every word)".

The history of Japanese belief in KOTODAMA is presumably as old as the Japanese language itself, which tells us (even today, more or less) that we can capture the spirit of any given entity by simply uttering the word signifying the entity. A name of someone or something was believed to have some magical power over the person or thing the name stood for. In fact, in ancient Japan (up until the early years of the Heian Era) the terms "事(KOTO: thing)" and "言(KOTO: word)" were so closely associated together that they were felt to be virtually the same thing. That is why it was thought blasphemous to call persons in high positions by directly referring to their names. Even today, calling someone by their real name is a privilege only allowed to someone so intimately near. When any other boys call a girl by affectionate but general nickname "花子ちゃん(HANAKO CHAN)", only her true love can intimately call her "花子(HANAKO)", which, in English, can be bravely translated into "HANAKO, my dear". Direct name-calling in Japan, while not strictly a taboo today, could still invoke feelings beyond the wildest imagination of Western folks.

－日本人が誰かさんを特定の「名前」や「代名詞」で呼ぶことを避ける本源的理由－

固定的な「人称代名詞」も持たず、かくも多くの代替可能表現があるばかりの日本語で、一体どうやって会話を成り立たせたらよいのか、と途方に暮れる英語人種に対しては、次の一言で事足りるであろう:「日本語の文章の大部分は、主語(subjects: I, we, you, he, she, it, they)や目的語(objects: me, us, you, him, her, it, them)抜きで完結し、主として動詞(verbs)とその付属語だけで成り立っている」。英語を母国語とする人々には全く信じられない話ではあるが、英語なら「(S)I (V)love (O)you」となる表現が、日本語ではほぼ常に「(V)好きです」で終わり、「(S)私は(O)あなたが(V)好きです」のような(S)主語(V)述語動詞(O)目的語の完全に整った形式の日本語になることは滅多にないのである。

英語世界で「主語や目的語の省略」が行なわれるのは極めて稀であるが、日本語世界で「主語や目的語がきちんと存在する事例」はそれに輪を掛けて稀なことである。本質的に言えば、特定の「名」で呼んだり呼ばれたりすることを、日本人は積極的に忌避しているのである。「そんなバカな！？」と思うだろうか？　確かに、インド・ヨーロッパ語族の人々にはおかしな話に響くであろう;が、「名を直接呼ぶことをはばかる」この日本人の態度は、「言霊(ことだま:個々の言葉のそれぞれに生来宿る魂)」と呼ばれる超自然的信仰に根ざした由緒正しき古来の習慣なのである。

日本人の「言霊」信仰の歴史は、恐らくは日本語の言語としての歴史そのものと同じくらい古いもので、それによれば、いかなる「存在」も、それを表わす「言葉」を口にするだけで、その精髄を我々は鷲づかみにできる、とされている。誰かや何かを表わす「名」は、その「名」が表わす人物・事物に対し、神秘的な霊力を有するものと信じられたのである。事実、大昔の日本では(平安時代初期に至るまで)「事(こと＝thing)」と「言(こと＝word)」とは実に密接に結び付いていたため、これら両語は実質的に同一のものを指す言葉と意識されていたのであった。それ故にこそ、高い位にある人々を呼ぶ際に、その「名」に直接言及することは不敬の振る舞いであると考えられた。今日でさえ、誰かさんをその「本名」で呼ぶのは、ごくごく近しい関係にある人物にのみ許された特権なのである。その他諸々の男子がある女の子を「花子ちゃん」と(親しげではあるものの、世間向けに過ぎない)愛称で呼ぶ中で、ただ一人彼女の恋人だけが(いかにもねんごろな感じで)彼女を「花子」と呼ぶことができるのである(この場合の「花子」を英語に訳せば「Hanako, my dear:花子、僕の愛しいひと」ぐらいまで大胆に解釈してもよいであろう)。人の名前を直接呼ぶことは、今日の日本では必ずしも厳格なタブー(禁令)ではないものの、それでもやはり西欧人の想像の到底及ばぬような微妙な感情的余波を引き起こし得る行為なのである。

When name-calling was thus consciously avoided, it was only natural that personal pronouns had no chance of development in the history of Japanese language. Moreover, by giving someone any definite pseudo personal pronoun, Japanese people will make their mental stance clear toward that person: whether they respect(eg.あなたさま:ANATA SAMA), feel affectionate to(eg.君:KIMI) or distant from(eg.おたく:OTAKU), or even positively hate(eg. てめぇ:TEMEE) that person, is made clear by the choice and use of a particular denomination. Rather than putting themselves in a possibly awkward position by improper name-calling, Japanese people instinctively avoid using any personal pronouns, with the logical consequence that Japanese sentences so frequently omit subjects or objects, only to be supplemented by the reader's imagination according to the context.

For Japanese learners of English, therefore, the first thing to remember is never to omit subjects or objects in English, which, in most cases, take the form of personal pronouns (I, we, you, he, she, it, they / me, us, you, him, her, it, them). The good news is, they are definitely fixed in English and so easy to understand that Japanese people will find little difficulty in mastering them, and once they get acquainted with their use, they can feel the freedom of English from those crazy variations of nuances and restrictions which make Japanese conversation too cramped and dishonestly unnatural to reach people of different social status.

The bad news is, people once liberated from such crazy chains will never want to get back to their old suffocating restraints of the Japanese, linguistic or otherwise. Those Japanese who have acquainted themselves with English freedom could no longer put up with suffocatingly absurd customs in their native country. A possible solution is that all Japanese, beyond any social status, should be able to communicate freely in English, not in order to desert Japanese but so that they can understand what it is like to be Japanese, and they will try consciously to make themselves better, linguistically or otherwise. Sounds impossible? Maybe... but it may turn out to be nothing compared to the difficulty foreign people find in deciding what pseudo personal pronoun to adopt in their Japanese conversation.

このように「名を呼ぶこと」を意識的に避ける日本語の歴史の中で、「人称代名詞」が発達する機会がなかったのは至極当然のことである。更に言えば、「人称代名詞めいた特定の呼び名」を誰かさんに宛がうことで、日本人は、その人物に対する自らの心的立ち位置を明らかにすることになってしまう。「あなたさま」と呼んで敬意を示すか、「君」と呼んで親愛の情を表現するか、「おたく」呼ばわりで敬遠するか、「てめぇ」と叫んで喧嘩腰の嫌悪感をあらわにすることさえも、特定の「呼び方」を選んで自らの口に乗せることで、日本人は、あからさまに表明することになってしまうのである。不適切な呼び名で相手を呼んだりすれば、厄介な立場に自らを追いやることになりかねないのだから、そんなことになるよりはむしろ、いかなる人称代名詞も使わずに避けたがるのが日本人の本能なのである。その当然の帰結として、日本語の文章では「主語」や「目的語」の省略が実に頻繁に行なわれ、欠落した「主語／目的語」の部分は、読者側が脈絡を読んだ上で思い描いた適当な語を補う、ということになるわけである。

それ故にまた、日本人が英語を学習する場合にまず忘れてはならないことは、英文中では「主語や目的語は決して省くな」ということである。多くの場合、英語の「主語(I, we, you, he, she, it, they)」・「目的語(me, us, you, him, her, it, them)」は「人称代名詞」の形態を取る。幸いなことに、英語の人称代名詞の形態は厳密に決まっていて理解するにも極めて容易なので、その習得に日本人が苦労することはほとんど全くないであろうし、ひとたび英語の人称代名詞の使い方に習熟してしまえば、英語がいかに自由奔放な言語であるかが実感できるであろう・・・それに引き替え日本語世界ときたら、頭がおかしくなりそうなほどたくさんの言い回しだの微妙な含みだの禁句だののせいで、窮屈で不誠実なまでに不自然な会話しか成り立たないから、社会的立場の違いを越えて他人と心を通い合わせることなんてできやしない、あぁ、英語にはそんな不自由がなくて、いいなぁ・・・と、肌身で感じることであろう。

ここで困ったことは、ひとたび阿呆な束縛の鎖から解き放たれた人々は、古くさくて息が詰まるような日本人の世の中の制限の数々へは(言葉の面でもそれ以外の面に於いても)二度と再び戻りたがらない、ということである。英語世界の自由度を知ってしまった日本人は、母国の窒息しそうな阿呆臭い決まり事にはもはや耐えられないと感じることであろう。考え得る解決策としては、全ての日本人が、社会的立場の枠を越えて、英語で自由自在に会話できる能力を身に付けてしまえばよい。日本語を捨てるためにではなく、日本人であることの意味を理解するために、英会話自在の境地に達すればよいのである・・・そうなれば彼らは、言葉の面でもそれ以外でも、自分達をより良い存在に変えて行くべく意識的に努力することになるはずなのだから・・・無理な話に聞こえるだろうか？　まぁ、そう感じる人もいるかもしれない。が、外国人が日本人との会話の中で適切な「疑似人称代名詞」を選ぶ際の難儀に比べれば、物の数にも入らぬほどの苦労と言えるかもしれない。

- Get acquainted with English through pronoun pronouncement -

If you are a complete beginner in the study of English, it is a very good practice to change anything you see into a pronoun(we, you, they, he, she, it... "I" will play no role in this practice) and instantly pronounce it. It seems easy enough, but it takes some getting used to before you are perfectly familiar with the notion of English pronouns. Shall we take some examples?

One of the commonest mistakes beginners make is "personal association of impersonal pronouns": to confuse an impersonal pronoun(it, they, its, their, them) with the person it is associated with. For example, where "Your lips look so charming. I feel like kissing <them>." is the correct English, beginners often say "...I feel like kissing <you>" simply because "your lips" belong to "you". Likewise, "My nose is running. <It> simply wouldn't stop" will be mistaken for "... <I> simply wouldn't stop" by novice learners of English. "Your lips" and "My nose" are objects of perception, not identical with the person they belong to.

This objectification process is initially difficult for Japanese people, who rarely make mental distinction between themselves and things or folks around them. You doubt me?... OK, then, what do you feel about this English: "Our company is in great danger now. <It> has to regenerate <itself>."... didn't you feel it strange and want to say instead "...<We> have to regenerate <ourselves>"? Identification of oneself with things or folks around them is so deep-rooted in Japanese consciousness that "pronoun pronouncement" is important for beginners.

To be able to paraphrase anything in the correct form of personal/impersonal pronoun(I, we, you, they, he, she, it) is the cornerstone of your command of English. Do consciously practice pronoun pronouncement while you are still awkward with English language. It won't take much effort, it won't take too much time, but it will certainly take you somewhere, when you are completely sure you can handle English pronouns instantly and instinctively.

－「代名詞発声練習」で英語慣れを作れ－

全くの英語初学者の場合、目にした物事全てを「代名詞(we/you/they/he/she/it・・・この訓練に“I”の出番はない)」に置き換えて即座に口に出して言ってみるのはとてもよい訓練になる。実に簡単そのものに思えるだろうが、英語を学ぶのが全く初めての日本人の場合、「代名詞」の概念に完璧に馴染むまでにはある程度の慣れが要る・・・いくつか例を挙げようか？

初学者が犯す間違いの典型的なものは、「非人称代名詞を間違って人称代名詞に関連付けてしまうこと」である：「非人称」の代名詞(it/they/its/their/them)を、それと関連性の高い「人物」と混同してしまうわけである。例えば、正しい英語では「Your lips look so charming. I feel like kissing 〈them〉.：君の唇はとっても魅力的で、＜その唇＞に思わず口づけしたい気分」となるべきところ、初心者の場合はちょくちょく(「your lips：君の唇」は「you：君」に属すものだからという単純な理由から)「I feel like kissing 〈you〉：＜君＞に思わず口づけしたい気分」になってしまうのだ。似たような感じで、「My nose is running. 〈It〉 simply wouldn't stop.：鼻水が出る。＜この鼻水＞、とにかくもう止まらない」を「〈I〉 simply wouldn't stop.：＜私＞、とにかくもう止まらない」と勘違いしたりするのが英語初心者というものである。「Your lips：君の唇」も「My nose：私の鼻」も、知覚的認識の対象であって、それら物体の属する人物と同一物ではないのである。

こうした「物事を客体として認識する過程」は、英語に不慣れな日本人には難しい；日本人というものは、自分自身と身の回りの物事・人々とを心理的に同一視していて滅多に区分して捉えたりしない人種だからである。お疑いか？．．．よろしい、それなら、次の英文を見て諸君はどう感じるだろうか？：「Our company is in great danger now. 〈It〉 has to regenerate 〈itself〉.：我が社は今大変な危機にある。＜それ＞は＜それ自体＞を刷新する必要がある」・・・何か変な感じがして「〈We〉 have to regenerate 〈ourselves〉：＜我々＞は＜自ら＞を刷新する必要がある」に言い換えたい気分に駆られないであろうか？・・・このように、自己と周囲の物事・人々との同一視体質は日本人の意識に深くこびりついているものだから、「代名詞にして言ってみる訓練」は初学者には大事である。

ありとあらゆる物事を正しい形態の「人称／非人称代名詞(I/we/you/they/he/she/it)」で言い換えできる能力は、英語駆使力の礎石である。まだまだ英語がぎこちない間は、「代名詞にして口に乗せる訓練」を意識的に実践してみることだ。さしたる努力も不要、さほど長い時間も要さないが、この訓練で「自分には英語の代名詞が瞬間的・本能的に処理できる」と完璧に確信できるようになった暁には、きっと英語学習にそれなりの手応えが得られるはずである。

3. Lack of future in Japanese tense

"時制(JISEI: tense)" is another dimension in which Japanese language is impossibly different from English. English consciousness is clearly divided by temporal distinctions into three tenses, namely, "現在(GENZAI: the present), 過去(KAKO: the past)" and "未来(MIRAI: the future)", each of which with possible accompaniment of "完了形(KANRYOU-KEI: the perfect tense)", while contemporary Japanese language is essentially lacking in the future and perfect tenses.

- The present and future have no boundary in Japanese -

Let us take English examples to see the temporal difference in their language, below which will come their Japanese equivalents:
過去形(KAKO-KEI: the past tense)
I worked yesterday.
私は昨日働いた(WATASHI WA KINOU HATARAITA)
現在形(GENZAI-KEI: the present tense)
I work every day.
私は毎日働く(WATASHI WA MAINICHI HATARAKU)
未来形(MIRAI-KEI: the future tense)
I will work tomorrow, too.
私は明日も働く(WATASHI WA ASU MO HATARAKU)

For each of the above-mentioned forms of the past, present and future, there can be "完了形(KANRYOU-KEI: the perfect tense)" in the form of "have+過去分詞(KAKO-BUNSHI: the past participle)" with "have" being changed into "had/have/has/will have" in accordance with the tense and the subject:
過去完了形(KAKO-KANRYOU-KEI: the past perfect tense)
I had worked eight hours by then.
その時点までに私は既に8時間働いていた(SONO JITEN MADENI WATASHI WA SUDENI HACHI JIKAN HATARAITE ITA)
現在完了形(GENZAI-KANRYOU-KEI: the present perfect tense)
I have worked three hours.
私は既に3時間働いた(WATASHI WA SUDENI SAN JIKAN HATARAITA)

3. 日本語時制に「未来」なし

「時制(tense)」もまた、日本語と英語が全くの異次元に属する領域の一つである。英語世界の意識は時系列の違いによって「現在(the present)」・「過去(the past)」・「未来(the future)」の3つの時制へと明瞭に区分され、その各々に「完了形(the perfect tense)」が付随する場合があり得る・・・一方、現代日本語には本源的に「未来」と「完了」の時制が欠落している。

ー日本語に「現在」／「未来」の境なしー

英語の「時制」の相違を確認するために例文を見てみよう。英文の後にはそれに相当する日本語表現も掲げておく。

過去形(the past tense)

I worked yesterday. 私は昨日働いた

現在形(the present tense)

I work every day. 私は毎日働く

未来形(the future tense)

I will work tomorrow, too. 私は明日も働く

上述の「過去・現在・未来」の各時制ごとに、「have+過去分詞(the past participle)」("have"の部分は時制及び主語に応じて"had/have/has/will have"に変化)の形を取る「完了形(the perfect tense)」があり得る:

過去完了形(the past perfect tense)

I had worked eight hours by then. その時点までに私は既に8時間働いていた

現在完了形(the present perfect tense)

I have worked three hours. 私は既に3時間働いた

未来完了形(MIRAI-KANRYOU-KEI: the future perfect tense)
I will have worked eight hours at 5 P.M.
午後5時の時点で私は8時間働いたことになる(GOGO GOJI NO JITEN DE WATASHI WA HACHI JIKAN HATARAITA KOTO NI NARU)

Now, the first and easiest thing for Japanese learners to consider is the English distinction between "現在形(GENZAI-KEI: the present form)" and "未来形(MIRAI-KEI: the future form)": simple addition of the auxiliary verb "will" before any given verb (in its "原形:GENKEI=root form") will change the present into the future tense. While in Japanese, there is not even a distinction between the present and the future, as can be seen in the translations above. The future in Japanese language is not shown by the "語尾変化(GOBI-HENKA: inflection)" of verbs but by the presence of "時の副詞(TOKI-NO-FUKUSHI: temporal adverbs)". If "明日(ASU:tomorrow)" is found within the sentence, the tense will be automatically interpreted as belonging to "the future", so that "私は明日働く(WATASHI WA ASU HATARAKU)" does not have to be meticulously written as "私は明日働くだろう(WATASHI WA ASU HATARAKU DAROU)".

- Volitional "will" and expecting "will" -

Precisely interpreted, the English auxiliary verb "will" can be translated into two types of Japanese expressions: volitional "つもりだ(TSUMORI DA)" and expecting(non-volitional) "だろう(DAROU)".

When the "will" is meant as volitional declaration, its Japanese equivalent should either be "つもりだ(TSUMORI DA)" or " " — nothing added. In fact, "つもり(TSUMORI)" in Japanese has a way of sounding more like a pretext than a declaration of firm will, so that, in normal contexts, volitionally imagined future in Japanese is rarely accompanied by "つもりだ(TSUMORI DA)". If you find a Japanese sentence "私は明日働くつもりだ(WATASHI WA ASU HATARAKU TSUMORI DA)", you may reasonably expect that the person speaking like that WILL NOT in fact BE WORKING tomorrow.

When English "will" has no volition in it but is meant as an objective expectation of future events, the Japanese equivalent is "だろう(DAROU)", as in the case of "It will rain tomorrow" translated into "明日は雨が降るだろう(ASU WA AME GA FURU DAROU)".

未来完了形(the future perfect tense)

I will have worked eight hours at 5 P.M. 午後5時の時点で私は8時間働いたことになる

さて、日本人学習者が考慮すべき事柄のうち、最初にして最も単純なものは、英語の「現在形」と「未来形」の相違である。任意の動詞(の原形=the root form)の前に助動詞“will”を付加するだけで、「現在」時制は「未来」に変わるのだ。一方の日本語には(上掲の翻訳文でもわかる通り)「現在」と「未来」の区別すら存在しない。日本語に於ける「未来」は動詞の「語尾変化(inflection)」ではなく「時の副詞(temporal adverbs)」によって示されるのである。もし文章内に「明日」とあれば、時制は自動的に「未来」に属するものと解釈されるので、「私は明日働く」の表現を御丁寧に「私は明日働く<だろう>」と書いたりしなくてよいのである。

－「意志」の“will”と「想定」の“will”－

厳密に解釈すると、英語の助動詞“will”を日本語訳する場合、二つの表現に分かれる:「つもりだ」という意志含みの場合と、「だろう」という想定上の(無意志の)場合とに二分されるのである。

「意志」の宣言として用いられている“will”を日本語にする場合、「つもりだ」と付け足すか、または何も加えずそのまま、となる。実際の日本語では、「つもり」の表現には「堅い意志の表明」というよりむしろ「言い訳」めいた響きがあるため、日本語の普通の文脈では、「意志含みの未来として想定される事柄」に「つもりだ」が付くことは稀である。もし「私は明日働くつもりだ」という日本文を見たら、そんなこと言ってる人はきっと「実際には明日働いていないだろう」と思ってまず間違いない。

英語の“will”が「意志」を含まずに未来の出来事の「客観的想定」として用いられている場合の日本語訳は、「だろう」となる(例:「It will rain tomorrow. 明日は雨が降るだろう」)。

In summary, the future tense in English language, while being expressed by the addition of the same auxiliary verb "will" before the root form of a verb, is divided into "volitional future"="つもりだ(TSUMORI DA)" and "simply expected(non-volitional) future"="だろう(DAROU)". In actual Japanese, volitional future is no different from the present tense, usually used without "つもりだ(TSUMORI DA)", and non-volitional future can often be used without "だろう(DAROU)" in case there is some temporal adverb to show that the sentence develops in the future, making it virtually identical with the present tense, too.

- English past tense has so many variations that conscious memorizing process is required -

In Japanese language, the past tense can quite simply be expressed by modifying the DOUSHI(verb) with such inflections as "た(TA)", "だ(DA)" or "した(SHITA)": eg. "He says so:彼はそう言う(KAREWA SOU IU) into He said so:彼はそう言った(KARE WA SOU ITTA)", "She dies:彼女は死ぬ(KANOJO WA SHINU) into She died:彼女は死んだ(KANOJO WA SHINDA)" or "We evacuate:我々は避難する(WAREWARE WA HINAN SURU) into We evacuated:我々は避難した(WAREWARE WA HINAN SHITA)". But in English, while most verbs can signify the past tense by the simple addition of "d" or "ed" at the end of its root form (規則変化:KISOKU-HENKA: regular conjugation), some verbs must take completely different forms (不規則変化:FUKISOKU-HENKA: irregular conjugation) to be used in the past tense (namely, the past form), in the perfect tense or in the passive voice (viz the past participle). Although their variations must respectively be memorized, they can loosely be grouped into the following four patterns:

(1)A - B - B: the past form and the past participle take the same form

eg. catch - caught - caught, hear - heard - heard, sit - sat - sat

(2)A - B - C: the past form and the past participle take different forms

eg. break - broke - broken, fall - fell - fallen, lie - lay - lain

(3)A - B - A: the present and the past participle take the same form

eg. become - became - become, come - came - come, run - ran – run

(4)A - A - A: the present, the past and the past participle all take the same form

eg. cut - cut - cut, let - let - let, read - read - read

かいつまんで言うと、英語の「未来」時制は、動詞原形の前に助動詞“will”を付け足すだけで表現されるが、更に「意志未来＝つもりだ」／「単なる想定上の未来(無意志未来)＝だろう」の2つに区分される。実際の日本語では、「意志未来」はふつう「つもりだ」抜きで使うので「現在時制」と何ら変わりはなく、「無意志未来」の場合でもその文章が未来の時点で展開することを示す「時の副詞」が含まれていれば「だろう」抜きで使うこともしばしばだから、これまたやはり「現在時制」と変わらない。

－英語の「過去時制」の形態変化は多種多様；なので意識して記憶する必要あり－

日本語で「過去時制」を表わす場合、動詞の語尾を「た／だ／した」等の語尾変化で修正するだけでよい。例を挙げれば、“He says so.:彼はそう言う”を“He said so.:彼はそう言＜った＞”に、“She dies.:彼女は死ぬ”を“She died.:彼女は死＜んだ＞”に、“We evacuate.:我々は避難する”を”We evacuated.:我々は避難＜した＞”に、といった具合である。これに対し、英語の場合、多くの動詞はその原形(the root form)の末尾に“d”または“ed”を付けるだけで「過去時制」を表わせる(＝規則変化: regular conjugation)一方で、一部の動詞では、「過去時制」で用いる「過去形」と「完了時制／受動態」で用いる「過去分詞形」とで、まるで異なる形態を取らねばならない(＝不規則変化:irregular conjugation)。こうした「過去形／過去分詞形」の形態変化はそれぞれ個別的に暗記せねばならないものであるが、大まかに分類すれば、以下の4種に区分することができる:

(1) A-B-Bパターン: 「過去形」と「過去分詞形」が同じ形態を取る

例 catch - caught - caught, hear - heard - heard, sit - sat - sat

(2) A-B-Cパターン: 「過去形」と「過去分詞形」が異なる形態を取る

例 break - broke - broken, fall - fell - fallen, lie - lay - lain

(3) A-B-Aパターン: 「現在形」と「過去分詞形」が同じ形態を取る

例 become - became - become, come - came - come, run - ran - run

(4) A-A-Aパターン: 「現在形」「過去形」「過去分詞形」が全て同じ形態を取る

例 cut - cut - cut, let - let - let, read - read - read

The more detailed list of these irregular conjugations can be found in most reference books or dictionaries. Now that you have known why it is necessary to learn them by heart, to make clear the temporal distinctions, do memorize them all by rhythmically singing "ring - rang - rung, sing - sang - sung, sink - sank - sunk[en], etc, etc..."

- Chinese language does not even have the past form -

Although Japanese language is structurally different from Chinese language, it borrows from Chinese its ideographic writing system: "漢字(KANJI=Chinese characters)". But, unlike Chinese, Japanese language is not composed solely of KANJI: it also has "かな(仮名:KANA)", phonographic writing system originally invented from Chinese characters in ancient Japan. It is this latter, KANA, which makes it possible for Japanese to act like English in its inflection to differentiate the present tense from the past, as seen in the examples "私は働く(WATASHI WA HATARAKU: I work)" and "私は働いた(WATASHI WA HATARAITA: I worked)". In this case, the addition of the KANA "た(TA)" functions as a symbol of the past, just like in English "ed" signifies the past tense.

But in the case of Chinese which is totally ideographic without any phonographic supplement for making inflection, verbs can't show any distinction between the present, the past and the future. A Chinese "我働" can mean either "I work (the present)", "I worked (the past)" or "I will work (the future)" in the same form, the distinction of which must be made from contextual judgment. More specifically, the Chinese character "了(LA)" works to signify either "the past"(過去:KAKO: I worked) or "the perfect"(完了:KANRYOU: I have worked) context, but it is merely a temporal adverb — a Chinese equivalent to "in the past" or "already" in English, not an inflected form of a verb. Verbs themselves can never change in Chinese language, due to the purely ideographic structure of their writing system.

こうした「不規則変化」については、たいていの参考書や辞書を開けばより詳細な一覧表が見つかるだろう。それらを覚え込まねばならない理由がわかったからには、時制の区分を明瞭に付けるために、“ring－rang－rung, sing－sang－sung, sink－sank－sunk[en]”みたいな感じで、不規則変化表はぜんぶリズムに乗せて口ずさみながら覚え込んでしまおう。

－中国語には「過去形」すら存在しない－

日本語は中国語とは構造的に異なる言語だが、日本語の「表意文字」による表記体系は、中国語からの借り物（＝漢字）である。しかしながら、中国語とは異なり、日本語は「漢字」のみから成るわけではない。日本語はまた、古代日本が中国語を元に独自に発明した「表音文字」による表記法（＝仮名：かな）をも有している。日本語が英語に似た語尾変化によって「現在時制（例：私は働く:I work）」と「過去時制（私は働いた:I worked）」を区分することが出来るのは、この後者（＝カナ）のおかげである。先の例で言えば、仮名文字“た”が「過去」の記号として機能しており、これは英語の末尾“ed”が「過去時制」を表わすのと全く同様である。

だが、「表音記号」を補って語尾変化を生じることが出来ない「全面的表意言語」である中国語の場合、動詞が「現在／過去／未来」の区別を表わすことは不可能である。中国語で「我働」と書けば、全く同一の形態で“私は働く:I work(現在)”／“私は働いた:I worked(過去)”／“私は働くつもりだ:I will work(未来)”のいずれかを表わすことになり、そのどれを表わしているかの区分は文脈から判断する必要がある。より具体的に言えば、中国語では「了（ラ）」の文字が「the past(過去:I worked)」または「the perfect(完了:I have worked)」のいずれかの脈絡を表わす記号となるのだが、この「了」は単なる「時の副詞」であり、“in the past:過去に於いて”または“already:既にもう”という英語表現の中国語版に過ぎず、「動詞」の末尾が語尾変化したものではない。中国語の表記形態はひたすら「表意文字」であるために、「動詞そのもの」の形態変化は不可能なのである。

In Japanese, the presence of KANA can modify "我働" into "我ハ働ク(WARE WA HATARAKU:I work)" or "我働カン(WARE HATARAKAN: I will work)" or "我働ケリ(WARE HATARAKERI: I worked, or I have worked)" as is well-known to all Japanese folks with ordinary educational background enough to have been painfully trained in "漢文(KANBUN, locally modified Chinese sentences)" at school.

Anyway, temporal distinctions are where the speakers of Chinese and Japanese languages need special attention and getting used to; they should be examined in more detail in the next section.

日本語の場合、「仮名」が存在するおかげで、「漢文(＝日本独自の形に修正された中国の文章)」をヒイヒイ言いながら学校で教え込まれた経験のある日本の普通の教養人なら誰もが知っている通り、「我働」を「我ハ働ク:I work」や「我働カン:I will work」や「我働ケリ:I worked / I have worked」に微調整できるわけである。

とにもかくにも、時制の区分は、中国語や日本語を話す人々の場合、特別な注意を払って習熟せねばならない領域である・・・ので、次項で更に詳しく吟味してみるのがよさそうだ。

4. The past and the future are equal with everyone, only the present divides us apart

- The gender-free characteristic of English -

Compared with such old Indo-European languages as French, Spanish or Italian, English language is relatively new. While taking over lots of linguistic elements from those traditional languages, English has given up lots of complexities of other European languages, making it far easier to master for foreign speakers.

Let's take French, for example, to see how simpler English grammar is. All examples below develop in the present tense and are shown in French/English combination.

The first point to consider is the absence of gender in English language.

Il est un monsieur. / He is a gentleman.

Elle est une fille. / She is a girl.

See the French difference between “un” and “une” according to the gender of the noun coming after them, as opposed to the fixed “a” of English indefinite article.

Il est le monsieur. / He is the gentleman.

Elle est la fille. / She is the girl.

Definite article is always “the” same in English, while French language coordinates “le” and “la” with the gender of the noun they modify.

Il est grand. / He is tall.

Elle est grande. / She is tall.

Take notice of the English adjective “tall” being “grand” or “grande” in French according to the gender of the subject. This sexual difference at the end of the same word is also seen in one's name: while “Jean” is a man, “Jeanne” is a woman.

In French language, each and every noun has its 性(SEI: gender) — “男性(DANSEI: masculine)” or “女性(JOSEI: feminine)”. It seems quite natural that “彼(KARE: il=he)” or “彼女(KANOJO: elle=she)” has gender, masculine or feminine, but even such apparently neuter nouns as “太陽(TAIYOU: the sun: masculine : le soleil)” and “月(TSUKI: the moon: feminine : la lune)”

4. 過去と未来は誰もが平等、現在のみが我等を分かつ

－男性・女性の「性別」がない英語の特性－

フランス語やスペイン語・イタリア語といった長い歴史を持つインド・ヨーロッパ言語に比べると、英語は比較的新しい言語である。これら伝統的諸言語から幾多の言語要素を引き継ぎつつも、英語は、他の西欧言語に特有の複雑な特性の多くを捨て去ることで、外国人にも遙かに修得し易い言語となっている。

例としてフランス語と引き比べる形で、英語の文法がいかに単純かを見てみることにしよう。以下に示す例文はみな「現在時制」で展開し、フランス語の後に英語を配する形で示してある。

最初の考慮点は、英語に於ける言語学的「性別」の不在である。

Il est un monsieur. / He is a gentleman.　彼は紳士だ

Elle est une fille. / She is a girl.　彼女は少女だ

注目してほしいのは、フランス語では直後の名詞の性別に応じて“un”と“une”の違いがあるのに対し、英語の不定冠詞の方は“a”で固定されている点である。

Il est le monsieur. / He is the gentleman.　彼が例の紳士だ

Elle est la fille. / She is the girl.　彼女が例の少女だ

定冠詞の場合、英語では常に“the”であるのに対し、フランス語ではその定冠詞が掛かる先の名詞の性別に応じて“le”あるいは“la”へと形が変わっている。

Il est grand. / He is tall.　彼は背が高い

Elle est grande. / She is tall.　彼女は背が高い

英語の形容詞“tall”が、フランス語になると主語の性別に応じて“grand”あるいは“grande”と形を変える点に注目。同一単語の語尾に於けるこうした性差は、人物の名前にも見られる：“Jean:ジャン”は男／“Jeanne:ジャンヌ”は女、といった具合である。

フランス語に於いては、一つ一つ全ての名詞に「性(gender)＝男性(masculine)／女性(feminine)」の違いがある。“彼:il=he”や“彼女:elle=she”といった語に「男性／女性」の性別があるのは至極自然に感じるが、“太陽:the sun:男性:le soleil”だの“月:the moon:女性:la lune”といった一見「中性的」な名詞でさえそれぞれ独自の性別を持って

have their own genders. The same adjective "背が高い(SE GA TAKAI: tall)" changes shapes according to the gender of the noun it modifies ("grand" for masculine pronounced as "GU_RAN" / "grande" for feminine pronounced as "GU_RAN_D"), even "不定冠詞(FUTEIKANSHI: indefinite articles: un/une... French equivalent of "a/an")" and "定冠詞(TEIKANSHI: definite articles: le/la... "the" in English)" are all gender-sensitive.

It follows from this that learners of French language has to memorize each and every noun along with his/her gender respectively...! English learners are free from such mnemonic nightmare, for grammatical gender is extinct in English. Although English indefinite article "an" is similar to French "un" (both meaning "one"), when it was found that "an" before "子音(SHIIN: consonants)" sounded rather mouthful (ng. "an man"), English bluntly gave up the original form of "an" and cut it down into "a" (eg. "a man"), with the result that there is no such English as "There is an man" (although it is possible to say "There is one man").

The only case English still uses the indefinite article "an" is before "母音(BOIN: vowels, not in spelling but in pronunciation)", such as "I have an appointment with an FBI agent". Beware of "an FBI agent" not being "a FBI agent"; if it's CIA, "an appointment with a CIA agent" will be just fine. Thus, the different use in English of "a" and "an" is solely determined by pronunciation, which can be decided without any difficulty, not according to the gender of the noun coming after "a/an" (or should we say "un/une"), which can never be correctly dealt with without remembering whether it's a "he" or "she". How studiously students of French must study!... Tough luck for them, and thank our lucky stars.

As for the English definite article "the", it can be indiscriminately used before any noun, quite unlike the French "le/la". The only difference English "the" can make is the three variations in its pronunciation ("ZI" only difference English "ZEE" can make is "ZA" three variations in its pronunciation). See how simple English is (or how complicated French is)?

いるのである。全く同一の形容詞「背が高い:tall」であっても、その修飾する名詞の性別に応じて形態を変える(男性用だと“grand:グラン”／女性用だと“grande:グランド”)。不定冠詞(英語の“a/an”に相当するフランス語の“un/une”)や定冠詞(英語の“the”に相当する仏語の“le/la”)ですら、全てみな「性別に応じての形態変化」を伴うのだ。

これ即ち、フランス語を学ぼうという人達は、個々の「名詞」を覚える際にはそれぞれが「男性／女性」いずれの性別に属するかをも同時に、一つ一つ別々に、覚え込まねばならない、ということになるわけである．．．！　こういう暗記に伴う悪夢のような作業は、英語学習者には必要ない:英語では「文法上の性別」は廃止されて跡形もないからである。英語の不定冠詞の“an:アン”はフランス語の“un:アン”に似ていて、どちらもその意味するところは“one:ワン＝1つの”であるが、「子音(consonants)」の前に“an”を置くと発音が口幅ったい(悪い例　“an man:アン・マン”)とわかった時点で英語はあっさりとその本来“an:アン”だった形を放棄して“a:ア”の形へと切り詰めた(例　“a man:ア・マン”)ので、その結果、英語にはもう“There is ＜an man＞.”のような表現はない(“There is ＜one man＞.:男が一人いる”と言うことは可能ではあるが)。

英語が今もなお不定冠詞に“an”を使う唯一の場面は「母音(vowels:但し、発音上の母音であって綴り字上の母音ではない)」の直前のみ:例えば“I have an appointment with an FBI agent.:FBIの秘密情報員と約束がある”といった場合である。“＜an＞ FBI agent:アヌ・エフビーアィ・エィジェント”であって“＜a＞ FBI agent:あ・えふびーあい・えーじぇんと”でない点に要注意;もしこれが“CIA”であれば、“an appointment with ＜a CIA agent:ア・シーアィエィ・エィジェント＞”で全く問題ない。このように、英語に於ける“a”と“an”の違いはもっぱら「発音」により決するものであって、“a/an”の(というか“un/une”の、と言うべきか？)直後に来る名詞の「性別」に応じて決まるものではないのだから、何の苦もなく“a”か“an”か決められる。これが性別感応型の変化だと、“男性”なのか“女性”なのかを覚えていない限り正しい決定など絶対に出来ないので、フランス語を学ぶ生徒の場合はそれはもう律儀に勉強しないといけないわけである・・・彼らには「お気の毒に」といった感じだが、英語を学ぶ我々としては「あぁよかった」と安堵の胸をなでおろしてよい話であろう。

英語の定冠詞“the”に関しては、フランス語の“le/la”とは全然違って、どんな名詞の前だろうがお構いなしに使ってよい語句である。英語の“the”に関してあり得る唯一の相違は、発音に見られる3つのバリエーションの違い(母音の前では短く“ズィ”／“the”という単語そのものを発音する際には長く“ズィー”／子音の前では“ザ”、と読む)だけである。英語がいかに単純か(あるいは、フランス語がいかに複雑か)、おわかりいただけたであろうか？

- English "be" is the most complicated of its kin, but is far simpler than its French counterpart -

Let us proceed to check the possible variation of what we call "be verb" in English in comparison with French: you will easily see how complicated French verbs can be according to the gender and number of subjects.

The 1st person (singular): Je suis a la TAMAGAWA JOUSUI. / I am at the edge of Tamagawa waterworks.

The 1st person (plural): Nous sommes a la TAMAGAWA JOUSUI. / We are at the edge of Tamagawa waterworks.

The 2nd person (singular): Tu es a la TAMAGAWA JOUSUI. / You are at the edge of Tamagawa waterworks.

The 2nd person (plural): Vous êtes a la TAMAGAWA JOUSUI. / You are at the edge of Tamagawa waterworks.

The 3rd person (singular masculine or impersonal):Il est a la TAMAGAWA JOUSUI. / He is at the edge of Tamagawa waterworks. / It is at the edge of Tamagawa waterworks.

The 3rd person (singular feminine): Elle est a la TAMAGAWA JOUSUI. / She is at the edge of Tamagawa waterworks.

The 3rd person (plural whether masculine or famine): Ils sont a la TAMAGAWA JOUSUI. / Elles sont a la TAMAGAWA JOUSUI. / They are at the edge of Tamagawa waterworks.

The rule for "be verb" in English is quite simple: if the subject is plural(We, You, They), use "are"(We are, You are, They are); if the subject is singular(He, She, It, I), use "is"(He is, She is, It is) with the sole exception of the 1st person accompanying "am"(I am). While in French language, the grandiose varieties of "suis, es, est"(singular) and "sommes, êtes, sont"(plural) must be handled meticulously according to the gender and number of the subject.

Such forbidding perplexities will be felt to be nothing, to be sure, once one gets acquainted with their use by practice after practice after years of practice. But the presence of gender-specific expressions shown above will be more than enough to convince you of the relative ease with which you could master the gender-free language of English, as opposed to French, Spanish or Italian which are all gender-sensitive.

ー英語の"be"は英語の動詞中では最も複雑、だが、フランス語版の"be 動詞"に比べれば遙かに単純ー

次は、いわゆる"be 動詞"というやつの取り得る形態変化について、英語とフランス語を比較対照してみよう:主語の「性別」及び「数」に応じてのフランス語動詞の変化の複雑さが、容易にわかるはずである。

一人称(The 1st person)単数(singular): 私は玉川上水にいます

Je suis a la TAMAGAWA JOUSUI. / I am at the edge of Tamagawa waterworks.

一人称(The 1st person)複数(plural): 我々は玉川上水にいます

Nous sommes a la TAMAGAWA JOUSUI. / We are at the edge of Tamagawa waterworks.

二人称(The 2nd person)単数(singular): あなたは玉川上水にいます

Tu es a la TAMAGAWA JOUSUI. / You are at the edge of Tamagawa waterworks.

二人称(The 2nd person)複数(plural): あなたがたは玉川上水にいます

Vous êtes a la TAMAGAWA JOUSUI. / You are at the edge of Tamagawa waterworks.

三人称(The 3rd person)単数男性・または非人称単数(singular masculine or impersonal): 彼(それ)は玉川上水にいます

Il est a la TAMAGAWA JOUSUI. / He is at the edge of Tamagawa waterworks. / It is at the edge of Tamagawa waterworks.

三人称(The 3rd person)単数女性(singular feminine): 彼女は玉川上水にいます

Elle est a la TAMAGAWA JOUSUI. / She is at the edge of Tamagawa waterworks.

三人称(The 3rd person)複数・男女問わず(plural whether masculine or famine): 彼らは玉川上水にいます

Ils sont a la TAMAGAWA JOUSUI. / Elles sont a la TAMAGAWA JOUSUI. / They are at the edge of Tamagawa waterworks.

英語に於ける"be 動詞"の規則は単純そのものである:もし主語が複数(We, You, They)ならば"are"(We are, You are, They are)を使えばよい;もし主語が単数(He, She, It, I)ならば"is"(He is, She is, It is)を使えばよいが、唯一の例外として、一人称の場合だけは"am"(I am)を使う・・・ただそれだけのことである。一方、フランス語では"suis, es, est"(単数の場合)及び"sommes, êtes, sont"(複数の場合)の壮大なる取り合わせの数々を、主語の「性」及び「数」に応じて几帳面にやりくりせねばならないわけである。

人を寄せ付けぬまでにややこしいこの種の複雑性も、何年も何年も練習に練習を重ねた末にその用法に習熟してしまえば、物の数ではない、ということになるかもしれない・・・が、上に示したような「性別ごとに異なる」表現の存在を見ただけでもう、フランス語・スペイン語・イタリア語といった(どれも「性別感応型」の)言語に比べ、性差のない英語という言語を習得するのがいかに容易なことか、はっきり実感できるはずである。

- English "be" is simple enough: "do" is simpler still -

While "be verb" in English has three possible forms(am/is/are) according to the subject, "do verbs" have only two forms: "do" or "does". All "do" verbs should basically be used in its "root form", a form written on the dictionary, with the only exception of the subject being in the 3rd person, singular and in the present tense, namely, "He/She/It": these three subjects, and these 3 only, demand that the "do" verb be inflected in the form of "does": eg. "I/We/You/They <think> so. He/She/It <thinks> otherwise".

- Apart from the present tense, all English verbs are perfectly equal in the past and the future -

Here is another piece of good news about English: such variations as "am/is/are"(be verb) or "do/does"(do verb) do not exist in the past and the future tenses of English language: inequality only exists in "the present"... how idealistically wonderful it sounds! There is perfect equality in the future and even in the past in the world of English!... Ooops! I've made a mistake: "perfect" equality does not exist in everything that is "not in the present tense", for "the present perfect tense" consists of such varied forms as "I/We/You/They <have> made a mistake" or "He/She/It <has> made a mistake". But then again, from grammatical point of view, "the present perfect tense" belongs not to the past but to the present, so that the "inequality exists only in the present tense" theory still holds true.

In the future or the past tenses, you don't have to worry about how to change the forms of English verbs according to the gender and number of subjects... Good news, isn't it? In the future tense, you don't have to make any change in the verbs and have only to add "will" immediately before them to make "I/We/You/They/He/She/It will make a mistake"!... Too simple to make any mistakes, don't you think?

The bad news is, although English verbs don't have to change their shapes according to the gender or number of subjects in the past and future tenses, there are three(3) cases where verbs have to take two(2) forms different from the root form. That is to say, (1)when used in the past, verbs have to take "過去形(KAKO-KEI=the past form: "made" as opposed to "make")"; (2)when

－英語の“be 動詞”も十分単純だが、“do 動詞”はもっと単純－

英語の“be 動詞”は主語に応じて3つの形態(am/is/are)があり得るのに対し、“do 動詞”には“do”か“does”かの2つの形態しかない。全ての“do”動詞は「原形(the root form)＝辞書に掲載されている形」で用いるのが基本だが、主語が「三人称・単数・現在」即ち“He/She/It”の場合だけは例外である：これら3つの主語(だけ)は、“do”動詞の語尾を“does”の形へと形態変化させる必要がある。例えば、“I/We/You/They ＜think＞ so.：私/我々/あなた(がた)/彼らはそう考える”のに対して“He/She/It ＜thinks＞ otherwise.：彼/彼女/それはそうは考えない”といった具合である。

－「現在」を除けば、英語の動詞は「過去」も「未来」も全て完璧に平等－

英語に関しては更にまた耳寄りな話がある。“am/is/are”(be 動詞)だの“do/does”(do 動詞)だのといった形態変化は、英語の「過去」や「未来」の時制中には全く存在しない：不平等が存在するのは唯一「現在」時制のみである・・・おぉ、何と理想的なその響き！　英語の「未来」には(否、「過去」にさえ)完璧なる平等が存在するのである！・・・ぉっと！　ちょい、間違えた：「パーフェクトな」平等性が「現在時制以外」の全てに存在する、というわけではないのだった：というのも、「現在完了形(the present perfect tense)」という時制は“I/We/You/They ＜have＞ made a mistake.：私/我々/君(たち)/彼らは間違いを犯した”あるいは“He/She/It ＜has＞ made a mistake.：彼/彼女/それは間違いを犯した”といった異なる形態の表現から成る「現在時制以外」の時制なわけだから。しかし、よくよく考えてみれば、文法的見地から言って「現在完了形」は「過去」ではなく「現在」の時制に属するものであるから、「不平等は現在時制の中にのみ存在する」という理屈は、相変わらず、成立するわけである。

「未来」あるいは「過去」時制の中では、英語の動詞を主語の「性」や「数」に応じてどのように変化させたらよいか、などと心配する必要はないのである．．．耳寄りな話であろう？　「未来」時制に於いては、動詞そのものには何の手も加えずにただ単にその直前に“will”を加えるだけで“I/We/You/They/He/She/It will make a mistake.：私/我々/君(たち)/彼ら/彼/彼女/それは間違いを犯すだろう”となるわけである！．．．単純すぎて間違いなど犯しようもない話、だとは思われまいか？

ここで耳の痛い話も少々・・・英語の動詞は「過去」と「未来」の時制の中では主語の「性・数」に合わせて形態変化する必要はないものの、動詞がその「原形」とは異なる(2種類の)形態を取らねばならぬ場合が3つほどある。即ち、(1)「過去(the past tense)」に用いる場合には、動詞の「過去形(the past form：例　“make”に対する“made”)」を使わねばならない；(2)「受動態(the passive voice)」で用いる場合には、

used in "受動態(JUDOUTAI=the passive voice)", verbs have to take "過去分詞形(KAKOBUNSHI-KEI=the past participle: "made" not "make")" preceded by "is/am/are/was/were/will be: eg. A mistake will be made"; and (3)when used in "完了形(KANRYOU-KEI=the perfect tense)", verbs have to take "過去分詞形(KAKOBUNSHI-KEI=the past participle: not "make" but "made") " preceded by "have/has/had/will have: eg. He had made enough mistakes to be fired".

Take the example of "making a mistake", again, so that there'll be no mistake in your perception of English inflection in various tenses.

未来(the future tense):

I/We/You/They/He/She/It will make a mistake.

過去(the past tense):

I/We/You/They/He/She/It made a mistake.

現在(the present tense):

三単現(SAN-TAN-GEN: the 3rd person, singular and the present):

He/She/It makes a mistake.

三単現以外の現在(the present in general = other than SAN-TAN-GEN):

I/We/You/They make a mistake.

In the past and future tenses, the gender or number of the subject has no influence on the form of the verb. The only tense you have to pay special attention to is "the present", but the rule is rather simple. With the exception of "三単現(SAN-TAN-GEN: the 3rd person, singular and the present)" requiring the inflection of "s/es" at the end of the "root form" of the verb, all English verbs (except "be verb: am/is/are") take the same form — the one appearing on the dictionary, called the "root form=原形:GENKEI".

- To master the general rule, conquer the exceptions -

There is an English proverb which says "The exception proves the general rule": to say "this is an exception" is to say "except for this (or these), everything else follows the same general rule". In the case above, the general rule that all "do verbs" take the "root form" in the present tense holds true with the sole exception of SAN-TAN-GEN(the third person, singular and the present) taking "s/es" inflection.

動詞の「過去分詞形(the past participle:例 “make”ではなく“made”)」を“is, am, are, was, were, will be”の後に置いて“A mistake will be made.:間違いが犯されるだろう”のような形で使わねばならない;(3)「完了形(the perfect tense)」で用いる場合には、動詞の「過去分詞形(the past participle:例 “make”ではなく“made”)」を“have, has, had, will have”の後に置いて“He had made enough mistakes to be fired.:彼は解雇されるまでに既に、クビにされても仕方ないほどたくさんの間違いを犯していた”のような形で使わねばならない。

ここでもやはり“making a mistake:間違いを犯すこと”を例に取って、様々な時制の中での英語の語尾変化について、間違いを犯すことのないようしっかり認識しておこう。

未来(the future tense):

I/We/You/They/He/She/It will make a mistake.

私/我々/あなた(がた)/彼ら/彼/彼女/それは間違いを犯すだろう

過去(the past tense):

I/We/You/They/He/She/It made a mistake.

私/我々/あなた(がた)/彼ら/彼/彼女/それは間違いを犯した

現在(the present tense):

三単現(三人称・単数・現在:the 3rd person, singular and the present):

He/She/It makes a mistake.

彼ら/彼/彼女/それは間違いを犯す

三単現以外の現在(the present in general):

I/We/You/They make a mistake.

私/我々/あなた(がた)/彼らは間違いを犯す

「過去」と「未来」の時制では、主語の「性・数」は動詞の形態に何の影響も及ぼさない。特別な注意を払うべき時制は「現在」のみである;が、「現在」時制のルールも至極単純である。「三単現＝三人称・単数・現在」の場合のみ動詞の原形(the root form)の語尾に“s/es”の語尾変化を求められるのを唯一の例外として、英語の動詞はすべて(と言っても“be 動詞”の“am/is/are”は例外だが)全く同一の形態、即ち、辞書に掲載されているあの形(「原形」と呼ばれる形態)を取るのである。

ー一般原則を修得するには、例外を征すべしー

英語の格言に「The exception proves the general rule.:例外は一般原則を証明する」というのがある。「これは例外である」と言うのは「この(または、これらの)例外を除いて、その他全ては同一の一般原則に従う」と言うのに等しい。上述の場合で言えば「三単現(三人称・単数・現在)が“s/es”の語尾変化を取る」という場合を唯一の例外として、一般原則「全ての“do 動詞”は、現在形では“原形”を取る」が成立しているわけだ。

In such cases, you have only to pay special attention to the exception, and the rest can be collectively dealt with as the general case. For example, the statement "To those who have passed the test, we'll give a phone call by Friday" contains the general message that "those who have not passed the test will never get a phone call from us by Friday", which also means "if you don't receive a phone call from us by Friday, be advised that you have failed the test". In this case, the exception is "receiving a phone call from us by Friday in case of passing the test" and the general rule is that "we will make no phone call by Friday to those who failed the test". General rule (making no phone call by Friday) is automatically proved by the existence of the exception (making a phone call by Friday).

This "Exception proves the general rule" formula is so important and handy that let us coin an original verb/noun "EXPROGER"(by Jaugo Noto, 2012) and put it to good use (free of charge, of course). In the case above, "SAN-TAN-GEN's s/es" EXPROGERS that "all English do-verbs in the present tense be used in the root form, without any inflection".

Still uncertain how to use "exproger"?... OK, then, how about this: "He is quite an exceptional Japanese who has command of English": if "he", who can command English, is quite exceptional as a Japanese, it follows that Japanese people in general have no command of English. "His exceptional command of English" has "exprogered" the general rule that "the Japanese folks cannot command English".

It is quite important for an English learner to be a good EXPROGERER, since the abundance of exceptions, or unique deviation from the general rule, is one of the notable characteristics of English language in comparison with such rigidly formal languages as French or Spanish.

- No EXPROGER needed for English future tense -

Where there is no exception, there is no proving the general rule by the exception. The future tense in English language is totally ruled by the simple principle that all verbs be preceded (in the "root form") by the auxiliary verb "will"... Well, there might appear to be an exception: in British or legal English, "shall" instead of "will" will often be used. But most of those "shall"s

こういう場合、特別な注意を払う必要があるのは唯一「例外」のみであり、それ以外の事例はまとめて「一般的事例」として取り扱えばよいだけの話である。例えば、「試験に合格した人達には金曜日までに電話します」と言った場合、「試験に合格しなかった人達には金曜日までに電話はしません」という意味内容を含み、同時にまた「金曜日までに電話がなければ、あなたは落第したものとお考えください」という意味をも表わしている。この場合、「試験に合格した場合には金曜日までに電話がある」というのが例外であり、「試験不合格者には金曜日までに電話することはない」というのが一般原則ということになる。一般原則(金曜日までに電話しない)の存在は、例外(金曜日までに電話する)の存在によって自動的に証明されているわけである。

この「例外により一般原則を証明する」方式はとても重要かつ便利なものなので、ここで我々も独自に"**EXPROGER**(...**EX**ception **PRO**ves the **GE**neral **R**ule)"なる「動詞/名詞」共用語を発明して(発明者=之人冗悟:2012年)、この語を便利に活用したいと思う(無論、使用料はタダである)。上述の場合、「三単現の"s/es"」は、「現在時制では、全ての英語の"do 動詞"は、原形で、語尾変化なしで使用のこと」という一般原則を、例外の側から証明している(EXPROGER している)ことになる。

"exproger"の使い方、まだピンと来ないであろうか?・・・よろしい、それではこんな文章はどうであろう:「彼は英語を駆使できる極めて稀な日本人である」:もし「彼(この人、英語が駆使できる)」が日本人としては極めて例外的だとすれば、「日本人は一般的に英語が駆使できない」ということになる。「彼の持つ例外的な英語駆使能力」が「日本人に英語の駆使能力はない」という一般原則を「exproger:例外の側から証明した」わけである。

例外の豊富さというか、一般原則からの珍しい逸脱例の多さというか、そのあたりが(フランス語やスペイン語等の厳格に形式的な言語と比較した際の)英語という言語の際立つ特徴の一つだから、英語学習者の場合、「EXPROGER の達人=例外の側から一般原則を解き明かすのが上手な人」となることが極めて重要なのである。

ー英語の「未来」時制にEXPROGER(例外からの一般原則証明)の必要なしー

例外が存在しない場面では、例外の側から一般原則を証明してみせる芸当は成立しない。英語の「未来」時制に於いては、「全ての動詞(の原形)の直前に助動詞"will"を置くこと」という単純明快な原則だけが支配する...もっとも、一つだけ例外っぽく見えないでもない例があって、「イギリス英語または法律英語の中では、"will"ではなく"shall"が使われる場合がしばしばある」のである;が、そうした"shall"の大部分は"will" could safely be substituted with "will"s. The use of "shall" to signify the future tense is not to be seen as an exception to the general rule, but as a special feature of British or legal English, only to be learnt by advanced speakers of English, not by novice learners.

- Past form and the past participle must be conquered by EXPROGER -

In the past tense, all English verbs take "過去形(KAKO-KEI=the past form: eg. "I finished/did my homework")"; in expressing the meaning of "受身(UKEMI=passive)", all English verbs take "過去分詞形(KAKO-BUNSHI-KEI=the past participle: eg. "His homework was actually finished/done by his sister")"; and when expressing the meaning of "完了(KANRYOU=perfect)", all English verbs also take "過去分詞形(KAKO-BUNSHI-KEI=the past participle: eg. "Have you finished/done your homework yet?")". The shape of the past form and the past participle are not influenced by the gender or number of subjects, always used in the same form, whether the subjects are "I/We/You/They/He/She or It". Simple, right?... Well, simple enough if all English past forms and past participles were created equal according to the single general principle.

In fact, the general rule of English as regards the past form and the past participle, namely, "d/ed added to the end of the root form of a verb"(eg. "finish - finished - finished") must be EXPROGERED by so many exceptionally formed past forms and past participles (like "do - did - done") that the long daunting list of such irregularly shaped past forms and past participles (called "不規則変化:FUKISOKU-HENKA=irregular conjugation") is one of the first ordeals all English learners stumble upon (and not a few never stand up again).

But this irregular conjugation is the only realm of English where each and every verb demands respective memorization of its unique forms (past form/past participle): other than those exceptional English verbs should simply be added "d/ed" at the end to form regular conjugations of the past form and past participle. You have only to learn by heart the irregular conjugations to EXPROGER the regular conjugations; although the number of the former is quite a lot, the latter are too much more numerous to remember respectively.

で言い換えても問題はない。「未来」時制を表わすのに"shall"を用いるのは、一般原則に対する例外と見るべきではなく、イギリス／法律英語ならではの特徴とみなすべきであり、英語の上級者だけが修得すればよいものであって、初学者が修得を目指すべき事柄ではないと言える。

―「過去形」及び「過去分詞形」は「EXPROGER:例外を以て一般原則を征す」必要あり―

「過去」時制に於いては、英語の動詞はすべて「過去形:the past form:例 I finished/did my homework.:私は宿題をした」を取る必要がある;「受身(the passive voice)」を表わす場合、英語の動詞はすべて「過去分詞形:the past participle:例 His homework was actually finished/done by his sister.:彼の宿題は実際には彼の姉により行なわれた」を取る必要がある;「完了(the perfect tense)」の意味を表わす場合、英語の動詞はすべて「過去分詞形:the past participle:例 Have you finished/done your homework yet?:宿題はもう終えましたか？」を取る必要がある。「過去形」及び「過去分詞形」の形態は、主語が"I/We/You/They/He/She/It"のいずれであろうと、その主語の「性・数」には影響されず、常に同一の形態を取る。単純な話であろう？・・・というか、まぁ、実に単純なはずなのである・・・もし英語のすべての「過去形」／「過去分詞形」が「たった一つの一般原則」に従って平等の形で作られるものであるならば・・・。

ところがそう単純には行かないのが現実であって、「動詞の原形の末尾に"d/ed"を付け足せばよい」(例 finish - finished - finished)という「過去形／過去分詞形」に関する英語世界の一般原則は、"do - did -done"のような「例外的な形で」形成される「過去形／過去分詞形」の幾多の事例によって「EXPROGER:例外面から一般則を証明」する必要があり、こうした「不規則変化(irregular conjugation)」と呼ばれる特異な形の「過去形／過去分詞形」の長く恐ろしげな一覧表は、すべての英語学習者が真っ先につまづく(そして、少なからぬ人々が二度と再び起き上がらぬ)最初の試練の一つとなっている。

だが、この「不規則変化」というやつは、個々の動詞がその独自な変化形(過去形／過去分詞形)を一つ一つ個別的に暗記することを強要する例としては、英語世界で唯一の事例なのである:こうした例外的な英語の動詞を除き、他の全ての動詞はただ単にその末尾に"d/ed"を加えさえすれば「規則変化の過去形／過去分詞形」を形成できるのだ。学習者はただ「不規則変化の数々」を暗記しさえすれば「規則変化」の一般原則を「EXPROGER:例外側から制覇」できるのである・・・前者(＝不規則変化動詞)の数が極めて多いのは確かだが、後者(＝規則変化動詞)の方はそれより遙かに膨大なのだから、一般則の側を御丁寧に一つ一つ暗記するわけにも行くまい。

When the variation looks complicated, let your attitude be simple: just EXPROGER, and the general rule will take care of the rest. If you haven't learnt by heart a particular verb as belonging to the irregular conjugation, you should automatically consider it to belong to the regular conjugation: all you have to do to make the past form/past participle is to add “d” or “ed” at the end of its root form.

Conversely, you must pay such special attention to “the exception” (irregular conjugation) as to be able to declare any given case to be “the general” (regular conjugation) because you have never memorized it as “an exception”.

違いがたくさんあって複雑そうに見える場合、それに対する自分の態度の方を単純明快にすることである:ただ単に「EXPROGER:例外的な場合をまず最初におさえることで、一般原則の存在を浮かび上がらせる」だけでよい、そうすれば残りはすべて一般原則の方が勝手に片を付けてくれる。ある任意の動詞について、もし諸君がそれを「不規則変化する動詞」として暗記していないようならば、それは「規則変化する動詞」に属するもの、と自動的に判断すればよい:諸君はただ「その原形の末尾に"d"または"ed"を付け加える」だけで「過去形/過去分詞形」を形成すればそれでよいわけである。

逆に言えば、「例外(この場合は、不規則変化)」に対しては、諸君は特別な注意を払う必要がある。任意の動詞を見た時に「自分はこれを"例外(不規則変化)"として暗記した覚えはないのだから、これは"一般則(規則変化)"であるに違いない」と自信を持って言い切れるほどに、徹底的に特別な注意を払っておかねば、「EXPROGER:例外制覇による一般原則の証明」は不可能なわけである。

5. Lack of plurality in Japanese nouns

- All Japanese nouns are singular by nature -

The notion of "単数(TANSUU: singular)" and "複数(FUKUSUU: plural)" is yet another twilight zone for Japanese learners of English. In Japanese language, all nouns are innately felt to be "the singular"; consciously plural form of any given noun (which not a few foreign speakers of Japanese invariably make) sounds singularly strange to Japanese ears. No Japanese ever says "私の＜本たち＞のコレクションを御覧ください:WATASHI NO <HON TACHI> NO KOREKUSHON WO GORAN KUDASAI: Let me show you my collection of books". In Japanese consciousness, "本(a book)" is always to be used in the singular, never to be treated as the plural.

- Nouns are born "plural" in Japanese language -

Even in cases where a Japanese noun seems to be used in the plural form, like "友だち(TOMODACHI: friends)" or "子ども(KODOMO: children)", the fact is that such nouns are not recognized as the plural forms of "友(TOMO: a friend)" or "子(KO: a child)". You can easily verify this fact by such expressions as "彼は私の＜友だち＞です:KARE WA WATASHI NO <TOMODACHI> DESU: He is <a friend of mine>" or "彼女には＜子供＞が一人います:KANOJO NIWA <KODOMO> GA HITORI IMASU: She has <one child>". These Japanese sentences would be impossible if "TOMODACHI" or "KODOMO" were the plural forms of "TOMO" or "KO". Such apparently plural forms of nouns are actually not "plural"; they take those forms not in order to show plurality, but because the Japanese folks feel they should be used in those forms and nothing else. In the natural consciousness of Japanese people, plurality never exists in "TOMODACHI" or "KODOMO".

To English speakers, Japanese "plural" nouns look not unlike such English words as "corps" or "months" in which plurality is obscure to see or hear. But the reality about Japanese plurality is far stranger than the wildest imagination of English speakers: the number(singular/plural) of Japanese nouns are not changeable but fixed — seemingly plural nouns are simply born that way, not made so from some singular forms. "木々(KIGI: trees)"

5. 日本語名詞に複数なし

－日本語の名詞はすべて「単数形」として生まれる－

「単数(singular)」と「複数(plural)」という概念もまた、日本人の英語学習者にとっては謎の領域である。日本語では、全ての名詞は生まれながらにして「単数形」と感じられる。任意の名詞をわざと「複数形」にしてみると(外国人の多くは日本語を話す時にまず確実にこの芸当をするわけであるが)、日本人の耳には何とも奇妙に響くものである。日本人なら誰一人「私の＜本たち＞のコレクションを御覧ください」などとは言わない。日本人の意識の中では「本(英語だと“books”)」は常に「単数」で使うべきものであって、「複数」として取り扱って「本たち」とすることなどあり得ないのである。

－日本語の場合「複数形」の名詞は「生まれながらにしてその形」－

日本語の名詞が「複数形」で使われているように見える場合、例えば「友だち(friends)」や「子ども(children)」のような名詞の場合であっても、実際にはこうした名詞は「友(a friend)」や「子(a child)」といった「単数名詞が複数化したもの」として認識されてはいない。この事実を確認するのは簡単である・・・「彼は私の＜友だち＞です＝He is 〈a friend of mine〉.」とか「彼女には＜子ども＞が一人います＝She has 〈one child〉.」とかの表現を見るがよい：もし「友だち」や「子ども」が「友」や「子」の「複数形」だとしたら、こうした日本文が成立する道理がないであろう？　こういう一見「名詞の複数形」っぽい表現は、実際には「複数形」ではないのである。これらの名詞がその形態を取るのは、「複数であることを示すため」ではなく、「そういう形で用い、それ以外の形では用いないのが自然」だと日本人が感じているからこそなのである。日本人の自然な意識の中では、「友だち」や「子ども」の中に「複数性」は存在しないのだ。

英語人種の目から見ると、日本語の「複数」名詞は、見た目や聞いた感じではその複数性がはっきりとはわからない点で、“corps(部隊)”や“months(数ヶ月)”といった英単語に似ていなくもない。しかし、日本語に於ける「複数性」の実態はもっと遙かに風変わりであり、英語人種のどんな突飛な想像も及ばぬほど異様なものである：日本語の名詞の数(単数／複数)は、可変性のものではなく、固定されているのである・・・一見「複数形の」名詞に見えるものは、最初からその形で生まれて来るだけであって、何らかの「単数形から」複数化したものではないのである。「木々(trees)」なる語は生まれながらにして「木々」なのであり、「木(a tree)」の複数形というわけでは必ずしもないの

are born “KIGI”, not exactly the plural form of “木(KI: a tree)”; the fact that “森(MORI: a forest)” or “林(HAYASHI: a wood)” can never take the plural forms of “森森(MORIMORI)” or “森たち(MORITACHI)” or “林林(HAYASHIBAYASHI)” or “林たち(HAYASHITACHI)” goes to show that Japanese plurality is an innate attribute of a given noun: it just has to be memorized, not to be tinkered with.

- Suffixes for plurality or mentality? -

Theoretically speaking, to signify plurality, Japanese language has such suffixes as “たち:TACHI: eg. 君たち(KIMITACHI: you)” or “ら:RA: eg. 彼ら(KARERA: they)” or “ども:DOMO: eg. 私ども(WATAKUSHIDOMO: we)”. But these expressions were originally meant to show mental attitude of the speaker, not as differentiating symbols of plurality. Exceptionally cultured Japanese should know the terminological fact that “たち(達:TACHI)” in Japanese is exquisitely associated with “どち(DOCHI)” meaning “どうし(同士: friends, colleagues, comrades, one's company, kin)” signifying affectionate respect for a group of people referred to with “たち:TACHI”. Compared with this, the suffix “ら(等:RA)” is rather insulting in nature, dealing with a bunch of folks as nothing to be respectively treated with respect.

No ordinary Japanese ever says “彼たち(KARETACHI)” because the plural form of “彼(KARE: he)” has been traditionally fixed in Japanese as “彼ら(KARERA: they)”. Those who use “彼たち(KARETACHI)” are using that expression for three possible reasons: (1)since the plural form of “彼女(KANOJO: she)” is generally “彼女たち(KANOJOTACHI: they)”, the masculine plural form should also be “彼たち(KARETACHI: they)” from the standpoint of sexual equality — VIVA [WO]MEN'S LIB!; (2)when everyone else in Japan sticks to “彼ら(KARERA: they)”, the novel expression of “彼たち(KARETACHI: they)” should sound so unique as to make the speaker stand out among the crowd — COOL!; and (3)they simply didn't know the traditional Japanese expression “彼ら(KARERA: they)” and thought it just fine to add the suffix “たち(TACHI)” at the end of “彼(KARE: he)” to form the plural form of “彼たち(KARETACHI: they)” — BOO!

である。「森(a forest)」や「林(a wood)」が「森森」だの「森たち」だの「林林」だの「林たち」だのといった複数形態を取ることなどあり得ない、という事実は、日本語に於ける「複数性」は、任意の名詞が生まれながらにして持つ生得的特性である、という事実を証明している。こういう「生来の複数名詞」はただもう暗記するより他に仕方がないのであって、形をいじって「単数形／複数形」をこしらえ上げることなどできない代物なのである。

ーこの接尾語は、「複数」のため？「心的態度」のため？ー

理屈だけを言えば、「複数」を表わすための接尾語として、日本語には「たち(例　君たち＝you)」や「ら(例　彼ら＝they)」や「ども(例　わたくしども＝we)」のような語がある。が、これらの表現は本来、「話者の心的態度」を示すために生まれたものであって、「複数性を示すための差別化記号」として生まれたものではない。たぐいまれなる教養を持った日本人であれば、「達」なる日本語は「どち＝同士: friends, colleagues, comrades, one's company, kin」と微妙な形で関連しており、「たち」として言及される一群の人々に対する親愛の情を込めた敬意を表わす語である、という言語学的事実を知っていることであろう。この「たち」に比べると、「ら(等)」なる接尾語には本来侮蔑的な響きがあり、複数の人間どもを「敬意を込めて個別的に取り扱ってやる必要もないような物の数にも入らぬ連中」として「一山いくら」的にまとめて取り扱う感じである。

普通の日本人なら決して「彼たち」などという言い方はしない: 日本語に於ける「彼＝he」の複数形は伝統的に「彼ら＝they」と相場が決まっているからである。人々がこの「彼たち」という言い回しを用いる理由として考えられるのは、次の3つのうちのいずれかである: (1)「彼女＝she」の複数形は一般に「彼女たち＝they」なのだから、男性側の複数形もまた「彼たち＝they」であるべきだろう、男女平等の観点からもそうするのが当然だろうーウーマンリブ(男女同権運動)万歳！; (2)他の日本人がみんな「彼ら＝they」という言い回し一辺倒の中で、「彼たち＝they」という風変わりな表現は独特な響きがあるから、それを口にすればみんなの中で自分だけ目立つじゃんークールだぜぃ！; (3)日本語に於ける伝統的な言い回しの「彼ら＝they」なんて知らなかったから、単数の「彼＝he」のお尻に単純に「たち」の接尾語くっつければ、「彼たち＝they」という正しい複数形が出来上がるだろう、とそう考えちゃっただけですぅーアホかっ！

If the last one happens to be the paramount reason why such a queer expression as “彼たち(KARETACHI)” should prevail in the present day Japan, the possible result of such linguistic anomalies might be that, some day, all Japanese nouns (which are essentially singular) could change shapes and mean plural freely by the simple addition of “たち(TACHI)” as the Japanese equivalent of “s/es” in English... I must warn you, however, that such is not the case with the contemporary Japanese: a noun is innately felt to be the singular, the forcibly pluralized form of which sounds too singular to be a legitimate Japanese.

Most Japanese people are totally ignorant of these linguistic facts of traditional Japanese language or their latent influence upon their own speech, but they could still discern the aggressively wild tone of “野郎ども:YAROUDOMO: those bastards” or hypocritically condescending tone of “私どもに言わせていただければ:WATAKUSHIDOMO NI IWASETE ITADAKEREBA: we humbly say that...”.

- There is no real notion of singular/plural in Japanese consciousness -

In summary, the apparently plural suffixes of Japanese language(たち:TACHI, ら:RA, ども:DOMO) are not really plurality modifiers but are meant as symbols of mental attitudes, ranging from disdain through humility to respect. It follows from this that the Japanese people have no actual distinction between the singular and the plural in their concept of nouns: their world is composed solely of the singular form. For them to migrate into the world of English, therefore, the concept of plurality has to be established wholly anew.

Conversely, learners of Japanese language from Indo-European speaking nations should make it a rule to “switch off” their attitude of counting up nouns, adding “s/es”(TACHI, RA, DOMO) at the end: all Japanese nouns are meant to be used in the singular, although sometimes seeming to be the plural.

もし主として上述の最後の理由から「彼たち」なる奇妙な言い回しが現代日本にはびこっているとするならば、言語学的に風変わりなこうした現象が進行したその果てに、ひょっとすれば、全ての日本語の「名詞(生来、単数形として生まれるもの)」が、いつの日か、英語に於ける“s/es”に相当する日本語としての「たち」を単純に付加することで、自由に形を変えて複数形を表わせる、ということになる日が来るかもしれない･･･しかしながら、今の時代の日本語では、そういうことにはなっていない、ということを念押ししておく必要があろう:名詞は生まれながらにして「単数形」の感覚であり、これを無理矢理「複数化」してしまえば、その響きの異様さはとてもまともな日本語とは言えないものとなる。

大方の日本人は、伝統的な日本語に於ける上述の言語学的事実を全く知らないし、そういう伝統的な日本語の特性が彼ら自身の喋り方にどのような潜在的影響を及ぼしているかも認識していない。が、そんな彼らでも、「野郎ども:those bastards」なる言い回しの攻撃的なまでに野蛮な響きや、「わたくしどもに言わせていただければ:we humbly say that…」の偽善的なまでにへりくだった調子は、ちゃんと見分けがつくはずである。

－日本人の意識の中に「単数／複数」の真の概念なし－

とどのつまりが、日本語の中で一見いかにも「複数化の接尾語」に見える語句(たち、ら、ども)は、実は複数化のための修飾語ではなく、心的態度を表わす記号であって、その範囲は「侮蔑」から「謙遜」を経て「尊敬」へとまたがっている。このことから、日本人は「名詞」の概念に於いて「単数(singular)／複数(plural)」の真の区別を有していない、ということになる:日本人の世界は「単数形」のみから成るものなのである。であるから、そんな日本人が日本語世界から英語の世界へと移行するためには、「複数の概念」を全く新たに構築せねばならない、という結論になる。

裏返して言えば、インド･ヨーロッパ言語を母国語とする人々が日本語を学習する場合、名詞の「数」を数え上げてはその末尾に“s/es”(たち、ら、ども)を付ける彼ら生来の態度の「スイッチを切る」習慣を身に付けるべきである:日本語の名詞は(たとえ「複数形」に見える時が時々あっても)すべて「単数」で用いられるべきものなのだから。

- English nouns had best be memorized not in the singular but as a pair of determinative/numerical adjective + plural form -

For Japanese people who have no real concept of plurality, here is one great tip for overcoming that lethal handicap and building up their vocabulary along with some useful expressions: never memorize "a noun" as is, but always learn it by heart coupled with such adjective modifiers as "some/lots of/a pair of/etc, etc." (eg. "some handkerchieves", "lots of photos", "a pair of trousers"), thereby imprinting nouns upon the memory in the plural, NEVER in the singular form.

Along with the concept of plurality, Japanese language is absolutely devoid of "冠詞 (KANSHI: articles)"; more specifically, "不定冠詞 (FUTEIKANSHI:the indefinite article: "a" and "an")" and "定冠詞 (TEIKANSHI:the definite article: "the")". That is why ordinary Japanese people are prone to use nouns in dually wrong ways: (1)in the singular form (the "raw" form written on the dictionary) and (2)without any indefinite/definite article: ng. "I'm not good at <computer>". For Japanese people unfamiliar with English, remembering or pronouncing or spelling an English word is "an accomplishment" in itself; their mental attention span is so limited that they are already satisfied when they can correctly remember/pronounce/spell "computer", and never realize that they have failed to add "a" or "the" before "computer". This type of incorrect English – a singular noun used without accompanying any article – is typical of Japanese folks, whose language has absolutely no indefinite/definite articles or actual concept of plurality.

The best cure for this linguistic propensity, again, is: "always remember/use nouns in the plural form, unless it is absolutely necessary to remember/use them in the singular form". This simply practical remedy is most effective when applied in the earliest stage of learning English. When a noun is stored up in your memory in the singular form – without accompanying "s/es" at the end – it MUST be a noun which CANNOT take the plural form (eg. "deer" or "John" or "mail" or "democracy" or any such nouns without the form or concept of the plural). If your memory presents you with a noun in the singular form, it must automatically follow that the noun is to be used in

－英語の名詞を覚える際は、「単数形」としては暗記せず、「限定詞／数的形容詞＋複数形」の組み合わせで覚えるのが最善のやり方－

「複数」の真の概念を持たない日本人のために、その致命的に不利な条件を克服した上で、便利な表現ともども語彙の構築にも役立つ素晴らしい秘訣を、一つ御紹介しよう:「名詞」をそのままの形で覚えることは絶対にせず、常に"some/lots of/a pair of 等々"の形容詞的修飾語と抱き合わせで暗記するのである。例えば"some handkerchieves:ハンカチ数枚"、"lots of photos:写真多数"、"a pair of trousers:ズボン一着"といった具合に、「名詞」は「複数形」で記憶に印象付けて、「単数形では決して覚えない」ようにするのである。

「複数」の概念同様、日本語には「冠詞(articles)」もまた完全に欠落している。より具体的に言えば、「不定冠詞(the indefinite article: "a/an")」及び「定冠詞(the definite article: "the")」に相当する語句が日本語には存在しない。そのせいで、普通の日本人は「名詞」の使い方を(1)単数形で(辞書に載っている"素のまま"の形で)使ってしまう;(2)不定冠詞／定冠詞抜きで使ってしまう;という二重の形で間違った用法に陥りがちなのである(ng.=NO GOOD:ダメ用例(×) I'm not good at <computer>.:私はコンピュータが得意ではありません)。英語に不慣れな日本人にとっては、一つの英単語を「思い出し」たり「発音し」たり「綴った」りすることそれ自体が「一つの偉業」なのだ;彼らの精神的注意力が及ぶ範囲は極めて狭いので、"computer:コンピューター"なる単語を正しく「思い出し／発音し／綴った」その時点でもう彼らは満足してしまい、その"computer"の前に"a"や"the"を付け加えるのを忘れたことなど、彼らにはまるで認識できないのだ。この種のマチガイ英語－何の冠詞も伴わずに名詞を単数形で使うような誤用－は、日本人には典型的に見られる;彼らの母国語には「不定冠詞／定冠詞」など影も形もないし、彼らは「複数」の真の概念をも持ち合わせていないのだから、そうなるのが当然なのだ。

こうした困った言語学的習癖を治す最高の特効薬は、繰り返しになるが、「単数形での暗記／使用が絶対的に必要な場合以外は、名詞は常に複数形で覚え、複数形で使うべし」ということである。単純だが実用的なこの治療薬は、英語学習の最初期段階で服用するのが最も効果的である。任意の名詞が、もし諸君の記憶の中に「単数形」で－その末尾に"s/es"を伴うことなき形態で－覚え込まれている場合、その名詞は「複数形を取ることが不可能な名詞」(例えば、"deer:鹿"とか"John:ジョン"とか"mail:手紙類"とか"democracy:民主主義"とか、「複数」の形態とも概念とも無縁の名詞)である「はずである」。もし諸君の記憶バンクから任意の名詞が「単数形」で出てきた場合、その名詞は自動的に「単数形でのみ使用すべき名詞」ということになる・・・それ以外の

the singular form only; anything else should come up to your memory in the plural form with "some" types of determinatives before them... this type of attitude is quite useful, indeed indispensable, for Japanese learners of English to overcome their innate lack of articles and plurality concept.

- The plural is generally preferred to the singular in English -

The plural forms of some English nouns, just like the "不規則変化 (FUKISOKU-HENKA: irregular conjugation)" of the verb, take totally different shapes than their singular forms (eg. "a child/children", "a mouse/mice", "an ox/oxen"). In such cases, the singular and the plural must both be paid equal attention to and stored up in your memory side by side, of course. But always remember: practical usefulness of the plural far exceeds the singular form of most nouns.

In actual English, people rarely use such expressions as "I am good at <the computer>" or "I am good at <a computer>"; they almost always say "I am good at <computers>". The plural is the most ordinary and most useful form of a noun. Learners of English ought to acquire the habit of preferring the plural to the singular form in the early stage of their studies. This is also true with French natives, who are in the habit of always using a noun coupled with such articles as "un/une/le/la/les/du/de la/des"; English speakers don't use "a/an/the" so frequently as French people imagine. The overuse of "the" is one of the most conspicuous characteristics of foreign speakers of English from traditional "article-tight" Indo-European language speaking nations.

For anyone other than native English speakers, it is the best practice to remember and use English nouns in the plural, except when the singular form is absolutely necessary.

全ての名詞が諸君の脳裏に浮かぶ際には、“some、みたいな何らかの”種類の「限定詞(determinatives)」を直前に伴った「複数形」で浮かんでくるはずなのだから・・・この種の態度は、日本人の英語学習者に生来欠落している「冠詞」及び「複数」という概念の空白を乗り越える上で、極めて有益(というよりむしろ、必要不可欠)な態度である。

－英語は一般に「単数」よりも「複数」を好むー

英語の名詞の「複数形」の中には、動詞の「不規則変化(irregular conjugation)」と全く同様に、その「単数形」とはまるで異なる形態を取るものがある(例えば、“a child/children:子供”、“a mouse/mice:ネズミ”、“an ox/oxen:雄牛”など)。こういう場合、「単数形」と「複数形」の双方に同等の比重で注意を払った上で、仲良く並べて暗記する必要があるのは当然のことだ。が、常に忘れず覚えておくべきことは、「大部分の名詞に関しては、単数形よりも複数形の方が実用的には遙かに役立つ」ということである。

実際の英語の中では、“I am good at 〈the computer〉.”とか“I am good at 〈a computer〉.”とかの表現は滅多に使わない;英語人種はほぼ決まって“I am good at 〈computers〉.:私はコンピュータが得意”と言う。名詞の形態としては「複数形」が最も一般的かつ実用的な形なのである。英語学習者は、その学習の初期段階から「単数形」よりも「複数形」を好んで用いる習慣を身に付けるべきである。このことは、フランス語を母国語とする人々に関してもあてはまる。彼らはフランス語の冠詞“un/une/le/la/les/du/de la/des”とペアになった「単数名詞」を常用する癖があるが、英語人種はフランス人が想像するほど頻繁には“a/an/the”を用いたりしないのだ。“the”を使いすぎるのは、「冠詞の縛りが厳格な」伝統的インド・ヨーロッパ言語を母国語とする国々出身の外国人英語使用者の最も顕著な特徴の一つである。

生来の英語人種以外のすべての人々にとって、英語の名詞は複数形で覚え、複数形で使う(単数形が絶対に必要、という場合だけは例外)というのが、最も良い心がけなのである。

6. English articles are too much for novice comprehension

- Indefinite/Definite article: its possible danger for beginners of English -

One of the reasons why the Japanese people are generally unable to comprehend and command English is their fuzzy notion (not so clever understanding) of "command of English". In their cramp consciousness, each and every lesson in English textbooks MUST be comprehended then and there, with full to high marks in exams to show their conquest... too foolishly arrogant an attitude that comes back to haunt them. So long as they are mental and social slaves to that attitude, they will put too much stress on preparing for the lessons (lest they should lose their face in the classroom) to place enough weight upon reviewing those lessons (to secure their footholds in the world of English).

As this author has pointed out at the beginning of this book, English lessons in Japan are not organized to facilitate the understanding of learners, but arbitrarily made for the benefit of schools and teachers. If learners tried desperately to conquer everything in English the way teachers order them to, they are sure to get stranded at quite an early stage of their ordeals.

One quite certain point of shipwreck is "冠詞(KANSHI: articles)": how to understand and use "a/an/the". This author can assure you that you will never be able to comprehend and command English indefinite/definite articles with relative freedom until English has become your second nature. In other words, most foreign speakers with adequate command of English are still awkward in their use of "a/an" and "the". Can't you believe it?... It's because you haven't fully understood the fundamental difference of English language from the traditional Indo-European languages like French or Italian.

- How tight with articles is where English differs drastically from the rest of European languages -

The French use of articles(un/une/le/la/les/du/de la/des) before nouns is the reflective action for French natives. In English, however, lots of nouns are used without "a/an" or "the" before them. "Dogs are faithful animals" is the

6. 英語の冠詞は難解すぎて初心者の手に余る

－不定冠詞／定冠詞・・・英語初学者にとってのその危険性－

日本人が概して英語の理解も駆使力も有さぬ主たる理由の一つは、「英語の駆使力」に関する彼らの薄ぼんやりとした概念(あまり賢明ならざる思い込み)である。彼らのせせこましい意識の中では、英語の教科書に出て来るレッスンは一つ一つみな全て、出て来たその場で理解して、その征服の証しとして満点(ならずとも高得点)を取って見せねばならない、ということになる・・・愚かしいまでに傲慢なこの態度、これがやがて巡り巡って彼ら自身の首を絞めることになる。彼らが(心理的・社会的な制約から)こうした態度の奴隷になっている限り、授業の予習に(教室内で恥をかきたくないばかりに)力点を置き過ぎて、終わった授業の復習に(英語世界での地歩を固めるために)十分な比重を置くこともできなくなるだろう。

筆者が既にこの本の冒頭で指摘した通り、日本の英語授業は、学習者の理解を促進するために編まれているのではなく、学校と教師の便宜のために恣意的に編成されているものである。センセイがたが学習者に「修得せよ」と命じてくる通りのやり方で英語の万事を必死に征服しようと足掻いたならば、そうした苦役のごくごく初期段階で、立ち往生するのが必定なのだ。

英語学習者が頓挫を来たす第一の確実な難関は、「冠詞(articles)＝“a/an/the”をいかにして理解し使いこなすか」の問題である。この筆者は断言できるが、英語の「不定冠詞／定冠詞」をどうにか自在に理解・駆使できるのは、諸君にとって英語が既に「第二の本性」となって後のことである。言い換えれば、英語がそこそこ話せる外国人でも、その大部分は相変わらず“a/an”及び“the”の使い回しがぎこちないまま、ということである・・・信じられない？・・・そう感じるのは、フランス語やイタリア語といった由緒正しきインド・ヨーロッパ言語と英語との根源的な違いを、諸君がまだ十分理解していないからである。

－「冠詞に関する厳密度」には、英語とその他の西欧言語の劇的違いが現れる－

フランス語の名詞の前に冠詞(un/une/le/la/les/du/de la/des)を置くのは、仏語国民にとっては反射的次元の行動である。ところが、英語の場合、名詞の多くはその直前に“a/an”も“the”も伴わぬ無冠詞のままで用いられる。“Dogs are faithful animals.:犬というのは忠実な動物だ”という「複数形英文」が最も普通の形であって、“The dog is a most commonplace English sentence; "The dog is a faithful animal" or "A dog is a faithful animal" or "Dogs are a faithful animal" is too pedantic to sound like normal English.

The relationship between articles and nouns is so airtight in French that articles(un/une/le/la/les/du/de la/des) can and should be taught at the earliest stage of French language lessons. This is also true with most traditional "article-tight" Indo-European languages.

But English is a black sheep among European languages, which has totally abandoned the meaninglessly complex notion of "gender" of nouns, with the result that the airtight consciousness of respective articles, which must change shapes according to the gender and number of the nouns coming after them, has also become unnecessary in English. This freedom has liberated English from such pedantic sentences as "The/A dog is a faithful animal".

And, it is this freewheeling propensity of English that has made it impossible for novice learners of English to comprehend and master "a/an" and "the"; the use of these articles is in mutually exclusive relationship with the use of plural forms, the comprehensive understanding of which takes so much time, so many years of conscious scrutiny and mountains of example sentences that the task is a total impossibility for beginners of English. Trust me, this is not peculiar to Japanese students of English; French, Italian or Spanish natives are also at a loss what to do with English articles.

- The freewheeling articles of English can freely be placed anywhere in English textbooks -

The problem of indefinite/definite articles is a handful even for professional English scholars, too. There is no easy way to efficiently learn or teach the comprehensive use of "a/an" and "the". But guidebooks to English usage must have articles about the article(indefinite/definite) somewhere. It is never possible to write a superb piece of article to enable learners to comprehend and command English articles at a single stroke. It is, therefore, possible for writers of English textbooks to place the article(s) on indefinite/definite articles anywhere in their books. As it happens, virtually faithful animal."や"A dog is a faithful animal."、あるいは"Dogs are a faithful animal." などの「冠詞＋単数形の英文」は、学者臭くて普通の英語っぽく聞こえない。

冠詞と名詞の関係は、フランス語に於いては極めて厳密なものだから、フランス語のレッスンの場合にはその最初期の段階で冠詞群(un/une/le/la/les/du/de la/des)を教えることが可能(かつ妥当)と言えるであろう。これはまた「冠詞にうるさい」伝統的なインド・ヨーロッパ言語の大部分に関してもあてはまることである。

しかるに、英語というのは西欧言語の中でも「白羊の群れから浮いた黒羊」みたいな外れ者であって、名詞の「性別」という無意味に複雑な概念を完全に放棄したのが英語であるから、「直後に来る名詞の"性"と"数"に応じて形態変化せねばならぬ個々の冠詞の決まり事に関する水も漏らさぬ鉄壁の意識」などという代物もまた、英語では必要なくなったわけである。この自由度の高さが、"The/A dog is a faithful animal."的な学者っぽく堅苦しい「冠詞主導型文章」から英語を解放してくれたわけである。

しかしその一方で、英語の持つこうした自由奔放な傾向が逆にアダとなって、"a/an"と"the"を理解し使いこなすことは英語の初学者には無理難題、の事態が生じたとも言える。冠詞が使われる場面では複数形は引っ込み、複数形を使うならば冠詞が引っ込む、という相互排除的関係もあって、その使い方を包括的に理解するには、多大な時間と、山ほどの例文と、それをまた分析的に意識して見る長年の経験が必要になるのだから、英語初心者には到底達成不可能な仕事と言える。嘘ではない、これは日本人の英語学習者だけの問題ではなくて、フランス語やイタリア語やスペイン語を母国語とする人々だってやはり、英語の冠詞の扱いにはほとほと手を焼いているのだ。

－英語の自由気ままな冠詞たちは、英語の教科書中のどこに置いたって構わない・・・はずー

「不定冠詞／定冠詞」の問題は、英語の専門家にとってさえもやはり手に余る難題である。"a/an"と"the"の包括的用法を効率よく学び教える楽なやり方など、どこにも存在しないのだ。それでも英語のガイドブックでは、どこかに「冠詞(不定冠詞／定冠詞)」の項目を置かねばならない。英語の冠詞を一発で理解し使いこなすことを学習者に可能ならしむるほどの超絶的に優れた記事を一つ書いてやる、なんて絶対に無理;である以上、英語の教科書を書く者としては、「不定冠詞／定冠詞」に関する記事(一章であれ複数章であれ)なんて、本の中のどこに置いたって、いいわけである。

all textbooks on traditional Indo-European languages (which are all tight with articles) begin with the explanation of articles (variable with the gender/number of nouns coming after). Isn't it natural, then, that textbooks of English (which is quite loose with articles but is still "an European language") should start out like French guidebooks with an article on articles, however impossibly complicated it may seem to beginners?... Now you must have known how unnatural and difficult (no, IMPOSSIBLE!) it is for English learners to try to master indefinite/definite articles at the beginning of their learning career.

- How to loosely comprehend indefinite/definite articles -

Such being the case, beginners of English should not pay too rigid attention to the problem of indefinite articles("a" and "an") and definite article("the"). The basic knowledge they should have about these articles is simply that:

(1)English articles ("a/an/the") never change shapes according to the gender of nouns coming after them like traditional Indo-European languages (English nouns have no such gender);

(2)a noun or nouns already talked about or thought about by the parties concerned should accompany the definite article "the", regardless of the number of nouns coming after;

(3)a singular noun coming up to the speaker's consciousness for the first time should accompany the indefinite article "a" (eg. "a pen"), with the exception of a noun beginning with vowel sounds accompanying "an" (eg. "an album", "an FBI intervention");

(4)a noun which is merely referred to as one of many possible things should accompany the indefinite article "a" or "an" (eg. "I'm just a passer-by");

(5)a noun or nouns meant as something special different from the rest should accompany the definite article "the" (eg. "She is the witness of the crime");

(6)nouns which cannot be counted (uncountable nouns: eg. "cake") can be accompanied by the definite article "the" (eg. "the chalk") but cannot accompany the indefinite article "a" or "an" (ng. "a chalk"), so they instead accompany such expressions as "a bulk of / a group of / a lot of / a set of / a sheet of / etc, etc." (eg. "a stick of chalk");

たまたま、伝統的インド・ヨーロッパ言語(どれもみな冠詞に厳しい言語である)の教科書はほぼみな決まって(直後の名詞の「性/数」に応じて形を変える)「冠詞」の解説から始まっている。ともなれば、英語の教科書としても(冠詞に関しては極めて緩〜いものの、それでもやはり「西欧言語」には違いないのだから)フランス語のガイドブックみたいに「冠詞に関する一章」から始まったって(たとえそれが初心者にとって無茶苦茶ややこしく見えたって)よいではないか?・・・という次第。これで諸君も「不定冠詞/定冠詞」の修得を英語学習の駆け出し段階で目指すことがいかに不自然かつ困難(というよりむしろ不可能!)であるか、確実に理解できたことであろう。

ー「不定冠詞/定冠詞」の緩〜い理解のしかたー

そういう次第であるから、英語初学者の場合、「不定冠詞(“a”と“an”)」と「定冠詞(“the”)」の問題については、あまり厳密に意識しすぎない方がよい。こうした冠詞に関して初学者がおさえておくべき基本的知識は、次のような単純なものでよいだろう:

(1)英語の冠詞(“a/an/the”)は、伝統的インド・ヨーロッパ言語のように直後の名詞の「性」に応じて形態変化することはない(英語はそうした「性別」を持たない);

(2)当事者たちの間で既に話題・念頭に上った任意の名詞(単数/複数)は、直後に来る名詞の「数」にかかわらず、「定冠詞“the”」を伴う;

(3)話者の意識に初めて上った単数名詞は、「不定冠詞“a”」を伴う(例 “a pen:ペン”)が、発音上の「母音(vowels)」で始まる単数名詞の場合は例外的に“an”を伴う(例 “an album:アルバム”、“an FBI intervention:アメリカ合衆国連邦捜査局の干渉”);

(4)想定される幾多の物事のうちの一つに過ぎぬもの、として言及されている単数名詞は、「不定冠詞“a”または“an”」を伴う(例 “I'm just a passer-by.:私は単なる一通行人に過ぎない”);

(5)その他の存在とは違う特別な何か、を意味する名詞(単数/複数)は「定冠詞“the”」を伴う(例 “She is the witness of the crime.:彼女が例の犯罪の目撃者だ”);

(6)数を数えることができない名詞(「不可算名詞(uncountable nouns)」例 “cake:ケーキ”)の場合、「定冠詞“the”」を伴うことは可能(例 “the chalk:その白墨”)だが、「不定冠詞“a”または“an”」を伴うことは不可能((×) “a chalk”)であるため、不定冠詞の代わりに“a bulk of:一山の / a group of:一群の / a lot of:幾多の / a set of:一組の / a sheet of:一枚の / 等々”の表現を伴う(例 “a stick of chalk:白墨一本”);

(7)nouns signifying the name of a person (eg. “John”) does not usually accompany articles, but the name of a group of persons (eg. “the Beatles”, “the Simpsons”) usually accompany the definite article;
(8)indefinite/definite articles(“a/an/the”) belong to what is called “限定詞 (GENTEISHI: determinatives)”, which modify and determine the attributes of nouns coming after them, and cannot be used along with other determinatives (eg. this, that, my, our, your, his, her, its, their, some, any, every, one, no, etc,etc.), for the co-existence of which are used such expressions as “a friend of mine (ng. a my friend)” or “this mistake of his (ng. this his mistake)” or “no business of yours / none of your business (ng. no your business)”;
(9)in normal speech, nouns should basically be treated in the plural (eg. “Men are mortal”), with the exception of a noun requiring individual treatment (eg. “A man's life is heavier than the earth”).

(7) 人物の名前を表わす名詞(例 “John:ジョン”)は冠詞を伴わないのが普通だが、一群の人物たちの集合体の名前(例 “the Beatles:ザ・ビートルズ”、“the Simpsons:シンプソン・ファミリー”)は定冠詞を伴うのが普通;

(8)「不定冠詞/定冠詞(“a/an/the”)」は、直後に来る名詞を修飾したりその名詞の特性を規定したりする「限定詞(determinatives)」と呼ばれる語の一種であり、他の限定詞(this/that/my/our/your/his/her/its/their/some/any/every/one/no その他諸々)と重複して用いることはできず、こうした表現どうしが共存するためには、次のような表現が用いられる:“a friend of mine:私の友人の一人((×) a my friend)”、“this mistake of his:彼が犯したこの間違い((×) this his mistake)”、“no business of yours / none of your business:あなたには関係のない事((×) no your business)”;

(9) 普通の会話の中では、名詞は「複数形」で扱うのが基本である(例 “Men are mortal.:人間はいつかは死ぬ定めである”)が、個別的扱いを要する単数名詞の場合は例外である(例 “A man's life is heavier than the earth.:一人の人間の生命は地球よりも重い”)。

7. Let "be" alone, and the rest will "do" their job

- "Be verbs" as opposed to "do verbs" -

There are moments when words fail us, i.e, when we cannot hit upon any suitable words to utter. At such moments, ordinary English speakers stammer "I, ah...", at a loss what "do verbs" to put in; Japanese people unacquainted with English stumble "I'm a...", instinctively clinging to the very first English sentence pattern they were taught at school.

I'm not saying this to show how shameful it is for a Japanese to stop at "I'm a..." (as shameful as it is); I'm just pointing out the fact that "I am" (more generally, "S+be") structure is one of the most basic patterns of English, and that anything other than "S+be" structure must invariably take the form of "S+do" structure. To put it another way, if you thoroughly know when to use "be verb" and exclude them all, all the rest can be construed as "S+do" structures. In yet another way, we can let "be" EXPROGER "do" verbs.

- "Be" of existence -

The most fundamental meaning of "be" is "existence", as can be seen in sentences like "God is (God exists)" or "He is no more (He is not living any more)". This type of "be" is the only case where the verb "be" stands alone and needs nothing else to complete its meaning. Except for this case, all "be" will accompany such elements as "補語(HOGO: complement)", "現在分詞(GENZAI-BUNSHI: the present participle)" or "過去分詞(KAKO-BUNSHI: the past participle)" to complete the meaning.

The so-called "there+be" construction also belongs to this "existential be": eg. "There is a book on the desk" (cf: A book is there on the desk).

- "Be" of equation: type-I(along with subjective complement) -

The most frequent and important function of "be" is "equalizing the subject(S) with the complement(C)"; mathematically speaking, "(S)=(C)" type of equation is meant by "S+be+C" structure: this is what we call "sentence pattern #2". This sentence pattern is so important that most schools will drill beginners in it, having them repeatedly pronounce such

7. “be 動詞”一つ除けばみな“do 動詞”

ー“do 動詞”の対立概念としての“be 動詞”ー

言葉がうまく出てこない瞬間(口走るべき適当な言葉がサッと口をついて飛び出して来てくれない場面)というのはあるものだ。そういう時、普通の英語人は“I, ah...(アィ、ァー・・・)”と口ごもる;英語に不慣れな日本人は“I'm a...(アィムァ・・・)”ってな感じでけつまづく;学校で「いの一番」に教わった英語の文型に本能的にしがみついて、墓穴を掘るわけだ。

筆者は何もここで、日本人が“アィムァ〜”でパタッと止まるあのザマがいかにこっぱずかしいことかをあげつらおうというのではない(まぁ、恥ずかしいことは間違いないのだが);ここで指摘したいのはただ、“I am”(より一般的な言い方をすれば、“主語+be 動詞”)構造というものが、英文の最も基本的パターンの一つである、という事実であり、そしてまた“主語+be 動詞”構造に属さぬ他の全ての英文は必ず“主語+do 動詞”構造を取る、という事実である。言い方を変えれば、“be動詞”を使うべき場面の全てを網羅的に知った上で、そうした場面をすべて除けば、残りはみな“主語+do 動詞”構造として解釈すればよいわけである。更に別の言い方をすれば、「“be 動詞”を用いるべき例外的場面をおさえることで、“do”動詞を用いるべき一般的場面の全てを“EXPROGER:例外把握による一般制覇”できる」わけである。

ー「存在」の“be 動詞”ー

“be 動詞”の最も根源的な意味は「存在」であり、これは “God is.(God exists.):神は存在する”とか“He is no more.(He is not living any more.):彼はもはやこの世にいない”とかの文例に見る通りである。この「存在」の意味で用いる“be 動詞”は、“be 動詞”の意味がそれ自体で完結する(=他のいかなる語句を伴う必要もない)唯一の事例である。この「存在」の事例以外の全ての“be 動詞”には、「補語(complement)」や「現在分詞(the present participle)」や「過去分詞(the past participle)」といった諸要素を伴わねばその意味が完結しない。

いわゆる“there+be 構文”もまたこの種の“存在の be 動詞”に属する。(例 There is a book on the desk. cf: A book is there on the desk.:一冊の本が机の上にある)

ー「等価」の“be 動詞”:タイプI=「主格補語(subjective complement)」を伴う SVC 型ー

最も頻繁に用いられ、かつ、最も重要な“be 動詞”の機能は、「主語(S:subject)と補語(C:complement)とを等価の関係で結ぶこと」である。数学的な表現をすれば、「(S)イコール(C)」型の等式を意味するのが「S+be+C」構造であり、これがいわゆる「第2文型」と呼ばれる英語の型である。この文型は極めて重要度が高いため、ほとんどの学校では

sentences as "I'm a student / This is a pen / He is a boy / She is a girl / We are friends / You are beautiful / They are kind / It is not true".

The (C)complement in this sentence pattern can take several kinds of "品詞(HINSHI: parts of speech)":

(1)名詞(MEISHI: noun): eg. This is my cell-phone.

(2)形容詞(KEIYOUSHI: adjective): eg. That is interesting.

(3)副詞(FUKUSHI: adverb): eg. He is away.

(4)前置詞句(ZENCHISHI-KU: prepositional phrase): eg. She is on the verge of nervous breakdown.

- "Be" of equation: type-II(along with objective complement) -

The equalizing function of "be" will also be seen in the "C" part of what we call "sentence pattern #5": S-V-O-C. The actual usage of this pattern, however, is so limited that all you have to memorize is the following two cases:

(1)S+consider/regard/deem+O+to be+C:

eg. He considered/regarded/deemed my story to be a fiction.

In this case, the "to be" part can be substituted with "as" and be written as follows:

eg. He considered/regarded/deemed my story as a fiction.

(2)S+let+O+be+C:

eg. If you say such a thing, you will let yourself be misunderstood.

Traditionally, the auxiliary verb "let" will accompany the complement "be misunderstood" without omitting the "be"; nowadays, however, "misunderstood" without "be" is also allowable with "let", so that you could say "you will let yourself misunderstood" without making yourself misunderstood.

- "Be" of progressive -

"Be" verbs followed by "現在分詞(GENZAI-BUNSHI: the present participle)" mean "進行形(SHINKOUKEI: the progressive form)" in the following three tenses:

学習者に"I'm a student.:私は学生です / This is a pen.:これはペンです / He is a boy.:彼は少年です / She is a girl.:彼女は少女です / We are friends.:私たちは友達です / You are beautiful.:あなたは美しいです / They are kind.:彼らは親切です / It is not true.:それは真実ではありません"といった文章を何度も何度も口に出して読ませることで、このパターンを反復練習させるわけである。

この文型中の「補語(C:complement)」に用いられ得る「品詞(parts of speech)」には、以下のような種類がある:

(1)名詞(noun):例 This is my cell-phone.:これは私の携帯電話です
(2)形容詞(adjective):例 That is interesting.:それは面白い
(3)副詞(adverb):例 He is away.:彼は留守です
(4)前置詞句(prepositional phrase):例 She is on the verge of nervous breakdown.:彼女の神経は今にもプッツンといきそうだ

ー「等価」の"be 動詞":タイプII＝「目的格補語(objective complement)」を伴う SVOC 型ー

"be 動詞"の「等号」としての機能はまた、いわゆる「第５文型:SVOC」の"C(complement)＝補語"の部分にも見られる;が、このパターンが実際に使われる場面は極めて限定的で、諸君としては以下の2つの場合を暗記しておけばそれでよい:

(1)「S+consider/regard/deem+O+to be+C」
例 He considered/regarded/deemed my story to be a fiction.:彼は私の話を作り話とみなした

この場合、"to be"の部分を"as"に置き換えて次のように書くことも可能である:
例 He considered/regarded/deemed my story as a fiction.

(2)「S+let+O+be+C」
例 If you say such a thing, you will let yourself be misunderstood.:そんなことを言うと、君、誤解されるぞ

由緒正しき正統文法では、助動詞の"let"は"be"動詞を省くことなき"be misunderstood"の形を伴う・・・が、最近では"be 動詞抜き"の"misunderstood"だけの形も"let"に関しては許容範囲とされているので、"you will let yourself misunderstood"と言っても誤解されることはないだろう。

ー「進行形」の"be 動詞"ー

"be 動詞"の後に「現在分詞(the present participle)」を続けると、以下に示す3つの時制に於ける「進行形(the progressive form)」の意味になる:

現在進行形(GENZAI-SHINKOUKEI: the present progressive form):
He is studying English now.
過去進行形(KAKO-SHINKOUKEI: the past progressive form):
He was studying English ten years ago.
未来進行形(MIRAI-SHINKOUKEI: the future progressive form):
He will still be studying English ten years from now.

- "Be" of passive -

"Be" verbs followed by "過去分詞(KAKO-BUNSHI: the past participle)" mean "受動態(JUDOUTAI: the passive voice)":
eg. I was hurt by his comment. (cf: His comment hurt me.)
eg. This fact is not known to everyone. (cf: Not everyone knows this fact.)
eg. The garden was covered with snow. (cf: Snow covered the garden.)
eg. Cider is made from apples, not from grapes. (cf: They make cider not from grapes but from apples.)
eg. His parents were killed in a car accident. (cf: A car accident killed his parents.)
eg. I was born and bred here in Tokyo.

As can be seen from the examples above, "動作主(DOUSANUSHI: the agent)" in the passive voice can be shown by several prepositions (by, to, with, from, in), of which the most frequently used one is "by".

Theoretically speaking, "受動態(the passive voice)" of "X is -ed by Y (eg. You are loved by her)" is an inverted statement of "能動態(the active voice)" of "Y - X" (eg. She loves you). Actually, any sentence in the passive voice is originally meant to be in the passive voice, and not exactly made as "a reflected image in a mirror" of the active voice. The last example "I was born and bred here in Tokyo" is there to prove it. No one will paraphrase it into the active voice "My mother bore me and my family bred me here in Tokyo". The reason why this latter sentence sounds strange is that the essential message of the original "passive" sentence was "where I was born and bred" while the "active" paraphrase puts undue stress upon "who bore and bred me".

現在進行形(the present progressive form):
He is studying English now.:彼は今英語を勉強しているところである
過去進行形(the past progressive form):
He was studying English ten years ago.:10年前、彼は英語を勉強していた
未来進行形(the future progressive form):
He will still be studying English ten years from now.:10年後も彼は相変わらず英語を勉強していることだろう

ー「受身」の“be 動詞”ー

“be 動詞”の後に「過去分詞(the past participle)」を続けると、「受動態(the passive voice)」の意味になる:

例 I was hurt by his comment.:私は彼の発言で傷付いた (cf: His comment hurt me.:彼の発言は私を傷つけた)

例 This fact is not known to everyone.:この事実は誰もに知られているわけではない(cf: Not everyone knows this fact.:誰もがみなこの事実を知っているわけではない)

例 The garden was covered with snow.:庭は雪で覆われていた (cf: Snow covered the garden.:雪が庭を覆っていた)

例 Cider is made from apples, not from grapes.:サイダーはブドウではなくリンゴから作られる (cf: They make cider not from grapes but from apples.:サイダーはブドウではなくリンゴを原料にして作る)

例 His parents were killed in a car accident.:彼の両親は自動車事故で死んだ (cf: A car accident killed his parents.:自動車事故が彼の両親の生命を奪った)

例 I was born and bred here in Tokyo.:私はこの東京で生まれ育った

上掲の例文からもわかる通り、受動態の「動作主(the agent)」は、何種類かの前置詞(by, to, with, from, in)を用いて明示することができるが、そのうち最も頻繁に使われるのは“by”である。

理屈の上から言えば、「受動態(the passive voice)」の“X is -ed by Y＝XはYによって―されている:例 You are loved by her.:君は彼女に愛されている”は「能動態(the active voice)」の“Y - X＝YはXを―している:例 She loves you.彼女は君を愛している”を引っ繰り返した言い回しである・・・が、実際には、受動態の文章はすべて、最初から「受動態として言われているもの」であって「能動態を鏡に映した逆向き文章として作ったもの」では必ずしもないのである・・・この事実を証明するのが、最後に示した例文の“I was born and bred here in Tokyo.:私はこの東京で生まれ育った”である。この文章を“My mother bore me and my family bred me here in Tokyo.:私の母は私をこの東京で出産し、私の家族は私をその東京で養育した”の能動態文章で言い換えようとする人など誰一人存在しないであろう。この後者の文章がおかしく感じられる理由は、元々の「受動態」の文章の言わんとするところは「私が＜どこで＞生まれ育ったか」であるのに対し、「能動態」での言い換えは「＜誰が＞私を産み、育てたか」に筋違いの力点を置いている点にある。

Although schools will drill you in “passive/active paraphrase”, be advised that pulling such a stunt is not always possible. Let “passive” be “passive” and forget about getting back to “active”.

One more thing to consider: in such expressions as “Be advised...” or “I was surprised”, the “be+advised” and “be+surprised” parts are not considered to be “be+the past participle” but as “be+adjective” combination, with the result that they are not deemed as “the passive voice”. There are as many such “adjectives derived from the past participles (eg. amazed, bored, excited, interested, etc,etc.)” as “adjectives deriving from the present participles (eg. amazing, boring, exciting, interesting, etc,etc.)”. Unless they strongly point to the latent agent (eg. We were bored by his long speech), these past participles can be deemed to be adjectives, not part of the passive voice (eg. We were generally bored in the concert).

- “Be” of perfect -

Although quite few in number, a “be” verb followed by “過去分詞 (KAKO-BUNSHI: the past participle)” can also mean “完了形 (KANRYOUKEI: the perfect tense)”: eg. “The sun is set”, “I'll be gone”. This “be+past participle” is an archaic form of “have+past participle”, which can also be seen in French language using “être”(be) instead of “avoire”(have) before the past participle. But the actual number of such expressions are too few for novice learners of English to studiously remember.

Now that you have seen all possible usage of “be verb”, let these instances EXPROGER the “realm of do verbs”... and stop making such awkward stammering statements as “I'm a...”.

学校では諸君に「受動態／能動態の言い換え」の反復練習を強いるだろうが、そういう離れ業が英語世界で常に成り立つわけではない、という現実は覚えておくことである。受動態は受動態のままで流し、能動態に書き戻すことなど考えぬのがよろしいのである。

考慮すべきことをもう一点："Be advised...:・・・という点を御承知おき願いたい"だの"I was surprised:驚いた"だのの表現に於ける"be+advised"や"be+surprised"の部分は、「be 動詞＋過去分詞(the past participle)」とはみなされずに「be 動詞＋形容詞(adjective)」の組み合わせとみなされるので、その結果、これらの表現は「受動態」とはみなされない。こういう「過去分詞由来の形容詞（例 amazed:驚いた, bored:退屈だ, excited:興奮した, interested:興味津々だ）」は、「現在分詞由来の形容詞（例 amazing:驚くべき, boring:倦怠を誘う, exciting:興奮を呼ぶ, interesting:興味を引く）」と同様、極めて多数存在する。潜在的な「動作主(the agent)」の存在を特に強く指し示す場面（例 We were bored by his long speech.:彼の長話に我々は退屈させられた）以外では、これらの「過去分詞」は「形容詞」とみなすことができ、「受動態の一部」とはみなさないのである（例 We were generally bored in the concert.:その演奏会全般に関し我々は退屈していた）。

－「完了」の"be 動詞"－

数は極めて少ないが、"be 動詞"の後に「過去分詞(the past participle)」を続ける形は、「完了形(the perfect tense)」を意味する場合がある。"The sun is set.:太陽はもう沈んでしまった"や"I'll be gone.:私はそろそろサヨナラしましょう"などはその例である・・・この種の「be＋過去分詞」は、「have＋過去分詞」の古形であって、同様の現象は、フランス語で過去分詞の前に"avoire(英語の have に相当)"ではなく"être(英語の be に相当)"を用いる例の中にも見られる・・・が、こうした表現が実際に用いられる場合はごくごく僅かなので、英語の初学者が丹念に覚え込む必要がある例とはいえない。

・・・さぁて、と、これで諸君は"be 動詞"に関して考えられる用法の全てを確認したわけであるから、これらの事例を以て「"do 動詞"の領域」を「EXPROGER:例外を制することで一般則をも制覇」すればよいわけだ・・・ついでに、「I'm a...(アィマァ・・・)」的なコッパズカシイ口ごもり方も、卒業するとよいだろう。

8. Always be aware of the duality of "-ing"(the present participle/gerund)

- "-ING" does not compose "the progressive form" alone -

A bird newly born is said to believe the first thing it sees to be its mother, be it a bird or a man, living or inanimate. Anyone, fowl or human, new to the world totally unknown is so unsure of it that anything it/he/she can grasp in the earliest stage of the world's exploration looks so reliable and important that beginners instinctively stick to it... and often get stuck in that blind belief.

The English inflection "-ing" is a typical "chick's mom" for English beginners in Japan. Since the first lesson they were given about "-ing" taught them that "a be verb followed by -ing(the present participle) is the progressive form", Japanese people unaccustomed to English instinctively believe "-ing" to always include some "progressive" nuance in it. This fallacy can quite easily be overcome by enumerating all possible usage of "-ing" in English, which broadly divides into two kinds – the present participle and a gerund – the detailed explanation of which coming up as follows:

- "-ING" used as the present participle -

(1)the progressive form of "-ing"(complete style) = "be+-ing"

eg. It is evident that we are losing the battle.

This is the most basic style of "the progressive form", which describes some action "in the making"; in other words, an action that is being taken now but is felt to be "temporary" (likely to stop sooner or later); it follows from this that something that is felt to be "permanent" (at least unlikely to stop any time soon) can not be expressed in the progressive form; ng. "My house is standing next to his" ("My house stands next to his" is the correct expression).

(2)the progressive form of "-ing"(adjective style) = "-ing+noun" / "noun+-ing"

eg. We are fighting a losing battle. (cf. a battle which we are losing)

8. "-ing"(現在分詞/動名詞)の二面性を常に意識せよ

ー"-ING"は「進行形」を表わすのみにあらずー

生まれたばかりの鳥は、(鳥であれ人であれ)最初に見たものを(生き物であれ無生物であれ)自分の母親と信じるもの、と言われている。誰しも(鳥類であれ人類であれ)全く未知の世界に降り立ったばかりの頃は、世の中のことがまるでわからぬために、その世界の探訪過程の最初期段階で自分がつかんだ物事は何であれ、実に頼もしく重要そうに見えるものだから、初心者はそれに本能的にすがりつく・・・そうしてしばしば、その盲目的信頼に足を取られて、身動きが取れなくなるのである。

日本の英語初心者たちにとって、上述の「ヒヨコのママ」となる典型的存在が、英語の語尾変化の"-ing"形である。彼らが"-ing"に関して受けた最初の授業では「"be 動詞"の後に"-ing"(現在分詞:the present participle)を続けると、進行形になります」と教わったので、英語に不慣れな日本人は、「"-ing"の中には常に何らかの"進行形"の含みがある」と本能的に信じ込んでしまうのだ。こういう誤った信奉を克服する方法は極めて簡単で、英語の"-ing"に関して考え得る全ての用法を列挙してしまえばそれでよい・・・その用法は大まかに言うと2種類に分かれる:「現在分詞(present participle)」と「動名詞(gerund)」である・・・以下、これら2つについて更に詳しく説明してみよう。

ー"-ING"の「現在分詞」としての用法ー

(1)「進行形(the progressive form)」としての"-ing"(完全型)="be 動詞+-ing"

例 It is evident that we are losing the battle.:我々がこの戦いで敗北しつつあるのは明白だ

これは「進行形」の最も基本的な形式で、「いま現在進行中」の何らかの動作を表わしている。言い換えれば、いま現在進行中ではあるけれども「一時的なもの」として(遅かれ早かれ停止するであろう、と)感じられる何らかの行動を表わしている。そのため、「恒久的なもの」(少なくとも、近々そうでなくなるだろう、とは思われないもの)と感じられる何かを「進行形」で表現することはできない。例えば"(×) My house is standing next to his."と進行形で書くことはできないわけで、非進行形の"My house stands next to his.:我が家は彼の家の隣に建っている"が正しい英文となる。

(2)「進行形(the progressive form)」としての"-ing"(形容詞型)="-ing+名詞" / "名詞+-ing"

例 We are fighting a losing battle.:我々は負け戦をしている (cf. a battle which we are losing:我々が敗北しつつある戦い)

eg. Late summer's heat waning day by day is sad news to the young, good news to the elderly. (cf. late summer's heat which is waning day by day)

This type of progressive form is relatively rare in English, which can be understood by paraphrasing that part with "関係代名詞節 (KANKEI-DAIMEISHI-SETSU: the relative pronoun clause)" including the complete style of the progressive form.

(3)attributive(non-progressive) form of "-ing" = "-ing+noun" / "noun+-+-ing"

eg. I love this singer for her soothing voice. (cf. her voice that soothes listeners; ng. her voice that is soothing listeners)

eg. Never be a newspaper-swallowing fool. (cf. a fool that swallows newspapers; ng. a fool that is swallowing newspapers)

This type of present participle does not include "progressive" nuance in it. In the examples above, the former ("-ing+noun") is so frequently used that most of the "-ing" in this combination are felt to be "an adjective" rather than "the present participle"; virtually nobody in the English-speaking world feels "an interesting story" to be a combination of "an+-ing(the present participle)+noun"; it definitely feels to be "an+adjective+noun". Though not all of these "-ing"s are listed in the dictionary as "adjective"s, when you see an "-ing+noun" combination, you had better see the "-ing" as an "adjective" rather than "the present participle".

The latter example("noun+hyphen+-ing" combination) is usually used with "-(hyphen)" in between the noun and the present participle, in which the noun functions as the object of the present participle coming after it. In the above-mentioned example "a newspaper-swallowing fool", there is contained "(S)A fool (V)swallows (O)newspapers" semantic structure.

Beware of the "number" of the noun: in the "newspaper-swallowing" type of combination, the noun preceding the present participle is always to be used in the singular form, never in the plural form. Do you know why?... The

例 Late summer's heat waning day by day is sad news to the young, good news to the elderly.:日々弱くなる晩夏の暑さは、若者には悲報だが、お年寄りにはよい知らせである (cf. late summer's heat which is waning day by day:日一日と衰えて行く夏の終わりの暑さ)

英語の「進行形」がこの形で使われる例は比較的少数である。このタイプに出くわしたら、完全型の「進行形」を内包する「関係代名詞節(the relative pronoun clause)」で言い換えて意味を取ればよい。

(3)「限定形容詞・非進行形型(attributive & non-progressive)」の"-ing"＝"-ing＋名詞" / "名詞＋-＋-ing"

例 I love this singer for her soothing voice.:私はこの歌手の、心安らぐような声が好きだ (cf. her voice that soothes listeners:聞き手の心を和ませるような彼女の声・・・(×) her voice that ＜is soothing＞ listeners:今現在聞き手の心を＜安らがせている最中の＞彼女の声)

例 Never be a newspaper-swallowing fool.:新聞の言うことを鵜呑みにする馬鹿には決してなるな (cf. a fool that swallows newspapers:新聞の言うことをうのみにする馬鹿・・・(×) a fool that ＜is swallowing＞ newspapers:今現在新聞の言うことを＜ウノミにしている最中の＞馬鹿)

このタイプの「現在分詞」には「進行形」の含みはない。上例では、前者("-ing＋名詞")のタイプが非常に頻繁に用いられるため、この種の組み合わせに於ける"-ing"は「現在分詞」というよりむしろ「形容詞」の感覚となる・・・"an interesting story:面白い話"という形を見て「an＋現在分詞の-ing＋名詞」と感じる人など英語圏には実際には一人もいない;誰が何と言ってもこれは「an＋形容詞＋名詞」と感じられる形なのである。こうしたタイプの"-ing"の全てが辞書に「形容詞」として掲載されているわけではないものの、「-ing＋名詞」の組み合わせを見たら、この"-ing"は「現在分詞」というよりは「形容詞」とみなした方が身のためである。

上に掲げた後者の例(「名詞＋ハイフン(-)＋-ing」の組み合わせ)は、「名詞／現在分詞」間に「ハイフン(hyphen)」を入れて使うのが通例で、この表現の中では「名詞」が直後の「現在分詞」の「目的語(object)」として機能している。上掲の"a newspaper-swallowing fool"中には"(S)A fool:馬鹿が (V)swallows:丸呑みする (O)newspapers:新聞の言うことを"という意味上の構造が含まれている。

名詞の「数」に注意したい:"newspaper-swallowing"式の組み合わせでは、「現在分詞」直前の「名詞」は常に「単数形(the singular form)」で用いられ、「複数形(the plural form)」では決して使わない。何故だかわかるだろうか？・・・理由は単純で、

reason is simple: the "newspaper-swallowing" unit is not a "noun" but an "adjective" modifying the following noun "fool". The only "品詞(HINSHI: parts of speech)" that can take "the plural" are "名詞(MEISHI: nouns)" and "代名詞(DAIMEISHI: pronouns)"; "形容詞(KEIYOUSHI: adjectives)" can never be used in the plural in English, which attribute automatically reduces "newspapers"(plural) to "newspaper"(singular) in "a newspaper-swallowing fool", just like in such expressions as "a two-lane street", "a four-door car" or "a six-member family".

(4)predicative(progressive) form of "-ing" = "S+V+O+-ing"

eg. I heard him saying that. (cf. He was saying that; I heard it.)

eg. I can't have you saying things like that. (cf. You are saying things like that; I can't leave it as it is.)

This is a rather complicated style of progressive form, used in the "補語(HOGO: complement)" part of S-V-O-C sentence pattern(#5). The "progressive" implication in the "O+-ing" part is clear to see in the former example ("he was saying that"). While, in the latter example, the O-C part ("you saying things like that") is not meant as a "dynamic" and "momentary" progressive form (ng. "you are saying things like that now") but as a "habitual" action over a certain span of time (cf. "you usually say things like that / you keep saying things like that / you are in the habit of saying things like that"). Be advised "the progressive form" contains such "long-span habits"; eg. He is always complaining about something (if not complaining right now).

“newspaper-swallowing”の部分は「名詞」ではなく「形容詞」として直後の名詞の“fool”を修飾しているからである。「複数形」を取り得る唯一の「品詞(parts of speech)」は「名詞(nouns)」と「代名詞(pronouns)」のみである。英語の「形容詞(adjectives)」が複数形で用いられることは決してないわけだから、その特性が自動的に“a newspaper-swallowing fool”に於ける“newspapers(複数)”を“newspaper(単数)”へと引き戻すわけである・・・これはちょうど“a two-lane street:二車線道路”や“a four-door car:4ドアの自動車”や“a six-member family:六人家族”の“lane/door/member”が“lanes/doors/members”のような複数形を取らない形容詞成文であるのと同じ理屈である。

(4)「叙述形容詞・進行形型(predicative & progressive)」の“-ing”＝“S+V+O+-ing”

例 I heard him saying that.:彼がそう言っているのを私は聞いた (cf. He was saying that; I heard it.:彼はそう言っていた、それを私は聞いた)

例 I can't have you saying things like that.:お前にいつまでもそんなこと言わせてはおかないぞ (cf. You say things like that; I can't leave it as it is.:お前はそういうことを言うが、俺は事態をこのまま放置しておくわけにはいかない)

これは「進行形」としてはかなり入り組んだ形式で、SVOC の「第5文型」の「補語(C:complement)」部分に「-ing」が用いられている例である。“O＋-ing”の部分に含まれる「進行形」の含みは、前者の例(“he was saying that:彼はそう言っていた”)の中にはっきりと見て取れる。一方、後者の例文では、“O-C”部分(“you saying things like that:お前はそういうことを言う”)は「動的(dynamic)」かつ「一時的(momentary)」な「進行形」の意味で用いられているわけではない((×) “you are saying things like that now:お前は＜たった今そういうことを言っている＞”);ここは一定の時間幅にまたがっての「常習的(habitual)」な行動としての「進行形」なのである(参考 “you usually say things like that:お前は普段そういうことを言う / you keep saying things like that:お前はそういうことを言い続けている / you are in the habit of saying things like that:お前にはそういうことを言う癖がある”)。「進行形」にはこの種の「時間幅の長い習癖」の用法も含まれることを覚えておきたい。(例 He is always complaining about something (if not complaining right now).:彼はいつも何かしら文句を言っている(たった今文句を言っているわけではないにせよ))

- "-ING" used as a gerund -

eg. Doing publicity and forcibly making consumers want to buy something is the main way of business today, which almost completely takes over making good products that consumers naturally want to buy. The only way to get over this detestable trend is the training of consumers wise enough not to get carried away by obtrusive hypes.

"動名詞(DOUMEISHI: a gerund)" is a unique form, which is partly "verb" and partly "noun". The weight between "verb" and "noun" can vary from one gerund to another. In the example above, the "verbal" characteristic of the gerund can be seen in "(V)doing (O)publicity", "(V)making (O)people (C)want to buy something" and "(V)making (O)good products": only verbs(transitive) can directly take objects(O) without the intervention of prepositions.

On the other hand, the "nounal" characteristic of the gerund can be seen in "takes over <making good products>": only nouns(and pronouns) can be the object of prepositions(in this case, "over"). And "the training of consumers" part is still more "nounal"; only nouns and adjectives can be modified by the definite article "the".

In fact, such originally "gerund" terms as "training", "cooking", "hearing" or "living" are not so much "verbals" as "nouns", even in the consciousness of Japanese people. In short, a gerund is a verb playing the part of a noun, sometimes to the point of "never appearing to have been a verb".

- Prepositions call for gerunds -

Whenever a preposition takes as its object not a noun but a verb, the verb must take the form of a gerund("-ing"). That is to say, any "-ing" that is used immediately after a preposition can be deemed as a gerund, not the present participle.

ー「動名詞」としての“-ING”ー

例 Doing publicity and forcibly making consumers want to buy something is the main way of business today, which almost completely takes over making good products that consumers naturally want to buy. The only way to get over this detestable trend is the training of consumers wise enough not to get carried away by obtrusive hypes.

「宣伝をして消費者に何かを無理矢理買いたい気分にさせる」のが今日のビジネスの主流であり、「消費者が自然と買いたい気分になるような良い製品作り」にほぼ完全に取って代わっている。この忌まわしい潮流を克服する唯一の道は、押しつけがましい誇大広告に流されないような賢明な消費者の錬成である。

「動名詞(a gerund)」というのは独特な形態で、“動詞(verb)”と“名詞(noun)”の性質を部分的に兼ね備えている。“動詞”と“名詞”のどちらに重きを置くかは「動名詞」ごとにまちまちである。上掲の例文では、“(V)doing (O)publicity”、“(V)making (O)people (C)want to buy something”、“(V)making (O)good products”の部分に「動名詞の“動詞的”性質」を見ることができる:「前置詞(prepositions)」を介さずに直接「目的語(O:object)」を取ることができるのは「動詞・・・正確には“他動詞(transitive verbs)”」だけなのだから。

一方、「動名詞の“名詞的”性質」を見ることができるのは“takes over <making good products>”の部分である:「前置詞(prepositions)・・・この例では“over”」の目的語たり得るのは「名詞(及び代名詞)」だけなのだから。“the training of consumers”の部分はさらにまた“名詞的”である:定冠詞“the”が修飾する語は「名詞」か「形容詞」かのいずれかだからである。

実際には、“training:訓練”、“cooking:料理”、“hearing:聞き取り”、“living:生活”といった「“動名詞”由来語」は(日本人の意識の中でさえ)“動詞”というより“名詞”の感が強い。早い話が、「動名詞」とは「動詞」が「名詞」の役割を(時として「元々は動詞だった」とはもはや感じられないほど見事に)演じたもの、である。

ー「前置詞」は「動名詞」を求めるー

「前置詞(prepositions)」がその目的語として「名詞(nouns)」ではなく「動詞(verbs)」を取る時、その「動詞」は「動名詞(a gerund=“-ing”)」の形を取らねばならない。即ち、「前置詞」の直後に用いられた“-ing”は全て「動名詞」であって「現在分詞(the present participle)」ではない、とみなすことができるわけである。

However, there is one preposition which needs special attention — "to", which has two faces: a simple preposition followed by a gerund("-ing"), and an infinitive(不定詞:FUTEISHI) followed by the root form of a verb("-").
eg. Although he used to be rather awkward in English, he is getting used to living in the States, linguistically or socially.

In the example above, the first "to"(in "he used to be") is used as an infinitive and requires the root form "be" after it. The second "to"(in "he is getting used to living") is a simple preposition requiring the gerund "living" after it.

Thus, whenever you see a "to" coupled with "動詞型(DOUSHIKEI: verbals)", not with nouns, you must be careful whether it is "a simple preposition" or "an infinitive", which can be determined by the form of the verbal coming after "to": "to(preposition)+-ing(gerund)" or "to(infinitive)+-(root)".

しかしながら、一つだけ、特別な注意を要する「前置詞」がある・・・"to"がそれで、この語には二つの顔がある:後続部に「動名詞(-ing)」を従える単純な「前置詞としての"to"」と、後続部に「動詞原形(-)」を従える「不定詞(an infinitive)としての"to"」の二面性があるのである。

例 Although he used to be rather awkward in English, he is getting used to living in the States, linguistically or socially.

昔の彼は英語がかなりぎこちなかったが、この頃は言葉の上でも社会的にも、彼はアメリカでの暮らしに慣れてきている

上の例文では、最初の"to"("he used to be"の部分)は「不定詞の"to"」として用いられているので後続部には「原形」の"be"の形を求める。二つ目の"to"("he is getting used to living"の部分)は単純な「前置詞の"to"」であるから直後には「動名詞」の"living"の形を求めている。

このように、"to"が「名詞型(nouns)」ではなく「動詞型(verbals)」と一緒に使われる場面では常に、その"to"が「単純な前置詞」なのか「不定詞」なのかに注意を払わねばならないが、"to"の後に来る動詞の形態を見ればその判定は可能である:「to+-ing」の形ならばそれは「前置詞としての"to"+動名詞の"-ing"」であり、「to+-」の形ならばそれは「不定詞としての"to"+動詞の原形」である。

9. It takes proficiency to discern the past participle from the past form

- 述語(JUTSUGO: Predicate) or 後位修飾語(KOUI-SHUUSHOKUGO: qualifier): a tough hurdle for novice learners to get over -

eg. Old schools revisited felt all so strange to me that I was beginning to wonder if I had really passed my life there.

The above-mentioned sentence could hardly be understood by novice learners of English in Japan; they couldn't make head or tail of "revisited felt" part, thinking of it as "two verbs intangibly combined in the past form".

Actually, no two English verbs can ever be used in tandem: no English verb can immediately follow another verb (except in such cases as "He helped me solve the problem" being abbreviated into "He helped solve the problem"). Only "助動詞(JODOUSHI: an auxiliary verb)" can follow a verb (eg. "Old schools do feel strange"), but then again, the verb followed by an auxiliary verb must always take the root form, never the past form or the past participle (this is also true with the above-mentioned "help solve the problem" type of structure, the verb following "help" being always used in the root form).

Too complicated to follow?... OK, here comes the answer: the true structure of the first example is "(S)<Old schools {revisited}> (V)felt all (C)so strange to me", in which the "verbal" part is the second "felt", and the first "revisited" is not the past form of "revisit" but the past participle modifying the preceding noun "old schools". Such terms modifying(=describing the attribute of) terms from behind are called "qualifiers: 後位修飾語: KOUI-SHUUSHOKUGO", as opposed to "modifiers: 前位修飾語: ZENI-SHUUSHOKUGO" which modify terms immediately after them.

The "＜名詞{後位修飾語}述語＞:<noun {qualifier} predicate>" structure is one of the most perplexing in English sentences, but here is a useful tip for getting over this puzzle: whenever you see "an apparently past form of a verb" followed by "another verb, whether in the past/present/future form",

9. 過去分詞と過去形の見分けには熟練の技が必要

ー「述語(predicate)」なのか「後位修飾語(qualifier)」なのか・・・初学者には乗り越えがたい高いハードルー

例 Old schools revisited felt all so strange to me that I was beginning to wonder if I had really passed my life there.

再び訪れてみた昔の学校はどれもみな私には馴染みのない場に思われて、自分は本当にそこで人生を過ごしてきたのだろうか、と疑問に感じ始めていた

上掲の文章は、日本の英語初学者にはまずもって理解できないものだろう。"revisited felt"の部分を「2つの動詞の過去形がワケわからん感じで結合してる」と考えるあたりから、何が何だかさっぱりわからん感じになるに違いないのだ。実際には、英語の動詞が二つ並んで用いられる例は一切ない:("He helped me solve the problem.:私がその問題を解決するのを彼が手助けしてくれた"という文章が"He helped solve the problem."という"me"抜き形へと切り詰められる事例などを除けば)いかなる英語の動詞も直後にまた動詞を連続して従えることなどあり得ないのだ。直後に動詞を従えることが出来るのは「助動詞(an auxiliary verb)」のみである(例 "Old schools ＜do feel＞ strange.:昔の学校は確かに不思議な感じがする")が、それでもやはり、助動詞直後に続く動詞は常に「原形(the root form)」であって「過去分詞形(the past participle)」の形など絶対にあり得ない(この点は、上述の"help solve the problem"型の構造でも同じであり、"help"に続く動詞は常に「原形」で用いられる)。

あんまりややこしすぎてついて行けない、って感じだろうか?・・・よろしい、それならそろそろ正解を出そう:最初に掲載した例文の正しい構造は"(S)<Old schools {revisited}:再訪された昔の学校> (V)felt all:みな感じられた (C)so strange to me:私にとって実に奇妙な感じに"であって、「動詞」部にあたるのは2つめの"felt"であり、1つめの"revisited"の方は"rivisit"という動詞の「過去形(the past form)」ではなく、「過去分詞形(the past participle)」として直前の名詞"old schools"を修飾しているのである。このような「ある語を後ろから修飾する(=その特性を具体的に描写する)語句」のことを「後位修飾語(qualifiers)」と呼ぶ(これは、「ある語を前から修飾する語句」の「前位修飾語(modifiers)」と対を成す呼び名である)。

"＜名詞{後位修飾語}述語＞:<noun {qualifier} predicate>"の構造は、英文の中でも最もややこしいものの一つであるが、このパズルめいた構造を乗り越えるのに役立つコツを教えておこう:「一見、動詞の過去形に見えるもの」がその直後に「別の動詞(過去形/現在形/未来形の如何を問わない)」を従えている場面に出くわしたら、最初

be sure that the first one is "not a verb in the past form, but the past participle of a verb" which qualifies the noun immediately before it. This is quite a powerful info which will advance your level of English from sheer beginner to intermediate.

But there is one exceptional case which defies even the advanced-class learners of English... Would you like to see it, or hate to see anything even more scary?... Anyway, I'll show you, whether you like it or not.

- SVOC developing around verbs of perception, with O coming in front: tough like hell for all but the erudite -

eg. Houses, cars and even humans she saw washed away by the Tsunami left a permanent impression upon her heart.

In this example, the "saw / washed" part is not "the past participle / the past form" combination but "the past form / the past participle"... Mind-boggling? It sure is, but don't be afraid, for the explanation is soon coming up, after three more example sentences developing around the famous (or infamous?) "知覚動詞(CHIKAKU-DOUSHI: verbs of perception)".

Verbs of perception used in the (V)verb part of SVOC sentence pattern(#5) requires the following three forms of verbals in the part of (C)complement:

(1)S+知覚動詞(perceptional verb)+O+原形不定詞(GENKEI-FUTEISHI: the root infinitive):

eg. She heard people shout "Run!"

(2)S+知覚動詞(perceptional verb)+O+現在分詞(GENZAI-BUNSHI: the present participle):

eg. She saw the Tsunami coming.

(3)S+知覚動詞(perceptional verb)+O+過去分詞(KAKO-BUNSHI: the past participle):

eg. She saw houses, cars and even humans washed away by the Tsunami.

Now, you see, the first example sentence is based on the last one's SVOC sentence pattern, with the word order inverted into O-SVC: the "(V)saw (C)washed" was "(V)the past form (C)the past participle" combination, with the "(O)houses, cars and even humans" part (which ought logically to be in

のやつは「動詞の過去形ではなく、過去分詞形」がその直前の名詞を「後ろから修飾」しているものだ、と決めてかかればそれでよい。この知識は効果抜群で、このことを踏まえておけば、諸君の英語の水準も全くの初心者から中級レベルへと一歩前進することだろう。

だが一つ、たとえ上級レベルの英語学習者でさえも手もなくひねられる例外的な場合がある・・・見てみたい？・・・それともこれ以上恐ろしげなやつなんて見たくない？(・・・ま、好むと好まざるとにかかわらず、いずにせよ次にお見せしちゃうわけだけど)

－知覚動詞を中心に展開するSVOCのOが冒頭に出た構文・・・博学の主以外には地獄のように大変なやつ－

例 Houses, cars and even humans she saw washed away by the Tsunami left a permanent impression upon her heart.

家々が、車が、人間さえもが、津波によって流されるのを彼女が目の当たりにしたあの光景は、彼女の心に消えない印象を残した。

この例では、“saw / washed”の部分は“過去分詞(the past participle) / 過去形(the past form)”の組み合わせではなく、“過去形 / 過去分詞”の組み合わせになっている・・・頭がこんがらがりそう？・・・確かにそんなややこしさだが、心配はいらない、説明はすぐに(・・・あと3つほど、かの有名な(というか、悪名高い？)「知覚動詞(verbs of perception)」絡みの例文を列挙したその後で)聞けるから。

SVOC(第5文型)の「(V)動詞」部分に「知覚動詞(verbs of perception)」が使われた場合、「(C)補語」の部分に「動詞型(vervals)」を用いる際には以下の3種の形態となる:

(1)S+知覚動詞+O+原形不定詞(the root infinitive):

例 She heard people shout “Run!”

人々が「逃げろ！」と叫ぶのを彼女は聞いた

(2)S+知覚動詞+O+現在分詞(the present participle):

例 She saw the Tsunami coming.

津波がやって来るのを彼女は見た

(3)S+知覚動詞+O+過去分詞(the past participle):

例 She saw houses, cars and even humans washed away by the Tsunami.

家々や車さらには人さえも津波に流されるのを彼女は見た

ということで、おわかりいただけたであろう、最初に挙げた例文は、最後の例文の「SVOC」構文を基盤に成立しており、その語順が「O－SVC」に変更されたものだったのである。“(V)saw (C)washed”の部分は“(V)過去形 (C)過去分詞形”の組み合せで、

between the (V) and (C)) placed at the beginning of the sentence as the focus of attention. And the whole "O-SVC" part ("(S)<(o)Houses, cars and even humans {(s)she (v)saw (c)washed away (by the Tsunami)}>") functions as the (S)subject of "(V)left (O)<a permanent impression (upon her heart)>".

- There is no such thing as (V)(V) in English sentence patterns -

I'm sorry to have troubled your brains with unrealistically complicated sentences. But those sentences are actually used (not only written but spoken!) in the world of English. My advice for you is simple: when you see a seemingly (V)(V)(dual-verb) combination, the former part is most likely to be "a qualifier in the form of the past participle". The odds that you encounter the far rarer and tougher sentence pattern of "O-SV(a verb of perception)C(the past participle)" are less than 100 to 1!

“(O)houses, cars and even humans”部(論理的には(V)と(C)の中間に位置するはずの部分)が文章の冒頭部に置かれて注目の的となっている。そしてこの「O－SVC」部の全体((S)<(o)Houses, cars and even humans {(s)she (v)saw (c)washed away (by the Tsunami)}>)がまた、“(V)left (O)<a permanent impression (upon her heart)>“に対する“(S)主語”として機能しているわけである。

－英語の文章に「(V)動詞(V)動詞」が連続するパターンは存在しない－

現実離れして複雑な文章の数々で諸君の脳味噌を悩ませて申し訳ない。だが、そうした文章たちもまた現実の英語世界で使われている(書かれている、のみならず、喋られている！)のだ。諸君に対する筆者の助言は、単純である：一見「(V)(V)(動詞二枚重ね)」の組み合わせに見えるものを見たら、その(V)(V)の最初の側はほぼ決まって「過去分詞の形を取った後位修飾語」である。遙かに珍しく難解な「O－SV(知覚動詞)C(過去分詞)」構造に諸君が遭遇する確率は、100分の1以下(！)であろう。

10. SPAT-5: five sentence patterns are a magical set of molds to comprehend English in

- A long, cynical failure story of KATA in Japan -

Since English is a quite assimilative language, it has acquired not a few words from Japanese. "型(カタ:KATA)" is one of them, and quite a popular one at that, probably because it signifies the very notion that most foreigners feel is symbolically Japanese — a pattern, form, mold or structure in which things or actions are created and interpreted.

In the world of English grammar, there is a very powerful set of KATA called "五文型(GOBUNKEI): Five(5) Sentence Patterns of English". This KATA was originally conceived by a British scholar Charles Talbut Onions and has long formed the backbone of traditional teaching of English in Japan. As such, when self-styled reformists of the miserably faulty Japanese English education sought scapegoats to point their blaming fingers at, the traditional importance set upon those Five Sentence Patterns of English was made a target of, along with many other KATA-DORI(型通り:rigidly formal) methodologies – possibly because they were felt to be too symbolically Japanese.

But the practical usefulness of this KATA for English learners in Japan is so great that it is downright foolish of some Japanese English educators to pervertedly go against teaching it. Their bigoted antipathy to anything with a flavor of "英文法(EIBUNPOU)" – English grammatical comprehension and teaching – is the very embodiment of KATA-DORI-NO-NIHONJIN: a typical Japanese making a villain of someone/something else to play the role of Captain Justice, only to perpetuate the problem by refusing to seek and solve the real cause of the problem.

When in 1982 the Japanese Ministry of Education (now pompously called "Ministry of Education, Culture, Sports, Science and Technology" or compactly dubbed "MEXT") decided to "abolish" official censorship of textbooks regarding English grammar, their original message to "liberate" English grammatical education from unduly rigid official restriction was misinterpreted by too many Japanese as a "death sentence" to teaching of grammar at school. The result was that the level of English literacy in Japan,

10. SPAT-5:5文型は英文理解の魔法の鋳型

－日本の"カタ(型)"を巡る長く皮肉な失敗物語－

英語は同化吸収力が極めて高い言語なので、英単語の中には日本語から生まれたものも少なくない。「KATA(カタ＝型)」もまたその一つであり、しかもとっても人気のある和風英単語の一つである・・・恐らくは、「物事や行動をそれに当てはめて創出・解釈するためのパターン・フォーム・鋳型・構造」という、大方の外国人が「いかにも日本的」と感じる概念そのものを表わすのが「カタ」だから、ということだろう。

英文法の世界には、「5文型(＝英文の5大パターン)」と呼ばれる大変強力な一群の「型」がある。このカタは元々英国人学者 Charles Talbut Onions(チャールズ・トルボット・オニオンズ)によって考案されて以来、長い間に渡って日本の英語教育の中で重要な役割を果たしてきた。それぐらい伝統的な「型」であっただけに、惨めなまでに欠陥だらけの日本の英語教育の「改革者」を気取った連中が「こんなことしてるからダメなんだ！」として非難の矛先にすべき相手を探した時、「5文型に重きを置きすぎる日本の英語教育の伝統」もまた、他の幾多の「型どおりの」方法論と並んで生けにえの一つとなった・・・恐らくは、そのあまりに見事にカタにはまった方法論的やり方が「いかにも日本的すぎる」と感じられたからだろう。

だが、この「型」は日本の英語学習者にとっては実用的に大いに役立つものだから、日本で英語を教える者がこの「5文型」をムキになって排斥するのは、まったく馬鹿げている。「英文法(＝英文の構成原理を理解し教えること)」の臭いのする物事にはすべて偏屈なまでに背を向けたがる連中の姿勢こそ、まさしく「型どおりの日本人」の典型なのだ・・・自分以外の誰かや何かを「悪者」に仕立て上げることで、自分が「正義の味方」を演じる・・・のだけれど結局は、問題の本当の原因の究明も解決もしようとしないのだから、その問題をいつまでもズルズル長引かせるばかり・・・そんな典型的な日本人の姿そのものである。

1982年に日本の文部省(今現在は「文部科学省」などと大仰な呼ばれ方をしている英式略称"MEXT＝Ministry of Education, Culture, Sports, Science and Technology"という名の省庁)が、「英文法」に関する公的教科書検定制度を「廃止」する決定を下した時、英語の文法教育を厳格すぎる公的制約から「解放」しようとするその本来の意図を、学校で文法を教えることに対する「死刑宣告」と誤解する日本人があまりにも多すぎた・・・結果、ただでさえ低かった日本人の英語読み書き能力は、「体系立った

without systematic grammatical comprehension, went even downward ever since the 80s. Too many Japanese, teachers and learners alike, possibly including "MEXT" folks themselves nowadays, by making a scapegoat of English grammar, fell victims to their own absurd fallacy that grammar was not necessary for English mastery. They were foolish enough to believe that they had been, up until the 1980s, unable to command English BECAUSE they had been too conscious of grammar. So, the Japanese bravely gave up EIBUNPOU(English grammar) altogether and went boldly into the world of "総合英語:SOUGOU-EIGO(?GENERAL? English)" or "生きた英語:IKITA-EIGO(English !ALIVE!)", only to commit collective suicide on linguistic and logical plane. Not that grammatical facts were forbidden to be taught in classrooms; it is only that they were provided as occasional "useful tips" on "as necessary" basis, and totally lost their integrity as a collective system of knowledge. Ever since then, for lack of consciously systematic teaching or training in English education, systematical comprehension, comprehensive thinking and action or responsible coherence in any action are all quite rare to find here in Japan. And the rest is history: decades of decay of this once prosperous nation.

Simply put, it didn't occur to shallow grammar-haters in Japan that they didn't have that privilege of so many Indo-European learners of English which enabled them to comprehend this foreign language in roughly the same grammatical KATA as their own. English language is as grammatically similar to French or Italian as it is structurally alien from Japanese language. Native speakers of Indo-European languages can take advantage of their innate linguistic KATA as the mold in which to interpret English. Japanese natives, on the other hand, have to "migrate" from their own NIHONGO-NO-KATA into "totally alien" English grammatical structure. Spanish, Italian or even French natives could become speakers of English, however broken, by randomly memorizing words and phrases in English without much thought to grammar; the same random memorizing effort leads Japanese nowhere without the logical backbone of structurally similar grammar.

文法理解」を失って、1980年代以降は更にまた輪をかけて低落してしまった。教師も学習者も、ひょっとすれば最近は“MEXT：文部科学省”自身をも含めて、あまりにも多くの日本人が「英文法」をやり玉に挙げて叩くことで「英語修得に文法など不要」という愚かな思い込みに陥り、その誤信により自らの首を絞めたのである。1980年代に至るまで自分達が英語をモノに出来ずにいたのは「文法を意識しすぎていたせいだ」な〜んて信じ込めちゃうほどに、彼らは阿呆だったわけである・・・かくて、日本人たちは大胆にも「英文法」を完全に放棄して「総合英語」の世界へ、あるいは「“生きた”英語」とやらへ、勇敢に乗り出した・・・とどのつまりが、言語学的にも論理的次元でも、集団自殺のテイタラクとなり果てたわけである。「教室内で文法上の事実を教えてはならない」という禁令があるわけではない：文法的な事柄などというものは「必要に応じて」時折もらえる「便利な一口情報」として提供されるばかりで体系的知識としての堅実な存在感を完全に喪失してしまった、というだけの話である。そうして80年代以降ずっと、英語教育に於ける意識的に体系付けられた教育も訓練も存在しないがゆえに、いかなる行動面に於ける「全体を見据えた上での思考や行動」も「首尾一貫した責任ある態度」も、ここ日本ではみな滅多に見られぬ有様となってしまった・・・そしてその後、どうなったか・・・それは「歴史」に語ってもらおう：かつて一度は繁栄を見たこの国が、数十年かけて腐り果ててきたその様を。

単純に言えば、インド・ヨーロッパ語圏の大多数の英語学習者の場合、自国語と大まかな点ではほぼ一緒の文法的「型」に当てはめてこの英語という外国語を理解できるという特権的立場にあるわけだが、そのような特権は自分達にはないのだという事実が、考えの浅い「文法嫌いの日本人」連中の頭にはまるで思い浮かばなかったわけである。英語は文法的にはフランス語やイタリア語に類似しているが、構造的に日本語とは似ても似つかぬよそ者言語である。インド・ヨーロッパ言語を母国語とする人々ならば、英語を理解するための鋳型として、自国語の「カタ」を有効活用できる。これに対し、日本語を母国語とする人々の場合は、彼ら独自の「日本語のカタ」から「まったくの余所者」である英語の文法構造へと「移住」する必要がある。ドイツ語やイタリア語を(どころかあのフランス語でさえも)母国語とする人々ならば、「文法」などさほど深く考えずに単語や言い回しを無造作に覚えまくるだけで(片言とはいえ)英語を話せるようにはなる・・・が、彼ら同様の行き当たりばったりの暗記努力をいくら重ねたとて、日本人には「構造的に類似した文法」という論理の背骨がないわけだから、どうにもなりはしないのだ。

Too lucidly simple to point out, right? The last thirty years of this miserable country would be more than enough to prove the absurd failure of that Japanese attitude which made too little of logical understanding and opted too much for mindlessly imitating the success of others essentially different from themselves, linguistically or otherwise. It is high time Japan woke up from such idle gainless sleep into stark reality: for them to master English, they have need of KATA, totally different linguistic structural molds to comprehend English in.

That is where the Five Sentence Patterns of English shines so graciously; so much so that let us thankfully benefit from it, devising for it a nickname *SPAT-5, meaning clear-cut(!SUPATTO!) understanding of English in five tangible molds.

**Be advised "SPAT-5" is an originally coined phrase by this author Jaugo Noto in 2012, and will not be understood by anyone who doesn't read this book.*

- The limitation of SPAT-5: five sentence patterns of English -

Since it is Japanese folks that this book is mainly written for, I must at first remind you of this plain fact, too plain for most people in the world to explain, that the value of KATA does not lie in its perfect application to everything but in its special usefulness in something. SPAT-5, Five Sentence Patterns of English, is not perfectly applicable to all English sentences. They cannot deal with "命令文:MEIREIBUN(imperative sentences)", "進行形:SHINKOUKEI(the progressive form)", "受動態:JUDOUTAI(the passive voice)" or "群動詞:GUNDOUSHI(group verbs)" as they are. These inapplicable objects must be changed into some other manageable forms: eg. imperative "Go" must be supplemented with the subject "you" and be treated as "(S)You (V)go"; "I was sleeping" is to be interpreted as "the progressive form of (S)I (V)slept"; "Caesar was killed by Brutus" needs to be translated into "the passive voice of (S)Brutus (V)killed (O)Caesar"; and "We've done away with the custom" should be treated as something like "(S)We (V)have abolished(='ve done away with) (O)the custom". This imperfection of SPAT-5

あまりに明快そのものの単純さで、いちいち指摘するまでもないこと、であろう？ 論理的理解を全く軽んじては何も考えずに他者の－それも自分達とは(言語学的にもその他の面でも)根源的に異なる余所様の－成功例の模倣に傾きすぎる日本の態度の愚かしい失敗の実証例としては、この惨めな国のこれまでの30年間は、十分すぎるというものであろう・・・もういいかげん、そうした不毛な惰眠から覚めてありのままの現実を見据える機は、熟しているはずだ：日本人が英語を習得するために、必要なものは「カタ」なのである。日本語とは全く異なる言語学的構造の鋳型に英文を当てはめて理解するための「型」が、日本人には必要なのである。

そこで燦然と輝くのが「英語の五文型(5 Sentence Patterns of English)」である・・・その威光の大きさに、我々は有り難くその恩恵に浴するとともに、5つのわかり易い鋳型にはめ込んで英語を明瞭に(！スパッと！)理解するためのものとして、この「五文型」には「SPAT-5(**S**entence **PAT**tern 5)」なるニックネームを献上しようではないか。

＊注意書き＊ "SPAT-5(すぱっとふぁいぶ)"とはこの筆者(之人冗悟：のと・じゃうご：2012)独自発案の造語につき、この本を読んでいない人には誰も何のことだかわからないであろうから、そのおつもりで。

－SPAT-5(英語の5大文型)の限界－

この本は主として日本人向けに書かれているので、ここでまず最初に次のような明瞭な事実(あまりに明瞭すぎて世界の人々には敢えて説明の必要もない事実)を念押ししておく必要があろう：「カタ」は、あらゆる物事に完璧に適用可能だから価値がある、のではなくて、一部の物事に特別有効だからこそ価値があるのである。英語の文章の5つの構造を表わす「SPAT-5」にしても、ありとあらゆる英文に対して100％適用可能ではない。SPAT-5 では、「命令文(imperative sentences)」も「進行形(the progressive form)」も「受動態(the passive voice)」も「群動詞(group verbs)」も、そのままの形では扱えない。これら適用対象外の事例は、SPAT-5 でも扱えるような他の形態へと直して解釈せねばならないのだ：例えば、「命令文」の"Go.：行け"の場合はそこに主語"you：君"を補った上で"(S)You (V)go.：君が行く"の形として扱わねばならない；"I was sleeping.：私は眠っていた"の文章は「"(S)I (V)slept.：私は眠った"の進行形」として解釈することになる；"Caesar was killed by Brutus.：シーザーはブルータスによって殺された"は「"(S)Brutus (V)killed (O)Caesar.：ブルータスがシーザーを殺した"の受動態」として解釈される；そして"We've done away with the custom.：我々はその風習を廃止した"の場合は「"(S)We (V)have abolished(='ve done away with) (O)the custom."のような(単独型動詞での)言い換え表現として取り扱わねばならない。「SPAT-5」のこうした

may be unacceptable to "型通りの日本人:KATA-DORI-NO-NIHONJIN", Japanese believers in the omnipotence of KATA, but other than that, most reasonable learners must find these molds quite useful in comprehending the seemingly endless patterns of English sentences. That said, let us proceed to the actual forms of SPAT-5.

- Actual explanation of SPAT-5: Five Sentence Patterns of English -

＜I: SV＞... a sentence requiring no object(O) or complement(C)

eg. (S)I (V)sing.

This 1st sentence pattern is the simplest, consisting of subject-verb combination only, without referring to any object or requiring any complement to complete the meaning.

It is well to remember that this sentence pattern(I) is not so often used as a simple combination of S-V. The reversed style beginning with the adverbs "There" or "Here" are more frequently used:

eg. There (V)is (S)a book on my desk.

eg. Here (V)is (S)something for you.

In both examples above, the adverbs placed at the beginning can be moved deep into the sentences to make "(S)A book (V)is there on my desk" and "(S)Something (V)is here for you".

The split structure shown below also belongs to the 1st sentence pattern:

eg. (S)The fact (V)is that she doesn't really love him.

Although many English learners/speakers regard the sentence above as "(S)The fact (V)is (C)that she doesn't really love him", it actually is a modified form of "(S)The fact that she doesn't really love him (V)is(=exists)"; but it might be just as well to regard it as S-V-C, if it makes it easier to comprehend the meaning of this complicated sentence. Grammar is there to serve the understanding, not to dictate how to understand something.

A little controversial interpretation of this 1st sentence pattern can also comprehend sentences which point at (O)objects by way of prepositions:

不完全性は、「型どおりの日本人（＝カタの万能性を信じて疑わない人々）」にとっては受け入れ難いものであろうが、こうした難点を別にすれば、まともな考え方ができる学習者の多くは、一見無限にも思える英文の構造を理解する上で、これらの「カタ」は極めて有益であると感じるはずである・・・と、ずらずら前口上を並べ立てた上で、そろそろ「SPAT-5」の実際の諸形態の考察に移ることにしよう。

－実際の「SPAT-5」の解説－

＜I: SV＞・・・「目的語(O:object)」も「補語(C:complement)」も必要としない文章

例 (S)I (V)sing. 私は歌う

この「第1文型」は最も単純なパターンで、「主語(S)－動詞(V)」の組み合わせのみから成り、「目的語(O)」に言及したり「補語(C)」を取ったりすることもなしにその意味が完結する。

この「第1文型」が「(S)主語－(V)動詞」の単純な組み合わせとして用いられる事例はあまり多くはない、という事実は覚えておくべきだろう。副詞の“There:そこに”や“Here:ここに”で始まる倒置構造の方が、単純型よりも頻繁に用いられる:

例 There (V)is (S)a book on my desk. 私の机の上に本が一冊ある

例 Here (V)is (S)something for you. ここにあなたへのちょっとした贈り物がある

上のいずれの例に於いても、冒頭部に置かれた副詞(There/Here)は文章の奥底に移動することが可能で、その場合は“(S)A book (V)is there on my desk.”及び“(S)Something (V)is here for you.”となる。

以下に示す分離構造もまた「第1文型」に属する:

例 (S)The fact (V)is that she doesn't really love him. 実際のところ、彼女は彼を心底愛しているわけではない

英語を学ぶ（話す）人の多くは、上の例文を“(S)The fact (V)is (C)that she doesn't really love him.”の構造だと考えるが、実際にはこれは“(S)The fact {that she doesn't really love him} (V)is(=exists)”の形態の修正版である・・・が、この構文を「S-V-C」とみなしたとて同じことであって、そうみなすことでこの複雑な文章の意味がわかり易くなるのであれば、何ら問題はない。「文法」は「理解を助ける」ためにあるのであって、「どのように理解すべきか命じる」ために存在するものではないのだから。

「第1文型」であるか否かに関しては少々議論が分かれるところだが、解釈のしようによっては「前置詞(prepositions)を介して目的語(O:objects)を指向する文章」もまた「第1文型」扱いが可能である:

eg. (S)She (V)looked at me.

In the sentence above, since the verb "look" is intransitive, it cannot directly refer to the object "me" in the form of "She looked me", and so it has need of the intervention of the preposition "at". It is therefore structurally correct to say that the sentence above belongs to S-V(1st) sentence pattern, not to S-V-O(3rd). But the fact still remains that the above-mentioned sentence needs the object "me" to complete its meaning, which makes it equally logical to regard it as S-V-O. Compare it with the example below:

eg. (S)She (V)looked (O)me in the eye.

These two sentences are as structurally different as they are semantically similar. In such cases, it will do more harm than good to dwell too much upon structural interpretation. Meaning matters more than structure: SV or SVO, "She" needs "me" as a target of her "look"; if that much is understood, there is no more structural interpretation or definition needed.

<II: SVC>... a sentence requiring a complement(C) but no object(O)

eg. (S)I (V)am (C)a singer.

This 2nd one is the basic and most frequently used sentence pattern of English, the essential meaning of which is equivalent to the mathematical equation "(S)=(C): subject equals complement", with (C)complement specifically defining the characteristic of (S)subject by the aid of (V)verb.

The verb most frequently used in this SVC pattern is what is called the "be verb", an English equivalent for the mathematical symbol "=(equal)". But it is to be noted that the so-called "do verbs" can also be used in this 2nd sentence pattern, if they (even loosely) comprehend the meaning of "(S) equals (C)", as in the examples shown below:

eg. (S)I (V)will become (C)a singer.

The example above is virtually identical with "(S)I (V)will be (C)a singer" and can naturally be interpreted as belonging to the 2nd sentence pattern.

例　(S)She (V)looked at me.　彼女は私を見た

上の文では、“look:見る”という動詞は「自動詞(an intransitive verb)」であるから、目的語(O:object)に直接言及する形で“She looked me”とすることはできない；がゆえに「前置詞(a preposition)」“at”の介在を必要とするわけである；であるがゆえに、上の文は「S-V(第1文型)」のパターンに属し、「S-V-O(第3文型)」ではない、と言うことも(構造的に見て)正しい；がしかし、それでも上掲の文章がその意味を完結させるには「目的語としての“me”」を必要とする、というのは揺るぎない事実なのだから、これを「S-V-Oの第3文型」とみなすことだって(論理的に見て)同じように正しいわけである。この文章を、次の例文と比較してみるがよい：

例　(S)She (V)looked (O)me in the eye.　彼女は私の目を見た

これら2つの文章は、構造的には異質でも、意味の上では同類である。こういう場合、構造的解釈にこだわり過ぎるのは有害無益というものだ。構造よりも意味の方が大事なのである：「SV」だろうが「SVO」だろうが、“She:彼女”には“me:私”が“look:見つめる”対象として必要なのである；そのことさえ理解できれば、構造的解釈だの定義だのをその上にさらに付け足す必要など、ないのである。

<II: SVC>・・・「補語(C:complement)」を必要とするが、「目的語(O:object)」は必要としない文章

例　(S)I (V)am (C)a singer.　私は歌手である

この「第2文型」は、英文の中でも最も基本的かつ最も頻繁に用いられる文型で、その意味の中核は、数学の等式「(S)＝(C)：主語は補語と等価である」に等しく、「補語(C:complement)」が「主語(S:subject)」の特性を「動詞(V:verb)」の助けを借りて具体的に定義する形である。

この「SVC」パターンで最もよく用いられる動詞が、いわゆる“be 動詞”であり、これは数学記号の“＝(イコール)”の英語版と言える語である。しかしながら、この「第2文型」では、“(S)＝(C)”の意味を(大まかにであっても)包含するならば、いわゆる“do 動詞”が用いられる場合もある、ということを覚えておくべきである(例えば次例のごとし)：

例　(S)I (V)will become (C)a singer.　私は歌手になるつもりである

上例は実質的に“(S)I (V)will be (C)a singer.”と同じであるから、当然「第2文型」に属するものと解釈し得る。

In the next example, while it is structurally impossible to say which sentence pattern of SPAT-5 it belongs to, it is to be essentially interpreted as a form of S-V-C:

eg. (S)I was born (C)a singer.

The main structure of the above-mentioned sentence “I was born” is in the passive voice and, as such, it defies structural interpretation according to SPAT-5: the rigid translation of it into “the passive voice of (S)My mother (V)bore (O)me” makes no sense at all. But there is certainly an “equal relationship(S=C)” between (S) “I” and (C) “a singer”, which can be certified by linking them with “be verb” to make “(S)I (V)am (C)a singer”. Therefore, SPAT-5 regards it as sentence pattern II: SVC. Likewise, the sentences below are also deemed to be S-V-C:

eg. (S)She (V)sank (C)crying into the sofa.

eg. (S)I (V)slept (C)naked in the bed.

eg. (S)He (V)came back home (C)a different man.

<III: SVO>... a sentence requiring an object(O) but no complement(C)

eg. (S)I (V)sing (O)songs.

This sentence pattern appears only with the so-called “do verbs” and never with “be verbs”, except in the case of the progressive form:

eg. (S)I (V)was singing (O)songs.

The essential difference between S-V-O and S-V-C lies in the relationship between (S)subject and (O)object: they are two different things (except in such sentences as “(S)She (V)killed (O)herself”), and the S-V-O sentence develops around the action of (S)subject against (O)object. On the other hand, in S-V-C(sentence pattern II), (C)complement is there to specify the characteristic of (S)subject. In other words, (C) is subordinate to (S): while (S) equals (C) in meaning, (C) does not exist on equal terms with (S) but as its attribute. Symbolically speaking, S-V-C sentence pattern(II) is a unilateral story of (S)subject alone, while S-V-O sentence pattern(III) is an interactive story between (S) and (O).

次の例は、「SPAT-5」のどのパターンに属するか構造的には断言できない形ではあるものの、本質的に言えば「S-V-C」形式として解釈すべきものである:

例 (S)I was born (C)a singer. 私は生まれながらの歌手である

上述の文章の中心構造の“I was born:私は生まれた”は「受動態」であるから、そのままでは「SPAT-5」による構造解釈は不可能である:これを律儀に解釈して「(S)My mother (V)bore (O)me.:我が母が私を生んだ“の受動態」などとしてもまるで無意味である。それでも「(S:subject) “I”」と「(C:complement) “a singer”」の間には「対等の関係(S＝C)」が存在することは間違いない:このことは、両者を“be 動詞”で結んで“(S)I (V)am (C)a singer”とすることで確証できる。それゆえに、「SPAT-5」ではこれを「第2文型:SVC」とみなす。同様に、以下に示す文章もまた「S-V-C」型と解釈される:

例 (S)She (V)sank (C)crying into the sofa. 彼女はソファーに泣き伏した

例 (S)I (V)slept (C)naked in the bed. 私はベッドに裸で寝た

例 (S)He (V)came back home (C)a different man. 彼は別人になって帰宅した

＜III: SVO＞・・・「目的語(O:object)」を必要とするが「補語(C:complement)」は必要ない文章

例 (S)I (V)sing (O)songs. 私は歌をうたう

この文章パターンでは、いわゆる“do動詞”のみを伴い、“be動詞”を伴うことはあり得ない。但し、「進行形(the progressive form)」の場合は例外である:

例 (S)I (V)was singing (O)songs. 私は歌をうたっていた

「S-V-O」と「S-V-C」の根源的な違いは、「主語(S:subject)」と「目的語(O:object)」の間の関係にある:「主語」と「目的語」は全くの別物であり(但し、“(S)She (V)killed (O)herself.:彼女は自殺した＝彼女は自分自身を殺した”のような文章の場合はその限りではない)、「S-V-O」型の文章は「(O:object)目的語」に対する「(S:subject)主語」の行動を中心に展開する。これに対し、「S-V-C(第2文型)」では、「(C:complement)補語」は「(S:subject)主語」の特性を具体的に規定するために存在する。言葉を換えて言えば、「(C:補語)は、(S:主語)に従属する」のである:「(S)主語」と「(C)補語」は意味の上では等しいが、補語(C)は、主語(S)と対等の関係ではなくて主語(S)の「属性(attribute)」として存在するのである。象徴的な言い方をするならば、「S-V-C(第2文型)は、主語(S)のみの一方的なお話」なのに対し、「S-V-O(第3文型)は、主語(S)と目的語(O)の双方向性の物語」なのだ。

The verbs to be used in this S-V-O sentence pattern(III) are "transitive", which means they can refer to (O)object without the intervention of any preposition. But the same verb can both be "transitive" and "intransitive", making the sentence pattern sometimes S-V-O and sometimes S-V:
eg. (S)You (V)must improve (O)your technique more.
eg. (S)You (V)must improve upon your technique more.

These two sentences, while structurally different, have practically the same meaning. In such cases, the most important thing is the objective awareness — the realization that the verb "improve" needs "your technique" as its object, whether it refers directly to the object or via some preposition. In that sense, the relationship between (V)verb and its (O)object should always be conceived as (V)-(O) relationship, regardless of the presence of prepositions between them.

＜IV: SVOO＞... a sentence requiring two (O)objects — (iO)indirect object and (dO)direct object — signifying the action of transfer or benevolence(sometimes malevolence) of (dO)direct object from (S)subject to (iO)indirect object
eg. (S)He (V)gave (iO)me (dO)some money.

The sentence above signifies the transfer of (dO)"some money" from (S)"He" to (iO)"me", and can be written in the form of S-V-O(sentence pattern III) as follows:
eg. (S)He (V)gave (O)some money to me.

The "destination" of the transfer is shown by the preposition "to". Although the act of "giving me some money" has an element of "benevolence", the action is essentially "transfer" and so calls for the vectorial preposition "to".
eg. (S)I (V)sing (iO)my baby (dO)a lullaby.

The sentence above can also be written in the form of S-V-O(sentence pattern III) as follows:
eg. (S)I (V)sing (O)a lullaby for my baby.

The action of "singing my baby a lullaby" is not made as "transfer" but as "benevolence", so it calls for the preposition "for".

この「S-V-O(第3文型)」で用いられる「動詞(verbs)」は「他動詞(transitive verbs)」である:即ち、「前置詞(prepositions)」の介在なしに「目的語(O:object)」に言及できる動詞である。しかし、全く同じ動詞が、ある時は「他動詞(transitive)」で別の時には「自動詞(intransitive)=前置詞なしには目的語を取れない動詞」である場合もあるので、それによって文型もまた「S-V-O」にも「S-V」にも変わることになる:

例 (S)You (V)must improve (O)your technique more.

例 (S)You (V)must improve upon your technique more.

君はもっと技術を向上させる必要がある

これら2つの文章は、構造的には異なるものの、実質的には同じ意味を表わす。こういう場合、最も重要なのは「目的語意識」－動詞“improve:改善する”には(直接言及しようが前置詞を介して間接的に言及しようがいずれにせよ)目的語“your technique:君の技術”が必要、という認識－である。この意味に於いて、「(V:verb)動詞」とその「(O:object)目的語」の関係は常に(途中に前置詞が存在する／しないの如何を問わず)「V(動詞)－O(目的語)関係」として認識すべきである。

<IV: SVOO>・・・2つの「(O:object)目的語」－「(iO:indirect object)間接目的語」と「(dO:direct object)直接目的語」－を必要とし、「(dO:direct object)直接目的語」が「(S:subject)主語」から「(iO:indirect object)間接目的語」へと「譲り渡される」かあるいは「善意(時に、悪意)により行なわれる」かのいずれかの行為を表わす

例 (S)He (V)gave (iO)me (dO)some money. 彼は私にいくらかのお金をくれた

上の文章は「(dO)直接目的語」の“some money:お金”が「(S)主語」の“He:彼”から「(iO)間接目的語」の“me:私”へと「委譲(transfer)」される意味を表わし、「S-V-O(第3文型)」の型を用いて次のように書くこともできる:

例 (S)He (V)gave (O)some money to me.

「委譲(transfer)」の行為の「行く先」は「前置詞」“to:～へ向けて”によって示される。“giving me some money:私にお金を与えること”という行為の中には「善意(benevolence)」の要素も含まれるものの、この行動は本質的に「委譲＝AからBへの移し替え」であるから、「ベクトル(→方向性)の前置詞」である“to”を伴うのである。

例 (S)I (V)sing (iO)my baby (dO)a lullaby. 私は赤ちゃんに子守歌を歌ってあげる

上の文章はまた「S-V-O(第3文型)」の型を用いて次のように書くことができる:

例 (S)I (V)sing (O)a lullaby for my baby.

“singing my baby a lullaby:赤ちゃんに子守歌をうたうこと”という行為は「委譲(transfer)」ではなく「慈善(benevolence)」として行なわれるものであるから、そこで必要な前置詞は“for:～のために”である。

The verbs to be used in this S-V-O-O(sentence pattern IV) can mostly be classified according to the preposition — "to" or "for" — needed in paraphrasing in S-V-O sentence pattern(III). But there are some exceptional verbs requiring prepositions other than "to" or "for":
eg. (S)He (V)asked (iO)me (dO)some questions.

The action of "asking me some questions" is made in order to "get something out of someone", so it requires the preposition "of" in S-V-O(III) paraphrasing:
eg. (S)He (V)asked (O)some questions of me.

The verbs "provide" or "supply" are similar in meaning to "give", but they basically require different prepositions than "to":
eg. (S)Many foreign countries (V)provide/supply (iO)Japan (dO)oil.
eg. (S)Many foreign countries (V)provide/supply (O)Japan with oil.
eg. (S)Many foreign countries (V)provide/supply (O)oil for Japan.
eg. (S)Many foreign countries (V)provide/supply (O)oil to Japan.

<V: SVOC>... a sentence in which the relationship between (O)object and (C)complement is to be interpreted as "a virtual interaction between (S)subject and (V)verb", to which "the structural S-V at the beginning of the sentence" refers as an intervening factor, in the capacities of a third-person, observer, instigator, promoter, etc,etc.
eg. (S)I (V)made (O)her (C)my secretary.

In the sentence above, the first relationship to consider is "(O)her(=she) (V)is (C)my secretary". This virtual S-V relationship is called "nexus", which is the very essence of S-V-O-C(sentence pattern V). The status of "(O/S)her/she (V)is (C)my secretary" is something that "(S)I (V)made", in which top priority is to be given to "(O)her-(C)my secretary"(virtual (S)she-(V)is (C)my secretary) relationship, not to "(S)I (V)made". Remember: you must first interpret the nexus(=virtual S-V relation) between (O)-(C) and then add (S)-(V) to it as an intervening supplement.

この「S-V-O-O(第4文型)」で用いられる「動詞(verbs)」は、「S-V-O(第3文型)」で言い換える場合に必要となる「前置詞(prepositions)」が“to:～へ向けて”であるかそれとも“for:～のために”であるかによって区分することができる場合が大半であるが、“to”でも“for”でもない別の前置詞を必要とする動詞も一部存在する:

例 (S)He (V)asked (iO)me (dO)some questions. 彼は私にいくつかの質問をした

“asking me some questions:私にいくつかの質問をすること”という行為は「誰かの中から引っ張り出す形で何かを手に入れる」ために行なわれるものであるから、これを「S-V-O(第3文型)」で換言する場合に必要になる前置詞は“of:～の中から”となる:

例 (S)He (V)asked (O)some questions of me.

“provide”や“supply”(意味はいずれも「提供する」)といった動詞は、意味の上では“give:与える”と同じだが、基本的に“to:～に向けて”とは異なる前置詞を必要とする:

例 (S)Many foreign countries (V)provide/supply (iO)Japan (dO)oil.

例 (S)Many foreign countries (V)provide/supply (O)Japan with oil.

例 (S)Many foreign countries (V)provide/supply (O)oil for Japan.

例 (S)Many foreign countries (V)provide/supply (O)oil to Japan.

多くの外国が日本向けの石油を提供している

<V: SVOC>・・・「“(O:object)目的語”と“(C:complement)補語”の関係」が「実質的に“(S:subject)主語”と“(V:verb)述語動詞”の関係」とみなされるべき構文で、この「実質的に(S)-(V)に等しい(O)-(C)」に対し、「文章冒頭にある“構造上の S-V”」は「第三者・観察者・教唆者・促進者・等々」の資格で関わる「介在要素」として言及する形となる

例 (S)I (V)made (O)her (C)my secretary. 私は彼女を私の秘書にした

上の文章で真っ先に考慮すべきは「(O)her(=she) (V)is (C)my secretary:(O)彼女は(C)私の秘書(V)である」の関係である。このような実質的「S(主語)－V(述語動詞)」関係は「ネクサス(nexus:対結)」と呼ばれ、この関係こそが「S-V-O-C(第五文型)」の中核となっている。「(O/S)her/she:彼女 (V)is:イコール (C)my secretary:私の秘書」という状態は、「(S)I:私が (V)made:作った」ものであり、この構造の中で第一優先順位を置くべきは「(O)her:彼女－(C)my secretary:私の秘書」(実質的に「(S)she:彼女-(V)is:イコール (C)my secretary:私の秘書」)の関係であって、「(S)I:私 (V)made:作った」の方の優先順位は低い。覚えておくことだ:まず最初に(O:目的語)-(C:補語)間に存在する「ネクサス(＝実質的 S-V 関係)」を解釈して後に、(S:主語)-(V:動詞)の部分を「介在型の補足要素」として(O)-(C)に付け足す、という手順を取る必要があるのが「SVOC(第五文型)」なのである。

S-V-O-C's difference from seemingly similar S-V-O-O is the presence/absence of “nexus(virtual S-V relationship)” between O-C/O-O:
eg. (S)I (V)made (iO)her (dO)some drink.

In order to prove that the above-mentioned sentence does not have S-V-O-C(sentence pattern V) structure, you have only to pick out “(iO)her (dO)some drink” part and try to interpret them as virtual S-V: since it is impossible to change it into “(S)She (V)is (C)some drink”, there is no “nexus” found between “(iO)her” and “(dO)some drink”, which makes it SVOO instead of SVOC.

S-V-O-C sentence pattern(V) is by far the most complicated and versatile structure of English, the mastery of which certainly takes much time, effort and getting used to, but will surely make learners confident of their growing command of English. Although I will not give further explanations or examples of S-V-O-C here, always remember to check “O-C” first and confirm the lurking “nexus” behind them, never to bother “S-V” until you have grasped the “virtual S-V relationship between O-C”.

一見似たように見える「S-V-O-C」と「S-V-O-O」の相違は、「O-C 間／O-O 間」に「ネクサス(nexus:実質的 S-V:主語－述語関係)」が存在する／しないの違いである:
例 (S)I (V)made (iO)her (dO)some drink. 私は彼女に飲み物を作ってあげた

上述の文章が「S-V-O-C(第五文型)」の構造を持たないことを証明するには、“(iO)her:彼女 (dO)some drink:飲み物”の部分を取り出してこれを「実質的 S-V:主語－述語関係」として解釈してみるだけでよい:この部分を「(S)She (V)is (C)some drink.:彼女は飲み物である」へと書き換えることはできないのだから、“(iO)her:彼女”と“(dO)some drink:飲み物”の間に「nexus:ネクサス(意味上の主語－述語関係:対結)」は存在せず、そのことからこの文型は「SVOC(第五文型)」ではなく「SVOO(第4文型)」ということになる。

第五文型「S-V-O-C」は、英語の文章構造の中でも最も複雑にして最も多彩なものであり、その修得には多大なる時間と努力と習熟を要するが、そうしてこの第五文型を修得した学習者には「自分も英語ができるようになってきたなぁ」という自信が付くのも確かである。S-V-O-C についてはもうこの場でこれ以上の説明も文例も提供することはしないが、いつでも常に“O-C:目的語－補語”に最初に注目してその背後に潜在する“nexus:ネクサス”を確認し、“O-C 間に存在する実質的 S-V 関係”をつかむまでは一切“S-V”には目もくれない心がけを決して忘れないことが大事である。

11. Backbone of English comprehension: 5 kinds of sentences, 6 sentential elements and 8 parts of speech

- The importance, or the limitation to the importance, of technical terms -

The importance of "a name" as a key to grasping something is never felt so dearly as in playing music. I believe most of you readers have heard and can remember the memorable introduction of "Let it be" by the Beatles. Not a few of you could even hum the tune a cappella. But very few of you could describe the opening stream of the music by way of chords like "C - Am - G - F... C - G - F - C"; fewer still are the exceptionally cultured people who can write the sound in notes. Without proper training in music, no one could ever read and play, let alone write, the notes.

You can hear, enjoy, and even play music without knowing anything about chords or notes; but the knowledge of what chords you are hearing or playing now will certainly help remember and re-create the music later on. And the more you grasp the sound via chords or notes, the more deeply ingrained in your memory the music will be.

The same can be said about what is called "technical terms" of linguistics. It is true that the knowledge of technical terms alone can take you nowhere, but once you get somewhere in the world of English, the point that is reached might as well be inscribed in your memory with some memento. Technical terms are to your comprehension of English what pictures taken here and there on the way are to your memory of a trip: the magical keys by which to recollect something from your memory.

But such keys are totally meaningless to those who have not made the trip. Only those who have themselves made the trip can make use of the keys in remembering and enjoying their actual memory of the trip. In this sense, talking about English in terms of esoteric terminology is just like being shown pictures of a stranger's trip you never made yourself: those who are talking or showing may be enjoying the experience, but you definitely can't. To enjoy a trip, you have to make the trip for yourself at first; likewise, to really comprehend English grammar, you initially have to make a trip in the world of English, not through technical terms but by way of example

11. 英語の五六八(イロハ):五つの文・六つの文章成分・八つの品詞

ー「専門用語」の重要性、または、その重要性の限界ー

何かをしっかり把握する鍵になるものとしての「名前」の重要性が最もひしひしと感じられるのは、音楽を演奏する時である。読者諸君の多くはきっと、ザ・ビートルズ(The Beatles)の“Let it be:レット・イット・ビー”のあの印象深い導入部(イントロ)を聞いたことがあるだろうし、頭の中で思い浮かべることもできるだろう。あの部分をアカペラ(無伴奏)で鼻歌みたいに口ずさむことさえできる人の数だって少なくないだろう。だが、あの曲の出だしの流れを「C－Aマイナー－G－F・・・C－G－F－C」という和音(コード)の形で表現できる人の数は非常に少ないだろうし、その音楽を楽譜の形で表記できるほど例外的に高い教養を持った人の数は更に少数である。然るべき音楽教育を受けない限り、楽譜を読んだり演奏したり(ましていわんや自分で書いたり)出来る人間など、いないのである。

コードも楽譜も何一つ知らないままでも、音楽を聴いたり楽しんだり、演奏することさえも、可能ではある;が、いま自分が聞いたり演奏したりしているコードは一体何か、それを知っておけば、後々その音楽を思い出したり再度演奏してみたりするのに、きっと役立つものである。そうして「音」を「コード」や「音符」を通して把握する場面が増えれば増えるほど、音楽はより深く諸君の記憶に刻み込まれるのである。

それと同じことが、言語学上のいわゆる「専門用語(technical terms)」に関しても言える。ただ専門用語を知っているだけでは二進も三進も(にっちもさっちも)行かないのは確かであるが、英語の世界でそれなりの進歩を遂げたなら、自分の到達点は、記憶の中に何らかの「記念碑」とともに刻み込んでおいたほうがよいだろう。諸君の「英語理解力」と「専門用語」の関係は、「旅」と「旅の途中のそこここで撮影した写真」の関係に似ている:記憶の中から何かを呼び覚ますための「魔法の鍵」となってくれるのである。

だが、そうした鍵も、旅をしていない人物には何の意味も持たない。自ら旅した人々だけが、実際の旅の記憶を思い出して楽しむための鍵として、これを有効活用できるのである。この意味で、得体の知れない専門用語を駆使して英語について論じるのは、自分がしたわけでもない他人の旅行の写真集を見せられる体験に似ている:喋ったり見せびらかしたりしている人達はその体験を楽しんでいるのだろうけど、旅したわけでもない諸君にとっては楽しいわけがない。旅行を楽しむにはまず、自ら旅する必要があるのだ。同様に、英文法を真に理解するためには、まず最初に英語世界の旅をする必要がある:専門用語の数々を通してではなく、多くの例文を通して、旅をしておかね

sentences. Once you have made the trip – when you have come to a full understanding of a certain pattern of English through some example sentence – a technical term fit for describing that pattern will make sense as an anchor to fix that particular knowledge in your intellectual reservoir. Technical terms without making trips simply make no sense at all: the authentic knowledge of English must be certified in the form of example sentences, with suitable technical terms put aside as captions.

What I've just written is a truism to all good linguists, taken so much for granted by them that it is needless, even absurd, to point it out as if it were a great truth to guide one to some hidden treasure. Still, I have to point it out here, because I know from years of teaching experience how many Japanese students of English are totally unaware of this truistic lesson: that English, unlike music or mathematics, cannot be talked about via chords, notes, symbols or formulas alone. Musicians and mathematicians can get proficient in their fields by getting used to the world of abstraction composed solely of technical terms: unless they can grasp the whole picture from a series of musical notes or numerical expressions, they are not considered proficient as musicians or mathematicians. English learners cannot get anywhere without actually making trips via countless numbers of example sentences inscribed in their memory with the humble aid of technical terms: unless you can instantly recite some example sentences coming up to your mind at the hint of some technical terms, your command of English is still immature.

That having been said, I can feel free to introduce you readers to the following, rather abstract kind of knowledge in English, which, nevertheless, will benefit you greatly. Without the help of these technical terms and knowledge, the abstract notion made possible by comprehending these seemingly esoteric sets of terminology, you are sure to get lost in the world of English. Grope your way by the aid of the following, and you'll stumble much less than you otherwise would. Trust me: I'm no mathematician or magician who tries to fascinate or hypnotize you; I'm a teacher of English who never tells you anything you need not know. What I'm going to write down below are all too important to forget: forget them, and forget about mastering English. They are the very backbone of your English comprehension.

ばならないのだ。その旅をし終えた後でなら－何らかの例文を通して英語のある種のパターンを完全に理解できたその時点で－そのパターンを表わす適当な専門用語が、そうした個別的知識を、諸君の知識の貯蔵庫へとつなぎ止める上で、初めて意味を成すわけである。旅もしないで専門用語だけ振り回してみても、全く何の意味もない:本物の英語の知識は、例文の形で確証する必要のあるものであって、その例文の脇には「然るべき専門用語」を添え書き的に置いておくのがよいのである。

・・・と、ここまで書いた内容は、語学の達者な人にとっては自明の理であって、あまりにも当然至極なものだから、そんなものをあたかも「人を秘宝へと導く偉大なる真理」であるかの如く大仰に指摘してみせるのは、「やらずもがな」を通り越して「アホかお前は！」の感さえ与える無意味さである。それでもなおかつ、この筆者がその言わずもがなの自明の理をここで指摘しておかねばならないわけは、長年に渡る教育者としての経験から、次のような自明の教訓をまるで知らない日本人の英語学習者がいかに多いかを知っているからこそである:即ち、音楽や数学とは異なり、英語は「コード」や「音符」や「記号」や「数式」のみでは語ることのできないものなのだ。音楽家や数学者ならば、専門用語のみから成る抽象的世界に慣れ親しむことで、その道の達人となることが可能である:一連の楽譜や数式を通して音楽的・数学的世界の全体像を把握することが出来ぬ限り、彼らは音楽家・数学者としては一人前とはみなされないのである。が、英語学習者の場合、専門用語のささやかなる助力をもって自らの記憶の中にしっかりと刻み込まれた無数の例文を通して「実際に旅する体験」をしないことには、どこにも行けはしない:何らかの専門用語を聞いた瞬間、それに触発されて何らかの例文が即座に脳裏に浮かび上がり、それが口をついて出て来ない限りは、諸君の英語駆使力も、まだまだ未熟なわけである。

・・・と、前口上も十分済んだところでようやく、筆者としては、読者諸君に対し、以下に示すようなかなり抽象的な種類の英語知識を紹介してもよいかな、という気分になるわけである。が、抽象的とはいえ、これらの知識は諸君に大いなる利益をもたらすものとなろう。これらの専門用語や専門知識、そしてこれら一見難解な用語群を包括的に理解することで得られる抽象的概念の手助けなしでは、諸君はきっと英語世界の迷子となること必定である。以下に示す様々な物事の助けを得ながら、手探りで進むがよい・・・そうすれば、そうした手助けなしで進む場合よりはずっと、転ぶ場面が少なくなるはずだから。どうぞ信じてくれたまえ、この筆者は数学者でもなければ、諸君に魅惑や催眠術の魔法をかけようとする魔術師でもなく、諸君が知る必要のない物事など一切教えたりしない英語教師なのだから。筆者が以下にこれから書き出す事柄はみな、重要すぎて忘れてもらっては困るもの揃いである:これらを忘れるというのなら、英語をモノにしようという野心も忘れるしかあるまい。これらは、諸君の英語理解力のまさに中核となる知識なのである。

- Five kinds of sentences in English -

From the standpoint of the purpose of speech, English sentences can be divided into the following five(5) kinds:

(1)平叙文(HEIJOBUN: declarative sentences): to say something in the affirmative

eg. She is beautiful.

eg. She has sung beautifully.

eg. She sings beautifully.

eg. She sang beautifully.

Declarative is the most basic form of all sentences.

(2)否定文(HITEIBUN: negative sentences): to say something in the negative

eg. She is not beautiful.

eg. She has not sung beautifully.

eg. She does not sing beautifully.

eg. She did not sing beautifully.

As for sentences developing around "be verb" or "'have' of the perfect tense", negative sentences can be made by simply inserting "not" at the end of the verb of declarative sentences.

When it comes to sentences developing around verbs other than "be/have", the process of making them negative is threefold: (I)if the sentence belongs to the present tense, according to the subject, divide the "verb" part into "does+verb"(He/She/It: the 3rd person singular = 三単現:SANTANGEN) or "do+verb"(I/We/You/They: other than the 3rd person singular); (II)if the sentence belongs to the past tense, regardless of the subject (He/She/It/I/We/You/They), divide the "verb" part into "did+verb"; (III)add "not" at the end of the "do/does/did" to compose negative sentences.

(3)疑問文(GIMONBUN: interrogative sentences): to ask about something

eg. Is she beautiful?

eg. Has she sung beautifully?

eg. Does she sing beautifully?

eg. Did she sing beautifully?

As for sentences developing around "be verb" or "'have' of the perfect tense", interrogative sentences can be made by simply inverting the position of the (S+be/have/has/had)(Subject+verb)

to (Be/Have/Has/Had+S) (Verb+subject).

No modulation other than the word order is necessary.

ー英語の文章の種類は5つー

発話の目的、という観点から見た場合、英語の文章は以下の5つの種類に分かれる:

(1)平叙文(declarative sentences): 何かを「肯定形で(in the affirmative)」言うための文章

例 She is beautiful. 彼女は美しい(be 動詞の現在形)

例 She has sung beautifully. 彼女は美しく歌った(do 動詞の完了形)

例 She sings beautifully. 彼女は美しく歌う(do 動詞の現在形)

例 She sang beautifully. 彼女は美しく歌った(do 動詞の過去形)

「平叙文」は、あらゆる文章中で最も基本的な形である。

(2)否定文(negative sentences): 何かを「否定形で(in the negative)」言うための文章

例 She is not beautiful. 彼女は美しくない

例 She has not sung beautifully. 彼女は美しく歌わなかった

例 She does not sing beautifully. 彼女は美しく歌わない

例 She did not sing beautifully. 彼女は美しく歌わなかった

"be 動詞"または"完了の have"を中心に展開する文章の「否定文」を作るには、「肯定文」の「動詞」の直後に単純に"not"を挿入するだけでよい。

"be/完了の have"以外の動詞を中心に展開する文章の「否定文」は、以下の3段階の過程を経て作る:(I)文章が「現在時制」の場合、「主語」に合わせて「動詞」を"does+verb"(He/She/It:三人称単数の場合)または"do+verb"(I/We/You/They:三人称単数以外の場合)の形に分割する;(II)文章が「過去時制」の場合、「主語」(He/She/It/I/We/You/They)の如何に関わらず、「動詞」を"did+verb"の形に分割する;(III)"do/does/did"の後に"not"を付ければ「否定文」が出来上がる。

(3)疑問文(interrogative sentences): 何かについて尋ねるための文章

例 Is she beautiful? 彼女は美しいですか？

例 Has she sung beautifully? 彼女は美しく歌いましたか？

例 Does she sing beautifully? 彼女は美しく歌いますか？

例 Did she sing beautifully? 彼女は美しく歌いましたか？

"be 動詞"または"完了の have"を中心に展開する文章の「疑問文」を作るには、「肯定文」の「主語＋be/have/has/had」の位置関係(主語 S＋動詞 V)を「Be/Have/Has/Had＋主語」(動詞V＋主語S)に入れ替えるだけでよい。語順の入れ替え以外の修正は一切不要である。

When it comes to sentences developing around verbs other than "be/have", the process of making them interrogative is threefold: (I)if the sentence belongs to the present tense, according to the subject, divide the "verb" part into "does+verb"(He/She/It: the 3rd person singular = 三単現 : SANTANGEN) or "do+verb"(I/We/You/They: other than the 3rd person singular); (II)if the sentence belongs to the past tense, regardless of the subject (He/She/It/I/We/You/They), divide the "verb" part into "did+verb"; (III)move the "Do/Does/Did" to the beginning of the sentence to compose interrogative sentences.

(4)感嘆文(KANTANBUN: exclamation sentences): to express wonder at something

eg. How beautiful she is!

eg. What a beautiful woman she is!

Exclamation sentences take two forms: beginning with "How" when stressing adjectives(eg. "beautiful") and starting with "What" when stressing nouns(eg. "a beautiful woman").

(5)命令文(MEIREIBUN: imperative sentences): to tell someone to do something

eg. Be beautiful.

eg. Let's play some music.

eg. Let me play the guitar.

eg. Let girls love and be beautiful.

Imperative sentences begin with the root form of a verb, without any subject. The imperative sentence usually takes the form of an order for "you" to do something (2nd person imperative).

Imperative sentences beginning with "Let's(=Let us)" or "Let me" are special in that they do not "tell you to do something" but "propose to you that we/I should do something". This may be regarded as "a pseudo 1st person imperative".

By using such auxiliary verbs as "let/make/have", it is possible to make "a pseudo 3rd person imperative" allowing or ordering "him/her/it/them" to do something, but, exactly speaking, the one who "lets/makes/has" "him/her/it/them" do something is still "you"(the 2nd person).

“be/完了の have”以外の動詞を中心に展開する文章の「疑問文」は、以下の3段階の過程を経て作る:(I)文章が「現在時制」の場合、「主語」に合わせて「動詞」を“does+verb”(He/She/It:三人称単数の場合)または“do+verb”(I/We/You/They:三人称単数以外の場合)の形に分割する;(II)文章が「過去時制」の場合、「主語」(He/She/It/I/We/You/They)の如何に関わらず、「動詞」を“did+verb”の形に分割する;(III)“Do/Does/Did”の位置を文章の冒頭に移動すれば「疑問文」が出来上がる。

(4)感嘆文(exclamation sentences): 何かに驚嘆する意を表わす文章

例 How beautiful she is! 彼女はなんと美しいのだろう!

例 What a beautiful woman she is! 彼女は何と美しい女性なのだろう!

「感嘆文」は2つの形態を取る:「形容詞(adjectives:例 “beautiful:美しい”)」を強調する時には“How”で始まり、「名詞(nouns:例 “a beautiful woman:美しい女性”)」を強調する時には“What”で始まる。

(5)命令文(imperative sentences): 何かをせよ、と誰かに命じる文章

例 Be beautiful. 美しくなれ

例 Let's play some music. 何か音楽を演奏しよう

例 Let me play the guitar. 私にギターを弾かせてください

例 Let girls love and be beautiful. 女性には恋をして美しくなってもらおう

「命令文」は、「主語」を伴わずに「動詞」の「原形(the root form)」で始まる。「命令文」は通例「“you:あなた”が何かをしなさい」(二人称命令文)の形態を取る。

“Let's(=Let us):我々は〜しようではないか”または“Let me:私に〜させてください”で始まる命令文は、「“you:あなた”が何かをしなさい」と“命じる”のではなく「我々/私が何かをすべきだ」と“提案する”点が特殊であり、この形態は「擬似的一人称命令文」と解釈することも可能である。

“let/make/have”等の「助動詞(auxiliary verbs)」を用いることで、「“him/her/it/them”が何かをすること」を許したり命令したりする「擬似的三人称命令文」を作ることも可能である;が、厳密に言えば「“he/she/it/they”が何かをすること」を“let:放任する/make:強要する/have:仕向ける”人物はやはり“二人称の you”なのである。

In short, the supposed subject of an imperative sentence is always “you” who are in front of the one who gives the order.

Aside from negative sentences, all the other sentences than declarative take inverted word order: none of them starts with (S)subject at the beginning. Simply put, beginners of English have only to get used to such word order inversion to get the knack of English communication. You can't go very far by such paraphrasing only, to be sure, but you can't go anywhere without being able to instantly switch between these five patterns of English sentences.

- Six elements of the sentence in English -

When we shift our attention from the purpose of speech of sentences to the function of words within a single sentence, we can divide an English sentence into the following six(6) different elements:

(1)主語(SHUGO: subject) = (S)

(2)動詞(DOUSHI: verb) = (V)

(3)目的語(MOKUTEKIGO: object) = (O)

(4)補語(HOGO: complement) = (C)

(5) 形容詞型修飾語 (KEIYOUSHIGATA-SHUUSHOKUGO: adjective modifier) = {ADJ}

(6)副詞型修飾語(FUKUSHIGATA-SHUUSHOKUGO: adverbial modifier) = (ADV)

Not all sentences have all those six elements in them. Some sentences are composed of (V)verb only (eg. Go! Run! Sing!), while others comprehend multiple elements inside. (eg. (S)<The singer {(o)whom (s)we (v)heard (c)shouting rock'n'roll (adv)(at the beginning of the concert)}> (V)sang (O)us (O){ADJ.}{a sweet, dreamy} lullaby.)

The roles of (S)subject, (V)verb, (O)object and (C)complement are all so essential and important that they are called the four(4) main elements of a sentence. All textbooks of English give you explanations, sketchy or detailed, about these 4 main elements and the 5 sentence patterns they can take (SPAT-5 as we call it in this book). These four, (S)(V)(O) and (C), since they are the “main” elements, are too clear-cut and easy to understand (once we make them out to be as such) to demand any comment here.

要するに、「命令文」の主語として想定される存在は常に「命令を出す者の眼前に存在する"you:君"」なのである。

「否定文」の場合を除き、「平叙文」以外の全ての文章は倒置語順を取り、文章の冒頭が「主語(S:subject)」で始まるものは一つとして存在しない。単純に言えば、英語の初心者が英会話のコツをつかむには、こうした語順の倒置に慣れさえすればそれでよいわけだ。そうした言い換えだけで英語がさほど上達するわけではないのは確かだが、これら5種類の英文のパターンを瞬時に切り替えることも出来ないようではどこへも行けやしないのもまた確かなことである。

－英文の6つの構成要素－

文章の「発話目的」から、単一文章内での「語句の果たす機能」へと視点を転じれば、英語の文章は以下の6つの異なる要素へと分解することができる:

(1)主語(subject) = (S)
(2)動詞(verb) = (V)
(3)目的語(object) = (O)
(4)補語(complement) = (C)
(5)形容詞型修飾語(adjective modifier) = {ADJ}
(6)副詞型修飾語(adverbial modifier) = (ADV)

文章の全てが上述の6要素の全てを包含するというわけではない。「(V)動詞」のみから成る文章(Go!:行け／Run!:逃げろ／Sing!:歌え)もある一方で、諸々の要素が複合的に絡み合う構造を内包する文章もある。(例　(S)<The singer {(o)whom (s)we (v)heard (c)shouting rock'n'roll (adv)(at the beginning of the concert)}> (V)sang (O)us (O){ADJ.}{a sweet, dreamy} lullaby. コンサートのオープニングでロックンロールを絶叫するのを聞いた例の歌手が、甘い夢のような子守歌を我々に歌ってくれた)

「(S)subject:主語」、「(V)verb:動詞」、「(O)object:目的語」、「(C)complement:補語」はどれもみな極めて中核的で重要なものなので、これらを「文の主要4要素」と呼ぶ。これら4要素とその構成し得る5大文章パターン(この本の呼び名で言えば「SPAT-5」)については、どの英語の教科書にもみな何らかの解説(おおざっぱなものから詳細なものまで)が載っているものである。これらの(S)(V)(O)(C)は"主要な"要素なのだから、スパッと明快で理解も容易(ひとたび我々がそれを"主要素"と見抜いてしまいさえすれば、の話だが)である以上、ここで一々何か述べるまでのこともあるまい。

The most difficult part of English interpretation lies in distinguishing those four main elements, (S)(V)(O) and (C), from the rest — the lengthy, misleading chunks of words which are not essential but merely accessory to the essence of the sentence: {ADJ: adjective} being accessory to some particular noun, and (ADV: adverb) to verb. These two superfluities are often so bulky that the very length of them is enough to discourage beginners from reading any further. Indeed, the success of reading, writing or listening to English lies in your skill at discerning the essential from the accessory. Those who are poor at instant detection of the essence are incapable of reading or listening comprehension of English.

The ability or inability to draw out the essence from floods of words or news or voices will determine not only whether you can use English at your command but if you can effectively utilize stimuli from the world, if not the world itself, at your command.

Believe it or not, the world of English, the whole wide world that spreads outside our puny Japanese-speaking island, is not so short and simple as your usually monosyllabic daily conversation with Japanese folks. To survive in the wave after waves of English-speaking oceans, you have to practice distinguishing the essence from the unessential, marking adjective modifiers (which modify nouns) with curly brackets{...} and encircling adverb modifiers (which modify verbs) with parentheses(...). This practice, if earnestly attempted amid duly complicated English sentences, will take beginners in Japan four to five years of intensive study to enable them to swim with confidence through the rough sea of English.

- Eight parts of speech in English -

In trying to distinguish among mountains of words that compose English sentences, the knowledge of "品詞(HINSHI: parts of speech)" is of the utmost importance. English parts of speech divide into the following eight(8) kinds:

(1)名詞(MEISHI) = noun(n.): a name to express someone/something

eg. apples, birds, cats, dogs, eggs, fools, girls, hotels, inns, jokes, etc,etc.

英文解釈で一番難しいのは、これら(S)(V)(O)(C)の“主要素”をその他の“主要ならざる要素”からいかにして切り分けるか、の部分である・・・文章の精髄を成す部分の単なる飾りとして存在するばかりで中核的ではない言葉の塊が長々と続いて読む者の誤読を誘うような“主要ならざる要素”には、特定の「名詞(nouns)」に付随する{形容詞＝ADJ(adjective)}と、特定の「動詞(verbs)」に付随する(副詞＝ADV(adverb))とがある。これら2つの「余分なもの」は、がさばる場合が実に多いので、その「長さ」だけですでにもう初心者は読み進むのも億劫になるものである。実際の話、英語の「読み」「書き」「聞き取り」がうまく行くか否かは、「本質的なものを非本質的なものから弁別する技能」の如何にかかっている。本質を瞬時に見抜く能力に欠ける人々は、英語を読み取ることも聴き取ることも出来はしないのだ。

言葉・ニュース・声の洪水の中から本質的なものだけを取り出すことが、出来るか出来ないか、その違いは、諸君が英語を意のままに使いこなすことが出来るか否かのみならず、外界からの刺激を(世界そのものを、とまでは言わないが)意のままに有効活用できるか否かの分かれ道ともなるであろう。

信じるも信じぬも諸君の勝手だが、英語の世界(＝日本語だけ喋るこのチンケな島国の外に広がる広大無辺な世界)は、諸君が日本人の御仲間連中と交わす素っ気ない日常会話みたいに短小で単純なものではないのである。英語という大洋の波また波の中を溺れず泳ぎ渡るためには、本質的なものと非本質的なものの弁別練習を積まねばならない:「名詞(nouns)」を修飾する「形容詞的{adjective}修飾語」は{カーリー・ブラケット:curly brackets＝中括弧}で括り、「動詞(verbs)」を修飾する「副詞的(adverb)修飾語」は(パレンセシス:parentheses＝丸括弧)で括る練習を積み重ねることである。この練習を(そこそこ複雑な構造を持った英文の真っ只中で真剣に)4年から5年程度精力的に行なえば、日本人の英語初心者も、英語の荒海の中を自信を持って泳ぎ渡ることが出来るようになるであろう。

－英語の8品詞－

英文を構成する山ほど大量の語句を弁別しようとする際には、「品詞(parts of speech)」の知識は最も重要なものとなる。英語の品詞は以下の8種類に分かれる:

(1)名詞 = noun(n.): 「誰か」や「何か」を表わす名前

例 apples:リンゴ、 birds:鳥、 cats:猫、 dogs:犬、 eggs:卵、 fools:馬鹿、 girls:少女、 hotels:ホテル、 inns:宿屋、 jokes:冗談、 その他諸々

(2)代名詞(DAIMEISHI) = pronoun(pron.): a general substitute for any particular noun or nouns
eg. I, we, you, they, he, she, it, one, some, none, any, nobody, everybody, etc, etc.
(3)形容詞(KEIYOUSHI) = adjective(adj.): a word to modify a noun
eg. absurd, beautiful, charming, detestable, erotic, fascinating, good, husky, interesting, jesting, etc, etc.
(4)前置詞(ZENCHISHI) = preposition(prep.): a function word used before a noun to show the relation of the noun to some other noun, verb, or adjective
eg. at, by, for, in, on, to, with, etc, etc.
(5)動詞(DOUSHI) = verb(v.): a word to express action, existence, state or occurrence
eg. avoid, bathe, come, die, end, fly, grow, have, invite, join, etc, etc.
(6)副詞(FUKUSHI) = adverb(adv.): a word to modify a verb, adjective or another adverb
eg. aside, beside, consequently, down, endlessly, forward, gladly, happily, inside, etc, etc.
(7)接続詞(SETSUZOKUSHI) = conjunction(conj.): a word to connect words, phrases, clauses or sentences
eg. and, although, but, because, so, then, yet, etc, etc.
(8)間投詞(KANTOUSHI) = interjection(int.): a word to express emotion which can stand alone and often stands out in the stream of conversation
eg. alas, bravo, cheers, damn, er, fuck, goodness, etc, etc.

Not a few English words can function in the capacities of several parts of speech. For example, "kid" can work either as a noun (eg. "Kids are lovely") or a verb (eg. "Don't kid yourself into believing such nonsense"). Many words work in the same form as both an adjective and an adverb (eg. "She is a fast runner"; "She runs fast"). Beginners will have a hard time of it distinguishing between a preposition and an adverb (eg. "The games will be held over the weekend"; "The game is over now"). To distinguish between these parts of speech, you have to pay conscious attention to the function of them in the sentence, which will sharpen your senses of grammatical comprehension.

(2)代名詞 = pronoun(pron.): 任意の「名詞」(単数／複数)の一般的代用表現
例 I:私、 we:我々、 you:あなた(がた)、 they:彼ら、 he:彼、 she:彼女、 it:それ、 one:人、 some:何か、 none:何一つ～ない、 any:何でも、 nobody:誰一人～ない、 everybody:誰でも、 その他諸々
(3)形容詞 = adjective(adj.): 「名詞」を修飾する語
例 absurd:愚かだ、 beautiful:美しい、 charming:魅力的な、 detestable:いまわしい、 erotic:色情的な、 fascinating:魅惑的な、 good:良い、 husky:低音の、 interesting:面白い、 jesting:冗談っぽい、 その他諸々
(4)前置詞 = preposition(prep.): 「名詞」と他の「名詞」「動詞」「形容詞」との間の関係を示す「機能語(a function word＝単体では意味を成さぬ、語句間の関係規定記号)」
例 at、 by、 for、 in、 on、 to、 with、 その他諸々
(5)動詞 = verb(v.): 「行動・存在・状態・発生」といった意味を表わす語
例 avoid:避ける、 bathe:入浴する、 come:来る、 die:死ぬ、 end:終わる、 fly:飛ぶ、 grow:大きくなる、 have:持つ、 invite:誘う、 join:加わる、 その他諸々
(6)副詞 = adverb(adv.): 「動詞」「形容詞」あるいは「他の副詞」を修飾する語
例 aside:脇に、 beside:横に、 consequently:結果的に、 down:下に、 endlessly:際限なく、 forward:前に、 gladly:喜んで、 happily:幸せに、 inside:内に、 その他諸々
(7)接続詞 = conjunction(conj.): 「単語(words)」「句(phrases)」「節(clauses)」「文(sentences)」どうしを結ぶ語
例 and:そして、 although:そうではあるが、 but:しかし、 because:何故ならば、 so:それ故に、 then:ということであれば、 yet:しかし、 その他諸々
(8)間投詞 = interjection(int.): 話の流れの中で独立的に(往々にして目立つ形で)存在する「感情」を表わす語
例 alas:あぁ、 bravo:素晴らしいっ、 cheers:乾杯、 damn:クソッ、 er:ぁー、 fuck:あーくそったれ、 goodness:ぅわっ、 その他諸々

異なる幾つもの品詞の機能を持つ英単語も少なくない。例えば“kid”という語は「名詞」としても働くし(例 “Kids are lovely.:子供はかわいい”)、「動詞」にもなる(例 “Don't kid yourself into believing such nonsense.:そんなたわごと信じるようなガキっぽいマネはするな”)。全く同一の形態で「形容詞」としても「副詞」としても機能する語も多い(例 “She is a {fast} runner.:彼女は{足の速い}走者である”は形容詞、“She runs (fast).:彼女は(速く)走る”は副詞)。初心者の場合、「前置詞」と「副詞」の区別には難儀することだろう(例 “The games will be held 〈over〉 the weekend.:それらの試合は週末にかけて行なわれる予定だ”は前置詞、“The game is 〈over〉 now.:ゲームはもう終わりだ”は副詞)。これらの「品詞」を見分けるためには、文章内でのそれぞれの果たす役割に注目する必要があり、その意識がまた諸君の文法理解力を研ぎ澄ましてくれることだろう。

- How to memorize and never fail to recollect eight parts of speech -

Things anchored in your memory by meaningful chains of association will hardly get lost. If you lose hold of any particular thing, try to draw in the chain of memory connected with it, and something else will come up to your mind, possibly accompanied by the thing you seem to have forgotten. That is why you should NEVER remember things item by item: you MUST always try to remember things in the web of meaningful association along with some others.

In trying to comprehend and memorize the eight parts of speech in English, the two main keys of recollection are "noun" and "verb".

Let us begin with the "noun", which naturally reminds us of its special version "pronoun"; a "noun" is modified by an "adjective"; and a "preposition" can only have a "noun/pronoun" as its object. Thus we have a chain of parts of speech centering around the "noun" as follows:

(1)名詞(MEISHI) = noun(n.)

(2)代名詞(DAIMEISHI) = pronoun(pron.)

(3)形容詞(KEIYOUSHI) = adjective(adj.)

(4)前置詞(ZENCHISHI) = preposition(prep.)

What stands in contrast with a "noun" is a "verb"; and a "verb" is modified by an "adverb". Here comes the simple pair centering around the "verb" as follows:

(5)動詞(DOUSHI) = verb(v.)

(6)副詞(FUKUSHI) = adverb(adv.)

The word that can connect "nouns", "pronouns", "adjectives", "prepositions", "verbs" and "adverbs" is a "conjunction":

(7)接続詞(SETSUZOKUSHI) = conjunction(conj.)

And a word which stands out solo with absolutely no regard to any other word is an "interjection":

(8)間投詞(KANTOUSHI) = interjection(int.)

Each of these eight parts of speech has its distinctive characteristics, which makes it imperative for learners to study and memorize them differently. How to deal with each part of speech in respective manners is to be detailed in the following section.

―8品詞をいかにして覚え、決して思い出し損ねることのないようにするか―

意味ある連想の鎖で諸君の記憶につなぎ止められた物事は、行方不明になることなどまずないものである。何か一つの物事が行方知れずになったなら、その物事と関連する記憶の鎖をたぐり寄せるべく努めてみれば、他の何物かが思い浮かんで、うまくすれば、失念していたっぽい物事も芋蔓式に念頭に浮かぶものである。なればこそ、物事を覚える際には、一個一個を独立した形で覚えるような真似は絶対にすべきではないのである:他の何かとの意味ある連想の蜘蛛の巣の上に絡め取るような形で物事を覚え込むようにするべきなのだ。

英語に於ける「8品詞(eight parts of speech)」を理解・記憶しようとする際に、記憶の主要な鍵となる2つのものは「名詞(noun)」と「動詞(verb)」である。

まずは「名詞(noun)」から見てみよう・・・「名詞」と言えば自然に思い浮かぶのがその特殊版と言うべき「代名詞(pronoun)」である・・・「名詞(noun)」は「形容詞(adjective)」によって修飾される・・・そして「名詞(noun)／代名詞(pronoun)」のみを目的語として取るのが「前置詞(preposition)」である・・・かくて、「名詞」を中心に展開する品詞の連想の鎖が、以下の如く成立する:

(1)名詞 = noun(n.)

(2)代名詞 = pronoun(pron.)

(3)形容詞 = adjective(adj.)

(4)前置詞 = preposition(prep.)

「名詞(noun)」と対称的な位置付けを有するのが「動詞(verb)」である・・・「動詞(verb)」は「副詞(adverb)」によって修飾される・・・こうして「動詞」を中心に展開する単純なペアリングが、以下の如く成立する:

(5)動詞 = verb(v.)

(6)副詞 = adverb(adv.)

“nouns(名詞)”、“pronouns(代名詞)”、“adjectives(形容詞)”、“prepositions(前置詞)”、“verbs(動詞)”、“adverbs(副詞)”の間をつなぐことが出来る語は「接続詞(conjunction)」である:

(7)接続詞 = conjunction(conj.)

そして、他の語句にはまったくお構いなしに一人で勝手に目立つ語句が「間投詞(interjection)」である:

(8)間投詞 = interjection(int.)

これら「8品詞」にはそれぞれ独自の特徴があるから、それぞれの品詞の学び方・覚え方は、各品詞ごとに異なるやり方でなければ具合が悪いことになる。それぞれの品詞をそれぞれなりのやり方で扱う方法については、次の項で具体的に述べることにしよう。

12. Respective manners of study and memorization for eight parts of speech in English

- 棒暗記(BOUANKI: Mechanical memorization) and 片言(KATAKOTO: broken) English are only good for nouns, pronouns and adjectives -

Of all the eight parts of speech, by far the most numerous and useful in conversation are nouns (including pronouns) and adjectives. Indeed, if you are totally ignorant of grammar, you could even then be able to communicate more or less with a foreigner in such manners as "You... beautiful... your cooking... good". This is also true with any other language than English; in French, "Vous... beau... votre cuisine... bon" should do something.

In English, thanks to the absence of "gender" in nouns, mechanical memorization and utilization of nouns and adjectives is far easier than in traditional Indo-European languages. In French, the same adjective(eg. "grand") varies according to the gender and number of the noun/pronoun it is used with like "Il est grand(He is tall) / Elle est grande(She is tall) / Les monsieurs sont grands(The men are tall) / Les filles sont grandes(The girls are tall)", while in English "tall" is simply "tall" with anything.

Still, there is something you should keep in mind when trying to memorize nouns and adjectives in English:

(1)Adjectives should be memorized in combination with some suitable nouns: eg. "an amazing story", "a beautiful woman", "a chilly winter's day", "a daunting task", etc,etc. Beginners should normally memorize an adjective with a noun in the singular form, in order to get used to instinctively switching between indefinite articles "a" and "an" according to the opening sound of the adjective being consonant or vowel.

(2)Nouns should always be memorized in their plural as opposed to singular forms, with "s/es" at the end and without "a/an/the" at the beginning: eg. "angels", "babies", "cuticles", "diaries", etc,etc. You must never remember nouns "as is", that is, in the singular form written on the dictionary without any article("a/an/the") (ng. "angel", "baby", "cuticle", "diary").

12. 8品詞ごとに異なる英語学習・暗記の作法

－棒暗記・カタコト英語で使えるのは名詞・代名詞と形容詞だけ－

8つの「品詞(parts of speech)」のうち、会話の中で最も頻繁に使われ最も役立つものは、「名詞(nouns・・・代名詞:pronounsをも含む)」と「形容詞(adjectives)」である。実際、文法を全く知らない場合でさえも、外国人との会話は「You:あなた... beautiful:きれい... your cooking:あなたの料理... good:おいしい」式のやり方で(ある程度までは)通じるはずである。これはまた英語以外のどんな外国語にも言えることで、フランス語でなら「Vous:あなた... beau:きれい... votre cuisine:あなたの料理... bon:おいしい」でそれなりに通じるであろう。

英語では、「名詞」に「性別(gender)」がないおかげで、「名詞」と「形容詞」を棒暗記して使うのは、伝統的なインド・ヨーロッパ言語の場合に比べて、遙かに容易である。フランス語の場合、同じ「形容詞(例えば"grand:背が高い")」でも、一緒に用いる「名詞／代名詞」の「性」と「数」に応じてその形態が次のように変わる(主語が変わるだけで、意味はすべて「背が高い」である):"彼＝Il est grand(He is tall). / 彼女＝Elle est grande(She is tall). / その男性たち＝Les monsieurs sont grands(The men are tall). / その少女たち＝Les filles sont grandes(The girls are tall).";英語の場合、"tall"は"tall"で、どんな語と一緒に用いても変わらない。

そのように単純な英語の「名詞」と「形容詞」ではあるが、それでもなお、これらを暗記する場合には、念頭に置くべきことがいくつかある:

(1)「形容詞」は何か適当な「名詞」との組み合わせで覚えるべし(例 "an amazing story:驚くべき話"、"a beautiful woman:美しい女性"、"a chilly winter's day:肌寒い冬の日"、"a daunting task:尻込みしたくなる仕事")。一般に初心者は「形容詞」を「名詞の単数形」との組み合わせで覚えるのがよい:それによって、「形容詞」冒頭部の音が「子音(consonant)」か「母音(vowel)」かによって変わる「不定冠詞(indefinite articles)」の"a"と"an"を、直感的に切り替える作法に慣れる練習になるからである。

(2)「名詞」は常に、「単数形(the singular)」ではなく「複数形(the plural)」で、末尾に"s/es"を付けた形(冒頭部に"a/an/the"を伴わない形)で覚えるべきである(例 "angels:天使"、"babies:赤ん坊"、"cuticles:表皮"、"diaries:日記"、その他諸々)。「名詞」を"そのままの形"で(辞書に書かれている通りの、冠詞の"a/an/the"を伴わない単数形、例えば"angel"、"baby"、"cuticle"、"diary"で)覚えることは決してすべきではない。

(3)Uncountable nouns (nouns which cannot be used in the plural) should be memorized in the singular form with some determinatives or numerical expressions before them: eg. “a piece of advice”, “a spoonful of butter”, “a slice of cake”, “beads of dew”, etc,etc. If you remember them “as is” (ng. “advice”, “butter”, “cake”, “dew”), you will easily fall into such erroneous expressions as “ng. too many advices, lots of butters, some more cakes or morning dews”.

Theoretically speaking, the number of nouns is infinite: you could invent any noun at will without limitation. All the other parts of speech (pronouns, adjectives, prepositions, verbs, adverbs, conjunctions, interjections) are more or less limited in their total number, but nouns have no limit to their possible number. You should exactly remember all English pronouns, you could attempt to remember all possible usages in prepositions, conjunctions or interjections; but you couldn't possibly remember all nouns; and, as for adjectives and adverbs, their total number is practically too large to remember.

Only fools try in vain to challenge the infinity. Never try to remember as many nouns as you happen to encounter in books or conversation. Unlike computers, your memory may not overflow with such useless floods of data, but your memory will certainly fail you: human brains will only remember useful information, and useless or harmful memories of the past will be magically drowned out from your life. Wise selection of words, which one to remember and which one to forget is especially important with nouns. Use your dictionary to measure the relative significance of a noun you happened to know in books or conversation, and decide whether to store it up in your permanent memory or lay your hand on it only temporarily. Most dictionaries for students will kindly mark words with some symbols signifying their relative importance.

The same can be said about verbs: you may try to mechanically remember all existing verbs in English, only to no avail. These two parts of speech — nouns and verbs — can only be wisely memorized and utilized by the selected (consciously selective) few.

(3)「不可算名詞(uncountable nouns)＝複数形で用いることのできない名詞」は、その「不可算名詞」直前に何らかの「限定詞(determinatives)」や「数量表現(numerical expressions)」を伴った「単数形」で覚えるのがよい(例 "a piece of advice:一つの助言"、"a spoonful of butter:スプーン一杯分のバター"、"a slice of cake:一切れのケーキ"、"beads of dew:数珠つなぎの露"、その他諸々)。もしこうした「不可算名詞」を"そのままの形で"(ダメな例 "advice"、"butter"、"cake"、"dew")覚えたりすれば、(×)"too many advices:多すぎる助言"、"lots of butters:大量のバター"、"some more cakes:あといくつかのケーキ"、"morning dews:朝露"といった間違い表現へとたやすく陥ることになるだろう。

論理的に言えば、「名詞」の数は無限であり、際限なく新たな「名詞」を造語することが可能である。「名詞」以外の全ての品詞(pronouns:代名詞／adjectives:形容詞／prepositions:前置詞／verbs:動詞／adverbs:副詞／conjunctions:接続詞／interjections:間投詞)の場合、その総数は(多かれ少なかれ)限られているが、存在し得る「名詞」の数には限りがない。英語の「代名詞」は全部正確に覚えておくべきだし、「前置詞／接続詞／間投詞」のあり得る用法全てを覚え込もうとするのもあながち不可能ではないが、「名詞」の全てを覚え込もうとしても絶対に無理な話である。「副詞」や「形容詞」に関しても、数が多すぎてその全てを覚えるのは現実的には不可能である。

「無限」に挑んで空しく果てるのは、愚か者の所業である。本や会話でたまたま出くわした「名詞」の全てを暗記しようとしてはならない。コンピュータと違って、諸君の記憶領域はそうした無意味なデータの洪水にさらされても「容量オーバー(メモリー・オーバーフロー)」で故障することはないかもしれないが、それでもやはりいざ思い出そうとした時にはきっと忘れているはずである:人間の頭脳というものは、有益な情報だけを覚え込み、過去に覚え込んだ無意味あるいは有害な記憶は人生の中から魔法のように消し去っているものなのだ。「名詞」に関しては、言葉の賢い選択(＝どの語を覚え、どの語は忘れ去るか)がとりわけ重要となる。本や会話でたまたま出会った「名詞」が、相対的にみてどの程度重要なのか、辞書を用いて測った上で、その「名詞」を恒久的記憶領域に蓄え込むべきか、それともほんの一時的におさえておくだけにとどめるかを決定することである。学習用辞典の多くは、語句の相対的重要度を何らかの記号付きで親切に明記してくれているものだ。

同じことは「動詞」に関しても言える:英語世界に存在する全ての「動詞」を機械的に覚え込もうと努力しても、結局は徒労に終わるだけである。これら2つの品詞(「nouns:名詞」と「verbs:動詞」)を賢く記憶し使いこなすことができるのは、選ばれた一部の人間たち(「言葉選び」を意識して行なう人たち)だけなのである。

As for other parts of speech — pronouns, adjectives, prepositions, adverbs, conjunctions and interjections — you will lose nothing by attempting to remember anything that you happen to meet. Their total number and possible usages or meanings are so large that you will naturally forget lots of them, but the more you try to remember, the better. At least, there is nothing in these parts of speech that you should consciously try not to keep in your permanent memory as in the case of nouns and verbs.

- Verbs must be learnt by heart in example sentences -

Poor linguists will invariably try to save intellectual energy, only to commit logical suicide in the end. Those who try to remember an English verb "as is" — who only lay their hands on the meanings in the dictionary in the raw form written on it — are wasting their time and intellectual resources. They could go nowhere by such haphazard methods, not at least in the world of English verbs.

When you try to remember and utilize verbs in English, you must stick to the following principles:

(1)Always remember a verb in some example sentence. A verb is only useful with usage, meaningless with meanings only. For example, remember the term(verb/noun) we invented early on in this book – EXPROGER: you can't make use of it by remembering its definition, "to prove the general rule by the exception(s)". You can only give it a full life in your memory by storing it up in your brains with such example sentences as "The relative ease and the universal popularity of English EXPROGER the difficulty foreign learners find in such gender-strict Indo-European languages as French, Spanish or Italian".

If you have read through the earlier parts of this book, the meaning of the above-mentioned example sentence must be clear... in case it isn't, I'll explain in detail: "English, while being a member of Indo-European languages, is an exceptional tongue which is totally gender-free. That is why it is relatively easy for beginners and generally spoken all over the world. With the exception of English, Indo-European languages like French, Spanish or Italian have strict rules about the gender of nouns, which makes it difficult for foreign learners to master such languages, thereby making them less popular than English."

これら以外の品詞(pronouns:代名詞、adjectives:形容詞、prepositions:前置詞、adverbs:副詞、conjunctions:接続詞、interjections:間投詞)に関しては、諸君がたまたま出くわしたやつを全て覚え込もうと頑張ってみても、まぁ悪くはないだろう。その数は膨大である上に用法も意味も多いのだから、その多くは自然に忘れてしまうだろうが、暗記の努力は大きければ大きいほどよい。少なくとも、これらの品詞に関しては(「名詞」や「動詞」の場合のように)わざわざ脳内の長期記憶領域に蓄え込むまでもない語として意識的に排除すべき語句は、ない。

ー動詞は例文の中で覚えよー

語学ベタな人間はみな一様に、知的エネルギーの節約努力をした結果、最終的には論理的自殺を遂げておしまい、という結末に終わる。英語の「動詞(verbs)」を"そのままの形で"覚えようとする者たちー辞書に載っている意味に、辞書に記載されたままの表記形で、漫然と触れただけで終わる人々ーは、自らの時間と知的資源の無駄遣いをしているのである。そんな行き当たりばったりのやり方では、少なくとも英語の「動詞」の世界では、どこへも行けやしないのだ。

英語の「動詞」を覚えて使おうとする場合、以下に記す原則を確実に守ることである:

(1)「動詞」は常に何らかの例文の中で覚え込むべし。「動詞」は用例あってこそ有益、意味のみおさえただけでは無益である。例えばの話が、この本の前の方で発明した例の単語(「動詞」/「名詞」共用語)の"EXPROGER"を覚えているだろうか?・・・この語句は、その定義「例外(単数/複数)により一般原則を証明すること」だけ覚えていても使いこなすことは不可能である。諸君の記憶領域内にこの語句を蓄えて生命を吹き込むことができるのは、次のような例文と共に覚え込んだ場合だけである:"The relative ease and the universal popularity of English EXPROGER the difficulty foreign learners find in such gender-strict Indo-European languages as French, Spanish or Italian. 英語が比較的簡単で全世界的に人気があるということは、フランス語・スペイン語・イタリア語といった「性別に厳密な」インド・ヨーロッパ言語を外国人が学ぶのがいかに困難かを、「性別のない」英語の特性が逆説的に証明しているようなものである"。

この本の最初の方を読破している諸君にとっては、上述の例文の意味は明瞭であるに違いない・・・が、万一明瞭でない場合に備えて、より詳しく解説すると、次のようになる:「英語は、インド・ヨーロッパ語族の一員ではあるものの、"性別を一切持たない"という点で例外的な言語である。それ故にこそ、初学者にとっても比較的容易で、世界中で話されてもいるわけである。英語を例外として、フランス語・スペイン語・イタリア語あたりのインド・ヨーロッパ言語たちは"名詞の性別"に関する厳格な決まり事を持っており、そのせいでこれらの言語を外国人が学ぶのは困難であるから、英語に比べてあまり人気がないわけである」。

Now, you know, verbs are only useful when memorized with example sentences. Trying to remember verbs with their definitions only will get you nowhere.

(2)Memorize verbs in the actual sentence pattern(s) (what this book calls "SPAT-5") in which they can be used. Some verbs can be used in SVOO(#4: eg. "She denied me entrance to her room") while others cannot (ng. "She prohibited me entrance to her room"; cf: "She prohibited me from entering her room"). If you are in the habit of remembering verbs with their meanings only, you may be able to wade through the relatively easier flows of SV or SVO, but you will soon get stuck in the narrower channels of SVOO or SVOC. So as not to get lost later on, try to remember verbs in their particular sentence patterns.

(3)Never try to save your efforts in paraphrasing a particular verb with "同意語(DOUIGO: synonyms)" or "反意語(HANIGO: antonyms)". English verbs have so many synonyms and antonyms that trying to remember them one by one, without any logical chain of association to collectively grasp and recollect many verbs in a single stroke, is too arduous to be practically possible. All good linguists instinctively know how easier it is (although seemingly harder) to remember many other related words along with any particular term.

Paraphrasing with synonyms and antonyms is also effective in avoiding wrong usage of words. Take the above-mentioned verb "deny" as an example. As I've already shown, it can be used in SVOO sentence pattern, unlike its synonym "prohibit". But, if you consult your dictionary, you will know that the verb "forbid" can also be used in SVOO (eg. "She forbade/denied me entrance to her room"). Without such knowledge of possible usage in some particular sentence pattern, you cannot make correct use of English verbs: your effort to memorize verbs is practically powerless without such useful example sentences.

Those who have no such knowledge will try to use verbs in "impossible" sentence patterns. As a result, some verbs which could not originally be used in a certain sentence pattern will come to get a license to it after a lapse of time with a certain number of "abusers". If you go deeper into your

これで諸君も「動詞」は例文込みで覚えてこそ役立つ語である、ということがわかったであろう。「動詞」をその語の定義のみで覚え込んでも、頓挫するだけである。

(2)「動詞」は、実際に用いられ得る「文型」(この本の呼び名で言うところの“SPAT-5”)の中で覚えるべし。「動詞」の中には「SVOO(第4文型)」で使えるものもある(例 “She denied me entrance to her room.:彼女は私を部屋に入れてくれなかった”)が、別の動詞はその文型では使えない((×) “She prohibited me entrance to her room.”ではダメ。参考までに、“She prohibited me from entering her room.”ならOK)。「動詞」をその語義のみで覚える癖のある諸君の場合、「SV(第1文型)」だの「SVO(第3文型)」だのの比較的泳ぎ渡り易い文型なら何とかなるかもしれないが、「SVOO(第4文型)」や「SVOC(第五文型)」といった幅の狭い海峡を前にした時には、行き詰まることになるだろう。後々道に迷うことのないように、「動詞」はそれぞれ固有の文型の中で覚える努力をすることだ。

(3)特定の「動詞」をその「同意語(synonyms)」や「反意語(antonyms)」で言い換える努力を決して惜しんではならない。英語の「動詞」には大変多くの「同意語/反意語」があるため、それらの語句を一個一個別々の語として覚え込もうとするのは(幾多の「動詞」を集合体的に一挙に把握し思い出すための論理的連想の鎖に絡めることもなしに暗記しようとすることは)、あまりにもシンドすぎて現実的には無理である。語学が達者な人ならみんな、どんな語句も、それに関連する幾多の他の語句ともども覚え込むほうが(一見するとより大変そうに思えるが)実際には楽であることを、本能的に知っているものだ。

「同意語/反意語」での言い換えはまた、言葉の誤用を避ける上でも有効である。上述した動詞“deny:与えない”を例に取って解説しよう。既に示した通り、この語は、同意語の“prohibit”とは異なり、「SVOO(第4文型)」での使用が可能である。しかし、辞書を引いてみたならば、“forbid”という動詞もまた「SVOO」で使えることがわかるだろう(例 She forbade/denied me entrance to her room.:彼女は私が彼女の部屋に入ることを許さなかった)。ある特定の文型で使用可能か不可能かに関するこうした知識を持ち合わせていない場合、諸君は英語の「動詞」を正しく使うことができない:この種の役立つ例文なしに「動詞」を暗記してみたところで、そんな努力など実質的に何の力も持たないのである。

こうした知識を持ち合わせない人々は、「動詞」を“あり得ない”文型の中で使おうとするものである。その結果、ある種の文型では本来使用不可能のはずの「動詞」が、ある程度の時間をかけて“誤用者”の数がそれなり以上の数まで膨れ上がるにつれて、次第に許容されるようになる。辞書の奥底へと分け入ってみれば、諸君は次のような

dictionary, you may find such example sentences as "The Japanese law forbids citizens to carry guns(*informal='from carrying guns')". You should know the reason why: because so many people who are in the habit of not memorizing a verb with example sentences are prone to associate the verb "forbid" with its synonym "prohibit" that they are liable to make an originally "impossible" paraphrase "The Japanese law prohibits(=forbids) citizens from carrying guns". While the reversed version "The Japanese law prohibits citizens to carry guns" is forbidden in English. You must know the reason why: because the number of people who use "prohibit" in such a wrong SVOC sentence pattern is so small that the dictionary does not have to show any linguistic respect for this "impossible" usage.

Since linguistics is based on popular usage, not on definitely fixed golden rules of grammar, the increase in the number of people who "abuse" some "impossible" usage will change "not allowed" into "informal" and eventually into "normal, if not formal". But since you learners of English are no collectors of statistical data in English usage, it is safe for you to try to remember English verbs in some "formal" example sentences listed in the dictionary.

- The vast seas of adverbs should be waded through by "where/how/when/why" distinction -

The number of English adverbs is so large that you will simply get lost if you blindly try to remember them as you happen to meet them. Keep in mind the following points whenever you see an adverb:

(1)Adjective-based adverbs need not be consciously memorized.

Although the name "adverb" derives from its function to "add on to verbs", the composition of most English adverbs is "adjective+ly". For example, a suffix "ly" added on to the adjective "quick" will make an adverb "quickly". Aside from such tricky adverbs as "hardly" or "supposedly", which can hardly be supposed to be "adjective+ly" versions of "hard" or "supposed", an adverb simply made by adding "ly" to any given adjective should basically be remembered as an "adjective", not as an independent "adverb". Just remember such adverbs as adjectives, and add "ly" at the end to use them as

例文を発見することになるかもしれない:“The Japanese law forbids citizens to carry guns(非標準=“from carrying guns”).:日本の法律は市民が銃を持ち歩くことを禁止している”。何故このような「非標準用法」が併記されているか、その理由がもう諸君にはわかったであろう:「動詞」を例文と共に覚える癖もない幾多の人々は、同意語である動詞“forbid”と“prohibit”を結び付けて考えがちであるから、彼らは両者を混同した“The Japanese law prohibits(=forbids) citizens ＜from carrying guns＞.”という(本来であれば“あり得ない”)言い換えに陥りがちなわけである。その一方で、この表現の裏返しの“The Japanese law prohibits citizens ＜to carry guns＞.”のような言い換えは、英語世界では禁じ手である・・・何故そうであるかも、諸君ならわかるはずだ:そのような間違った「SVOC(第五文型)」の中で“prohibit”を使う人間の数はごく少数なので、辞書側としては、この“あり得ない”用例に対し何らの言語学的敬意を表すべき必要もないからである。

言語学は、一般人がどのような形で言葉を使っているかの実態に基づく学問であり、絶対不可変の文法の黄金原則に基づく固定的な決まり事ではないのだから、“あり得ない”はずの何らかの用法も、それを“誤用”する人々の数が増えるにつれて、“不許可”から“非標準”へ、やがては“正式ではないが、一般的”へと格上げされて行くのである。しかし、諸君は「英語学習者」であって「英語の用例の統計データの収集家」ではないのだから、英語の「動詞」を覚えるに際しては、辞書の中に掲載された“正式な”例文の中で暗記するよう努めるほうが安全である。

－副詞の広大な海は“where:何処／how:如何／when:何時／why:何故”の区分で渡り切れ－

英語の「副詞(adverbs)」の数は実に膨大だから、出くわすたびに闇雲に覚え込もうとしていたのでは、道に迷うだけである。「副詞」を見た時は常に、以下の諸点を念頭に置いておくことである:

(1)「形容詞ベースの副詞」は意識して暗記するまでもない。

“adverb”という呼び名は“add on to verbs:動詞に添加する”という「副詞」の機能に由来するものではあるが、多くの英語の「副詞」の組成は“adjective+ly＝形容詞末尾に ly 語尾を付けたもの”である。例えば、形容詞の“quick:素早い”に「接尾語(suffix)」の“ly”を付け足せば、副詞の“quickly:素早く”が出来上がる。“hardly:ほとんど～ない”や“supposedly:本来ならば～のはず”といった(“hard:きつい”や“supposed:想定上の”といった形容詞に“ly”を付けた語句としては到底見なせない)油断ならない副詞は別にして、任意の「形容詞」に“ly”を付けただけの「副詞」は、基本的に「形容詞」として

adverbs as necessary. You should save such meaningless efforts as to try to remember these "add-on" types of adverbs respectively with as much respect as their "original adjectives", as your conscious memory bank is not without limitation.

(2)Be always aware which of "where/how/when/why" an adverb belongs to.

An adverb always belongs to one of the four semantic categories - where, how, when, and why. You should also remember that English adverbial expressions are normally used in that order(1:where > 2:how > 3:when > 4:why), as you can see in the following example:

eg. I went (to my office) (by bicycle) (yesterday) (because the bus was on strike).

One of the most effective ways beginners can get used to English is to make "5W1H interrogative sentences, including Who, What, Where, How, When, Why" out of EVERY English sentence they happen to meet, such as:

cf. Who went to the office by bicycle yesterday?

cf. What did you do yesterday?

cf. Where did you go by bicycle yesterday?

cf. How did you go to your office yesterday?

cf. When did you go to your office by bicycle?

cf. Why did you go to your office by bicycle yesterday?

By constantly and instantly making such interrogative sentences out of each and every English sentence they see in textbooks, beginners can get the knack of English composition and develop their categorical sense of adverbs simultaneously. Whenever you add an adverb to your memory bank, be sure to label it with one of the four categories: where, how, when and why.

暗記すればよく、独立した「副詞」として覚える必要はない。こうした「副詞」は「形容詞」として覚えておくだけにしておいて、「副詞」として用いる必要が生じた時だけ語尾に"ly"を付け足して「副詞」扱いすればそれでよい。こうした「形容詞アドオン(add-on)型副詞」を、その原型となった「形容詞」と同等の敬意を払いつつ個別的に暗記しようとするがごとき無意味な努力は、せぬがよろしい;諸君が意識して覚え込める脳内記憶領域の容量は、無尽蔵というわけではないのだから。

(2)ある「副詞」が"where:何処/how:如何/when:何時/why:何故"のいずれに属するかを常に意識せよ。

「副詞」は常に、"where:どこ/how:いかに/when:いつ/why:なにゆえ"という4つの意味別カテゴリーのいずれかに属する。そしてまた、英語の「副詞的表現」は、一般にその順番で(即ち、1)where > 2)how > 3)when > 4)why の順で)用いられることも覚えておくべきだ(例えば次例のごとし):

例 I went (to my office＝場所) (by bicycle＝手段) (yesterday＝日時) (because the bus was on strike＝原因・理由).

バスがストライキ中だったので、昨日は私は自転車で職場まで行った

初心者が英語に慣れる上で最も有効な手段の一つは、偶然出会った全ての英文を材料に「"Who:誰/What:何/Where:何処/How:如何/When:何時/Why:何故"から成る「5W1H 疑問文」を(以下の参考例のような形で)作ってみることである:

参考例 Who went to the office by bicycle yesterday? ＜誰が＞昨日職場へ自転車で通いましたか?

参考例 What did you do yesterday? あなたは昨日＜何を＞しましたか?

参考例 Where did you go by bicycle yesterday? あなたは昨日自転車で＜何処へ＞行きましたか?

参考例 How did you go to your office yesterday? あなたは昨日職場へ＜どうやって＞行きましたか?

参考例 When did you go to your office by bicycle? あなたが職場へ自転車通勤したのは＜いつのこと＞ですか?

参考例 Why did you go to your office by bicycle yesterday? あなたが昨日職場へ自転車で行ったのは＜何故＞ですか?

初心者が教科書で出会う英文の一つ一つについてこうした疑問文を絶えず(それも反射的に)作るように心がけておくと、英作文のコツがつかめると共に、「副詞」の分類意識も同時に磨くことができる。「副詞」を脳内記憶領域に加える際にはいつも、"where:場所/how:方法/when:時間/why:理由"のいずれか一つのラベルを貼っておくことを忘れないようにすることだ。

This distinctive attitude in adverbial categorization is also essential to refining your ability in reading, listening or writing. Of "5W1H", human mind will easily detect and be aware of "Who" and "What": they are rarely long, and will usually be used in such conspicuous sentential elements as (S)subject, (O)object or (C)complement: who but the sloppy could ever miss them? On the other hand, adverbial parts of sentences are often very long, sometimes to the point of being boring. They are usually unessential elements of sentences, meant to serve as accessories to some verb, only to serve as red-herring to beginners. So as not to get hypnotized by such attention-distracters, a long, boring or even misleading adverbial part of the sentence should always be labeled either as "where(PLACE)" or "how(MANNER)" or "when(TIME)" or "why(REASON)" and treated simply, or should be simply dismissed as flabby part simply making the sentence too fat to embrace!... Remember, the way you treat adverbs – that bulky element far too long for their unessential role in sentences – will decide whether you can really enjoy reading sentences, or you'll simply join in reading sleepers...zzz.

- Pronouns and auxiliary verbs had better be memorized all at once -

Unlike Japanese which has no definite "代名詞(DAIMEISHI: pronouns)", the number and usages of English pronouns are definitely fixed and relatively few. Aside from such personal/impersonal pronouns as "I, we, you, they, he, she, it", English language has such pronouns as "all, any, each, few, none, one, same, some, such, that, this, those, what, when, where, which, who, whom, whose, etc,etc.".

The number of "助動詞(JODOUSHI: auxiliary verbs)", specialized versions of English verbs which serve only to add some meaning to other verbs, is also fixed and few — twelve(12) in all to be exact: "be, can, dare, do, have, may, must, need, ought, shall, used, will".

こうした「副詞」のカテゴリー分けをする選別的態度はまた、英語の読解・聴取・作文の能力に磨きをかける上で必要不可欠である。「5W1H(Who:誰/What:何/Where:何処/How:如何/When:何時/Why:何故)」のうち、“Who:誰”と“What:何”については、人間の頭脳はこれを容易に突き止め意識するものである:これらの語句は大抵短いし、「(S:subject)主語」や「(O:object)目的語」や「(C:complement)補語」といった際立つ文章要素の中で用いられるのが普通である・・・そんな目立った語句を見落とす者が(よほどずさんな人はともかく)いるわけがあるまい？ これに対して、文章中の「副詞的成文」は大変に長い(時として倦怠感を誘うほどに長い)場合が多い。こうした「副詞」は文章内では主要ならざる要素であって、何らかの「動詞」の添え物として働くだけで、結果的には初心者の目をくらます厄介な存在となるのがオチなのである。こうした「注意を逸らすもの」の催眠術にかからぬように、文章内の長く退屈で誤読可能性すらある「副詞的成文」には常に、“where(PLACE:場所)”／“how(MANNER:方法)”／“when(TIME:時)”／“why(REASON:理由)”のいずれかのラベルを貼り付けて、ササッと軽くあしらっておくべきである・・・あるいは、文章を抱きかかえる気にもなれないほど肥え太らせるだけの「しまりのない贅肉部！」としてひたすら無視してしまえばよいのである・・・覚えておきたまえ、諸君が「副詞」を－文章内では大した役割を果たすわけでもない割には異様なまでに長すぎるあのガサばる要素を－どのように取り扱うか、その巧拙こそが、文章読解体験を心底楽しめるか、それとも単に読んでるうちに眠たくなって何が何だか理解できずに終わる哀れな読者の仲間入りすることになるか、それを決する決め手となるのである。

－代名詞・助動詞は一気覚えが得策－

固定された「代名詞(pronouns)」を持たない日本語とは異なり、英語では「代名詞」の数もその用法も厳格に固定されており、その数も多くはない。“I/we/you/they/he/she/it”といった「人称代名詞(personal pronouns)」や「非人称代名詞(impersonal pronouns)」以外にも、英語には次のような「代名詞」が存在する:“all:全て/any:何でも/each:おのおの/few:少数/none:何一つ～ない/one:者/same:同じもの/some:一部/such:そうしたもの/that:それ/this:これ/those:それら/what:何/when:いつ/where:どこ/which:どっち/who:誰(主格)/whom:誰(目的格)/whose:誰の/その他諸々”。

他の「動詞」に何らかの意味を添えるためにのみ機能する特殊な動詞である「助動詞(auxiliary verbs)」の数もまた固定されており、その数は少ない。正確に言えば以下の12個である:“be、can、dare、do、have、may、must、need、ought、shall、used、will”。

Although the number and usages of pronouns and auxiliary verbs in English are rather large and daunting for beginners, they should still be memorized in a stroke: not on “as necessary” basis, but in a series of systematic studies on their possible usages. In other words, studies of pronouns and auxiliary verbs ought to be dealt with as a set of grammatical knowledge as opposed to a part of random vocabulary building.

- Conjunctions and interjections could be memorized at a sweep, only to little avail -

Unlike in the case of pronouns and auxiliary verbs, you should not try to remember conjunctions and interjections in a single stroke: their memorization should be merely haphazard and need not be systematic. Their limited number may make it possible to list them all in a small book for you to mechanically remember, but their overlapping meanings and minute differences in nuance will make such attempts practically futile.

For example, a group of conjunctions that bind two clauses in contradictory relationship will contain such words or phrases as “although, and yet, but, though, whereas, and yet”. To try to remember them may look fruitful, but in fact, it's totally no use: these conjunctions appear so many times in English sentences that you have absolutely no need to consciously remember them.

Besides, the part of speech “conjunction” does not include such words and phrases as “but then again, conversely, however, nevertheless, notwithstanding, still, while” — these are all termed “adverb” while meaning the same thing as “although, and yet, but, though, whereas, and yet”. Such terms, conjunction or adverb, should be naturally stored up in your memory as you encounter them in English sentences. They stand out in the streams of contexts so outstandingly that they will easily stay in your linguistic memory without any conscious effort on your part, or without having their obvious roles in the sentence pompously pointed out in cheap, cheeky textbooks on “how to read English”.

The only meaningful effort you can make regarding conjunctions (or adverbs) is to associate relatively rare words and expressions with some other familiar conjunctions or adverbs. For example, an archaic conjunction

英語の「代名詞」及び「助動詞」の数と用法は、初心者にとってはかなり多くて尻込みすることであろうが、それでもやはり一挙に覚えてしまうのがよい。“必要に応じて折々学べばよい”というやり方ではなく、「代名詞」「助動詞」の用法としてあり得る全てのものを“一連の体系的学習の中で覚え込んでしまう”べきなのである。言葉を換えて言えば、「代名詞」と「助動詞」の学習は、「行き当たりばったりの語彙構築努力の一環として」ではなく「まとまった文法的知識の一環として」取り扱うべきなのである。

ー接続詞・間投詞の一気覚えは可なれど効果薄しー

「代名詞(pronouns)」や「助動詞(auxiliary verbs)」の場合とは異なり、「接続詞(conjunctions)」や「間投詞(interjections)」は一挙に覚えようとはしないほうがよい:その覚え方はただ無計画の行き当たりばったりでよく、体系的に暗記する必要はない。「接続詞」も「間投詞」もその数は限られているから、全部を小さな本の形で一覧表にして機械的に覚え込めるようにするのも不可能ではないが、これらの語句の多くは意味が重なる上に微妙なニュアンスの違いなどもあるから、一覧形式での機械的棒暗記努力は実質的に無益になるだろう。

例えば、二つの「節(clauses)」を逆接の関係で結ぶ一群の「接続詞」の中には、“although, and yet, but, though, whereas, yet”等の単語や成句が含まれる。これらを覚え込むのは一見有益に見えるものの、実際には全く無意味である:こうした「接続詞」は英文の中で物凄く多くの回数出現するものなのだから、意識して覚え込む必要など全くないのである。

さらにまた、「接続詞(conjunctions)」という品詞の中には“but then again, conversely, however, nevertheless, notwithstanding, still, while”等の単語や成句は含まれない:これらはみな「副詞(adverbs)」に分類される語句なのである・・・が、その意味するところは先に列挙した「接続詞」の “although, and yet, but, though, whereas, yet”と同じである。こういう語句は、それが「接続詞」であろうが「副詞」であろうが、英文の中で遭遇するたびに自然な形で諸君の記憶の中に蓄えられるべきものである。こうした語句は文脈の流れの中で大変際立つものであるから(諸君の側で意識的努力を払わずとも、文章内でのその明々白々な役割に関して“英語をいかにして読むか”的な安っぽく厚かましい教科書に得意そうに指摘してもらわずとも)諸君の言語学的記憶領域の中に容易に留まってくれるものである。

「接続詞(あるいは、副詞)」に関して諸君が行なうことの出来る唯一の意義ある努力は、比較的珍しい単語や表現を、何か別の馴染みのある「接続詞」あるいは「副詞」と関連付ける努力である。例えば、“albeit:〜ではあるが”という古風な接続詞は、次のよ

"albeit" had better be comprehended and memorized along with such expressions as "Be it ever so humble, there's no place like home ; Although it may be humble, home is the best place in the world". Contradictory "and" (eg. "The commander knew we couldn't win; and, he ordered us to fight on") should not be comprehended as a strange usage of "and" but as an abbreviated form of "and yet".

As for interjections, mechanical memorization and random exclamation are quite fitting for this part of speech. You could store them up in your vocabulary in totally haphazard ways and shout them out from time to time... at your own risk, that is. Such interjections as "Bullshit!", "Fuck!", "Goddamn!", "Holy shit!" or "Holy smoke!" are all appealing to English beginners because they can be used with absolutely no regard to grammar (and to others' feelings, too). For this reason, this author is quite sure of the popularity of a short seminar on "How to draw attention by simple exclamation of interjections", especially among those who miserably failed to master English. But this author is too busy and too decent to engage in such vulgar business. Interjections ought simply to be learnt by heart totally by chance, as you happen to encounter them and find them interesting (or shocking). Systematic categorization and memorization of all interjections in English, though possible, seems anything but fruitful and downright absurd. You may cry "Eureka!" at the idea at first, but will soon shout "Enough!" after you actually practice chanting "Alas!", "Bravo!", "Cheers!" or "Boo!"

- Prepositions could never be learnt at a sweep; learn idioms by heart, and prepositional comprehension will naturally come with them -

Of all English parts of speech, by far the most difficult to master is the preposition. It is difficult for Japanese learners for three reasons.

うな言い回しと共に理解し記憶するのがよい:「Be it ever so humble, there's no place like home. ; Although it may be humble, home is the best place in the world. たとえいかに粗末であろうとも、我が家こそは世界で一番素晴らしい場所である」。逆接の"and"(例 The commander knew we couldn't win; and, he ordered us to fight on. 司令官は、我々が勝てないことを知っていた;にもかかわらず、彼は我々に戦闘続行を命じた)の場合は、"and(=基本的には'そして'の意を表わす'順接'の語)"の不思議な用例として理解するよりも、"and yet(='それでいてしかし'の'逆接'の成句)"の短縮版として理解するほうがよい。

「間投詞(interjections)」に関しては、棒暗記した上でデタラメに叫んでみる使い方が、この品詞の場合、実にお似合いだと言える。まったくの行き当たりばったりで語彙に加えては、折々叫んでみればよいだけの語、それが「間投詞」なのである(・・・但し、叫んだ結果がどうなるかはこの筆者の知ったことではないので、自己責任でお試しあれ)。"Bullshit!:バカ言え"だの"Fuck!:こなくそっ"だの"Goddamn!:くたばりやがれ"だの"Holy shit!"あるいは"Holy smoke!"(いずれも"Holy God!:聖なる神よ"と叫ぶのをはばかる"Holy Spirit!:聖なる精霊よ"を更に冗談めかして"H-S"の頭文字が一緒というだけの理由から"Holy shit!:聖なるクソよ"だの"Holy smoke!:聖なる煙よ"だのと叫んだだけの間投詞)はみな、文法というやつに(そして、他者の感情に対しても)一切何のお構いもなしに使ってよい語句なので、英語初心者にとっては魅力的なものである。この理由ゆえに(筆者としては確信できるのだが)「間投詞を叫ぶだけでいかにして他人の注意を引き付けるか」などと銘打った短期集中講座を開催すれば(特に英語習得に惨めに失敗した人々の間では)さぞや大人気になること間違いなかろう・・・が、この筆者は、そのようなさもしい所業にいそしむには、いささか多忙にして品行方正すぎるので、やらない。「間投詞」は、たまたまそれに出くわして面白い(あるいは、けしからん)と感じるたびごとに、全く偶発的な形で覚えればそれでよい。英語の「間投詞」の全てを体系的に分類して覚え込むことは、不可能ではないが、ちっとも有益ではなくまったくバカげているように思う・・・そういうアイディアを思い付いた当座ならば"Eureka!:おぉっ、これだっ!"と叫びたくもなろうが、実際に"Alas!:あぁ～"だの"Bravo!:すっげー"だの"Cheers!:カンパーイ"だの"Boo!:ばーか"だのの数々を連呼しながら特訓する段になれば、早晩、"Enough!:うげぇ～～"と叫ぶのが関の山である。

ー前置詞の一気修得は無理、前置詞理解は熟語暗記の自然的副産物と心得よー

英語の「品詞(parts of speech)」の中でも、習得困難なものの断然第一位は「前置詞(prepositions)」である。日本人の学習者にとっては、以下の3つの理由から困難なのである:

(1)Japanese language has no equivalent of prepositions. The nearest in Japanese to English prepositions are "助詞(JOSHI: postpositional particles)" such as "て(TE), に(NI), を(WO), は(WA)". They are not unlike English prepositions in simplicity in form and multiplicity in meaning, but their position in the sentence and actual usage are too different to be deemed as equivalents. English prepositions are a total stranger to Japanese learners, making them the toughest hurdle to get over in all English words.
(2)A preposition belongs to what is called "a function word", devoid of meaning in itself and only meaningful in relation to some other words, thereby making it difficult or even impossible to comprehend "as is", making it imperative to remember it in some example sentence, which makes it harder still for Japanese learners to conquer who are in the habit of "just seeing, not speaking" English without any regard to such minute and seemingly meaningless words as prepositions.

You could remember nouns, pronouns, adjectives, adverbs, conjunctions and interjections the way they are presented in the dictionary and put them to practical use more or less; but you simply couldn't do that with verbs and prepositions. They need remembering in example sentences, which makes them harder (indeed impossible) to master for Japanese learners who like to study abstractions and to absorb fragmentary information but positively hate to read aloud, type in and correctly recite sentences.
(3)Most prepositions have multiple usages and are also used in the capacities of other parts of speech in the same form. Take your time and look up in the dictionary such prepositions as "as", "for", "of"... the number of their respectively categorized usages – labeled "conjunction", "adverb", "pronoun" and "preposition" like so many floors in a department store – is daunting enough, and the floods of example sentences in the form of idiomatic expressions will drown out your will to swim through their semantic streams. How could you ever conquer such impossibly diverse seas of meanings?

The answer is simple and sober: it will take you years of memorizing idiom after idiom to come to practical understanding of English prepositions. Each preposition has its own manners of connection or arrangement in relation to other words; verbs and nouns have some particular prepositions with which

(1)日本語には「前置詞」に相当する語がない。日本語の中で英語の「前置詞」に最も近いものは、“て、に、を、は”等の「助詞(postpositional participles)」である。これらの語は、形は単純だが意味が複雑多岐に渡る点に於いて、英語の「前置詞」に似ていなくもないが、文章内での位置も実際の用法もあまりにも異なりすぎていて、両者を同等扱いするわけには行かない。英語の「前置詞」は日本の学習者にとっては全く“見知らぬ他人”なのであって、それがこの「前置詞」をあらゆる英単語の中で最も制覇困難な障害物と化しているわけである。

(2)「前置詞」はいわゆる「機能語(a function word)」と呼ばれる語であり、それ自体には何の意味もなく、他の何らかの語句との関係の中に於いてのみ意味を持ち、それ故にこうした語句を“そのままの形で”理解するのは困難であり(あるいはいっそ不可能とすら言ってよく)、例文の中で覚えることが必須となるわけであるが、そのためにますます日本人学習者(英語を“ただ見てるだけで、口に出して読まない”習癖を持ち、あまりにも短くて一見意味なさそうに感じる「前置詞」なんて語には一切何の敬意も払わない人達)が「前置詞」を制覇するのは困難、というわけである。

「nouns(名詞)/pronouns(代名詞)/adjectives(形容詞)/adverbs(副詞)/conjunctions(接続詞)/interjections(間投詞)」といった語句であれば、辞書で紹介されている通りの形で覚え込んで実用に役立てることも(程度の差こそあれ)可能ではある;が、「動詞」と「前置詞」に関しては到底そういうわけには行かない。これらの品詞は例文の中で暗記する必要があるから、日本人の学習者(抽象的な概念を学んで断片的情報を吸収するのは好きだが、文章の数々を声に出して読んだりタイプライターで打ち込んだり正確に思い出して口に乗せて吟じたりするのは大嫌いな人々)にとって、これらの語句を習得するのは、より困難(というかむしろ不可能)なわけである。

(3)大抵の前置詞には幾つもの用法がある上に、同一の形態で別の品詞としても用いられる場合がある。少し時間を取って、“as”だの“for”だの“of”だのの「前置詞」を辞書で引いてみるとよい・・・それぞれの語ごとに(「接続詞」だの「副詞」だの「代名詞」だの「前置詞」だのとまるでデパートの売り場みたいに)カテゴリー分けされた用法の数の多さだけでも既に十分威圧的だが、「熟語的表現(idiomatic expressions)」の形で居並ぶ例文の洪水の前には、意味の流れを泳ぎ渡ってやろうとする諸君の意志も「溺死」してしまうことだろう。この絶望的なまでに多種多様な意味の大海を、いったいどうやって征服したらよいというのか?

その答えは、単純かつ地味なものになる:英語の「前置詞」を実用的に理解できるに至るまでには、何年もの年月をかけて「熟語(idioms)また熟語の暗記過程」を経なければならないのだ。それぞれの「前置詞」には、他の語句との関係の中で、独自の結合

they can combine to compose some particular meaning. Such formal relationship (called "collocation") is definitely fixed in English, without the knowledge of which you couldn't get proficient in this language.

With the help of really good guidebooks, you could master the whole realm of English grammar in a couple of years; but you could only get reasonably proficient in English collocation in a decade, if not a couple of decades. Never attempt in vain to conquer English prepositions the way you try to master other parts of speech. Some books, schools or teachers may prompt you to make that futile attempt, but don't kid yourself into believing that such a stunt is practically possible: they simply make you remember something just in order that they can test your performance in remembering something, not in order for you to master everything. To attempt to systematically master everything in prepositions via lessons given by your schools or teachers is the most daunting yet futile thing this author can ever think of: they may help to some extent, but will leave you helpless and powerless in the end. The only teacher that enables you to really master prepositions is idiomatic expressions: to learn them by heart in the form of innumerable example sentences which will come up to your memory whenever inspired by some particular preposition.

For example, the meaning of "derivation/deprivation" in the preposition "of" should be stored up in your brains not as an abstract item of knowledge but in such concrete forms as "Clear the street of snow", "May I ask a favor of you?", "She comes of a noble family" or "You expect too much of me". Be a little more imaginative and add "f" to "of", and you will get "off", which will remind you of the handy expression "spin-off", a thing coming out from something with which it was originally bound together. Now, you get the knack of "of" of derivation/deprivation.

I cannot emphasize and repeat this often enough: that the knowledge of English prepositions will grow up with your store of idioms and collocations in your brains. Take your time; haste only makes waste.

の作法や並び方の決まり事がある。「動詞(verbs)」や「名詞(nouns)」にはそれぞれ、ある特定の意味を表わす際に結び付くことのできる「前置詞」が決まっている。こういう形式的な関係、いわゆる「連語関係(collocation)」と呼ばれるものは、英語の中では厳格に固定されており、この知識なしには英語に熟練することなど不可能なのである。

「英文法」の全領域の修得は(本当に優れたガイドブックの助けを借りれば)2～3年で可能であろう・・・が、英語の「連語関係(コロケーション)」にそこそこ習熟するまでには十年はかかる(何十年もかかる、とまでは言わないが)。英語の「前置詞」を、他の品詞の場合と同様のやり方で征服しようなどと無益な努力を払ってはならない。一部の本や学校や先生方は、そうした無益な努力を諸君に強いるかもしれないが、そういう離れ業が現実的に可能であるなどという甘い考えを、諸君は抱いてはならない:そのテの本やガッコやセンセが諸君に何かを「覚えろ」と強要するのは、その何かを諸君が「どの程度しっかり覚えたかをテストする」ためにそうするだけであって、諸君に全てを修得させるためにするわけではないのだから。学校や先生が提供するレッスンを通して「前置詞」の全てを体系的に修得しようとする試みは、この筆者の知る限り、最も大胆にして不毛なる営みである。頑張ればある程度の役には立つだろうが、最後の最後には諸君は途方に暮れて自らの無力さを思い知って終わり、である。「前置詞」の真の修得を可能にしてくれる唯一の教師は「熟語表現(idiomatic expressions)」のみである。「熟語」を、何らかの「前置詞」に触発された際にはすっと記憶に浮かび上がってくるような無数の例文の形で暗記することを通してのみ、真の「前置詞」修得は可能になるのだ。

例えば、“of”という前置詞の中に含まれる“derivation:由来／deprivation:奪取”の意味を脳内に蓄えるためには、抽象的な知識の一項目としてではなく、次のような具体的例文の形で記憶するべきである:“Clear the street of snow.:路上の雪を片付けろ”、“May I ask a favor of you?:あなたにお願いをしてもいいですか？”、“She comes of a noble family.:彼女は高貴な家系の出身だ”、“You expect too much of me.:君は私にあまりに多くを期待しすぎる”。少しだけ想像力を働かせて、“of”の後に“f”を加えてみれば、“off”の形になって、“spin-off:スピンオフ”＝「元来一緒にくっついていた物事の中から、分離する形で生じた何か」を思い出すことだろう・・・という感じで、諸君は“of”の「由来／奪取」のコツがつかめるわけである。

このことは何度声を大にして繰り返してもまだ足りないことなので、念押ししておく:英語の「前置詞」の知識は、諸君の脳内に於ける「熟語(イディオム)」と「連語(コロケーション)」の知識と共同歩調で増えて行くものである。時間をかけて取り組むことだ;焦って一気に身に付けようとしても、結果は無益に終わるだけである。

- Noun/verb/adjective/adverb all combine together to count as one word -

With the exception of pronouns, prepositions, conjunctions and interjections whose forms are fixed and unchangeable, all the other English parts of speech are interchangeable with other parts of speech. It's a good idea to comprehend all these parts of speech as one single entity.

Just imagine yourself trying to remember "image", "imagery", "imagination", "imagist", "imagine", "imaginable", "imaginal", "imaginary", "imaginative", "imaginably", "imaginarily" and "imaginatively" respectively, as though they were twelve different words unrelated with one another. Try to remember them all in a single stroke, and your effort will be twelve times less than if you tried to remember them one by one. The apparent difficulty you find in comprehending all these twelve at a time for the first time may seem too forbidding to tackle, but the end result is well worth the effort: the minute difference between "imaginable", "imaginal", "imaginary" and "imaginative" can best be understood by dealing with them at a time and always trying to think of any one adjective in conscious contrast with the others.

Trust me: the more you remember, the less likely you are to forget — that is the paradoxical truth of vocabulary building. Those who try to remember the least are quite likely to forget the most.

Many nouns are used as verbs in the same form (eg. "How about a drive?" ; "Would you like to drive my car?"), and any given verb can generally take the form of a noun by adding some suffix (eg. "How can you treat me so bad?" ; "I protest your cruel treatment") or by changing a part of it (eg. "You never fail to please me" ; "The pleasure is mine"). Most adjectives can be used as adverbs by the simple addition of the suffix "ly" at the end, while some can be used both adjectively and adverbially in the same form (eg. "I'm a slow reader" ; "Speak a little more slowly" ; "You drive too slow").

ー名詞形・動詞形・形容詞形・副詞形、全部まとめて1英単語と心得よー

「pronouns(代名詞)、prepositions(前置詞)、conjunctions(接続詞)、interjections(間投詞)」といった形態的に固定されていて不変の品詞を除き、全ての英語の品詞は他の品詞へと形を変えることができる。こうした品詞はみな「一つの統合体」として包括的におさえておくのが良い考えである。

ちょっと想像してみてほしい:“image:イメージ”、“imagery:画像”、“imagination:想像力”、“imagist:写象主義者”、“imagine:想像する”、“imaginable:思い描くことができる”、“imaginal:想像力の”、“imaginary:架空の”、“imaginative:想像力豊かな”、“imaginably:およそ思い描ける限り”、“imaginarily:あくまで想像上の話として”、“imaginatively:想像をたくましくして”といった語句の数々を、お互い何の関係もない12個の別々の単語であるかの如く個別的に覚えようと頑張っている自分の姿を・・・これらの語句を全て一挙に覚えてしまえば、一つ一つ別々に覚え込もうとした場合の12分の1の労力で済むだろう。これら12語をみないっぺんに理解しようとする際には、最初こそ、ちょっと見、大変な困難を感じるであろうが、最終的に得られるものの大きさを思えば、その努力に十分値するはずである。“imaginable”、“imaginal”、“imaginary”、“imaginative”といった語句の間に存在する微妙な相違は、これらの語句をいちどきにまとめて取り扱い、どれか一つの形容詞を思い浮かべる時には他の形容詞と意識的に比較対照するようにしてこそ、最もよく理解できるのである。

信じてほしい、より多くを覚えるほうが、より忘れ難くなるものなのである・・・これは「ボキャビル(vocabulary building:語彙構築)」に於ける逆説的真理なのだ。最小限の事柄しか覚えようとしない人は往々にして最も多くの事柄を忘れるものである。

「名詞(nouns)」の多くは同じ形で「動詞(verbs)」にも使われる(例 “How about a drive?:ドライブしませんか?”、“Would you like to drive my car?:君、僕の車を運転したいかい?”)。一般的に、任意の「動詞(verbs)」を「名詞(nouns)」の形態に変えるには、何らかの「接尾語(suffix)」を付けたり(例 “How can you treat me so bad?:どうして君は僕をそうひどく扱うことができるんだい?”、“I protest your cruel treatment.:君のひどい扱いに、僕は抗議する”)あるいはその形態の一部を変えたりすればよい(例 “You never fail to please me.:あなたはいつも必ず私を喜ばせてくれます”、“The pleasure is mine.:いえいえ、私の方こそどういたしまして”)。「形容詞(adjectives)」の多くは、その末尾に“ly”を付けるだけで「副詞(adverbs)」として用いることができ、中には全く同一の形態で「形容詞的(adjectively)」にも「副詞的(adverbially)」にも用いられるものもある(例 “I'm a slow reader.:私は読むのが遅いんです”、“Speak a little more slowly.:もうちょっとゆっくり話しなさい”、“You drive too slow.:君の運転は遅すぎる”)。

These noun/verb and adjective/adverb interchangeability should be naturally acquired in the process of your vocabulary building, never to be learnt as an academic fact taught in some particular section of an English guidebook; such knowledge will get you nowhere, for they are only written as a scholar's notebook. Never try to read and learn: you simply can't. Remember and learn.

- English vocabulary without being braced with synonyms and antonyms is a mere castle in the air -

The abundance of synonyms and antonyms is one of the most outstanding characteristics of English language. In contrast, Japanese language, whose words and phrases are basically composed as combinations of several "漢字 (KANJI: Chinese characters)", is relatively poor in synonyms and antonyms. Or rather, any given word or expression in Japanese has its particular synonymous and antonymous expressions strictly fixed in the consciousness of Japanese people. Since the number of Chinese characters is strictly limited – a Japanese with average education is supposed to know as few as 1,945 KANJI to lead a decently intellectual life in Japanese language – synonymous or antonymous expressions in Japanese can never be expected to grow much in number.

That is why Japanese learners of English rarely try to remember any given English word in conscious connection with its synonyms or antonyms. They are therefore too prone to use the same word or expression again and again to be deemed as intelligent speakers of English with adequate vocabulary. It is not enough to store up words in your memory bank the way you feed computers with data after data; it is the associated connection of different words and phrases – synonyms, antonyms and paraphrases – that makes you rich in your linguistic resources.

Save your efforts with relation to synonyms, antonyms and paraphrases... and you are sure to first lose your face as an intellectual and eventually to lose your vocabulary for lack of relevant linguistic association. Save your face and memory by buying the effort of binding lots of words and phrases together whenever you try to remember any particular word or phrase.

こういう「名詞／動詞」間、あるいは「形容詞／副詞」間の相互乗り入れ的性質は、「ボキャビル(語彙構築)」過程で自然に身に付けるべきものであって、英語のガイドブック中の特定の項目の中で「学術的事実」として学ぶべきものでは決してない;そんな知識を仕込んだところで、諸君としては全くラチがあかない(だってそれは「学者サンの覚え書き」として書かれているだけなのだから)。「読んで、学ぶ」態度は捨て去ることだ:そんなこと、できっこないのだから・・・「覚えよ、さすれば自然に身に付かん」の態度で行きたまえ。

－同意語・反意語の筋交いも入れぬ英語語彙は、砂上の楼閣、と覚悟せよ－

「同意義(synonyms)」と「antonyms(反意語)」の豊富さは、英語という言語の最も際立つ特性の一つである。これとは対照的に、日本語という言語では、その単語も熟語も基本的には何文字かの「漢字」の組み合わせから成るものだけに、「同意語／反意語」は(英語との相対比較上)貧弱である。というよりむしろ、日本語の中の任意の単語や成句に関しては、その「同意表現」／「反意表現」として日本人が意識するものが厳格に固定されている、と言ったほうがよいだろう。「漢字」の数にははっきりとした制限があるのだから(平均的教育を受けた日本人がそこそこ知的な日本語生活を送るために知っているべきとされる「漢字」の数は、わずか1945字に過ぎない)、日本語に於ける「同意表現／反意表現」の数だって、そうそう増やすことなど期待出来っこないのである。

そういうわけで、日本人の英語学習者は、任意の英単語をその「同意語」／「反意語」と意識的に結び付けて暗記する努力を、ほとんど滅多に払わない。それゆえ彼らは、まったく同じ単語や表現を何度も何度も繰り返し使いがちなので、十分な語彙を持った知的英語人種とみなしてもらうまでには至らないわけである。単語を記憶領域に溜め込む際に、コンピュータに次から次へとデータを放り込むのと同じやり方をするだけでは十分とは言えない;「同意語(synonyms)」「反意語(antonyms)」「言い換え表現(paraphrases)」といった、異なる単語や言い回しとの連想を通して結び付けておくことこそが、諸君の言語学的資産を豊かに増やすことにつながるのである。

「同意語」「反意語」「言い換え表現」に関しては、努力を惜しんだら最後、まずは「知識人としての面目」を失い、やがては「意味ある言語学的連想の欠如」ゆえに「語彙」の方をも確実に失うことになる。ある一つの単語や言い回しを覚える際に、他の多くの単語や言い回しと結び付けて覚える努力を積極的に買って出ることで、諸君の「面目」と「記憶」とを失わない道を選びたまえ。そうして豊かに増やしたボキャブラリーは、

Vocabulary thus enriched will bear interest at some point, where you feel it much more interesting to say one thing in many different ways by way of ample alternatives stored up in your brains that are ready to come into your mouth at your command. Once you get that rich in your vocabulary and joy of English, your success is fully guaranteed: you are guaranteed to be an authentic master of English.

やがてどこかで「利子を生む」ことになり、その時点で諸君は、一つの事柄を(脳内に溜め込まれ、諸君の命令一下、いつでも口をついて出て来る状態にある、豊富な代替表現を用いて)多種多様な言い方で表現することの面白味をより一層感じることだろう。英語の語彙と喜悦がそこまで豊かになったなら、諸君の成功は完全に約束されたも同じこと:諸君は確実に、本物の英語の達人になれるはずである。

13. Be always aware what you are studying – terms (vocabulary), idioms (collocations), sentence patterns (SPAT-5), constructions, grammar, or anatomical interpretation of English sentences

- Those who succeed always know what they are doing; those who don't don't know what they are being made to do -

Let us begin this section with a question typically found in Japanese college entrance examination, featuring abnormally faulty English sentences artificially made so by the examiner to be corrected by examinees.

Correct errors (if any) in the following English sentences:

One of Japanese Anime-character that is popular for all the world is Tezuka Osamu's "鉄腕アトム(TETSUWAN ATOM)", translating into English in "Astroboy". The fact was interesting that his original name is not literarily translated as an "Iron-armed Atom" but to the "Astroboy". While this sounds futuristic and tinged with the optimistic hope in future, but the former wouldn't simply, for that remind us of a inhuman robot powered on inside nuclear reactor, who feels rather danger to Japanese after that terrible unclear powerplant disaster of 2011.

...The following is the correctly modified English, with respective parts needing correction, insertion or deletion being numbered and highlighted with (as many as 31!) [square brackets]:

One of (1)[the] Japanese Anime-character(2)[s] that (3)[is→are] popular (4)[for all the world→all over the world] is Tezuka Osamu's "鉄腕アトム(TETSUWAN ATOM)", (5)[translating→translated] (6)[into→in] English (7)[in→into/to] "Astroboy". The fact (8)[was→is] interesting that (9)[his→its/the] original name (10)[is→was] not (11)[literarily→literally] translated (12)[as → into/to] (13)[an...to be deleted] "Iron-armed Atom" but to (14)[the...to be deleted] "Astroboy". While this sounds futuristic and (15)[tinged→is tinged] with (16)[the...to be deleted, or to be replaced with "an"] optimistic hope (17)[in→for] future, (18)[but...to be deleted] (19)[the former→that] (20)[wouldn't simply→simply wouldn't], for (21)[that→it] (22)[remind→reminds] us of (23)[a→an] inhuman robot (24)[powered on→powered by / working on] (25)[inside nuclear reactor→a nuclear reactor inside / an inner nuclear reactor], (26)[who→which] feels rather (27)[danger→dangerous] to (28)[Japanese→the Japanese / Japanese people] after that terrible (29)[unclear→nuclear] (30)[powerplant→power plant] disaster (31)[of→in] 2011.

13. 単語(語彙)、熟語(連語)、文型(SPAT-5)、構文、文法、解剖学的英文解釈法・・・自分がいま何を学んでいるのかを常に意識せよ

ー成功する人は常に自分がしていることの意味を知っている;成功しない人は自分がやらされていることの意味を理解していないー

この項は、日本の大学入試に典型的に見られる設問から始めよう:出題者側でわざと(異常なまでに)間違いだらけの英文を用意しておいて、解答者に訂正させるという例のやつである。

以下の英文を(誤りあらば)正せ:

One of Japanese Anime-character that is popular for all the world is Tezuka Osamu's "鉄腕アトム(TETSUWAN ATOM)", translating into English in "Astroboy". The fact was interesting that his original name is not literarily translated as an "Iron-armed Atom" but to the "Astroboy". While this sounds futuristic and tinged with the optimistic hope in future, but the former wouldn't simply, for that remind us of a inhuman robot powered on inside nuclear reactor, who feels rather danger to Japanese after that terrible unclear powerplant disaster of 2011.

・・・正しく書き直された英文を以下に示す。訂正・追加・削除の必要のある箇所はそれぞれ(何と31カ所も!)[大括弧]を振って番号入りで目立たせてある:

One of (1)[the] Japanese Anime-character(2)[s] that (3)[is→are] popular (4)[for all the world→all over the world] is Tezuka Osamu's "鉄腕アトム(TETSUWAN ATOM)", (5)[translating→translated] (6)[into→in] English (7)[in→into/to] "Astroboy". The fact (8)[was→is] interesting that (9)[his→its/the] original name (10)[is→was] not (11)[literarily→literally] translated (12)[as→into/to] (13)[an...to be deleted] "Iron-armed Atom" but to (14)[the...to be deleted] "Astroboy". While this sounds futuristic and (15)[tinged→is tinged] with (16)[the...to be deleted, or to be replaced with "an"] optimistic hope (17)[in→for] future, (18)[but...to be deleted] (19)[the former→that] (20)[wouldn't simply→simply wouldn't], for (21)[that→it] (22)[remind→reminds] us of (23)[a→an] inhuman robot (24)[powered on→powered by / working on] (25)[inside nuclear reactor→a nuclear reactor inside / an inner nuclear reactor], (26)[who→which] feels rather (27)[danger→dangerous] to (28)[Japanese→the Japanese / Japanese people] after that terrible (29)[unclear→nuclear] (30)[powerplant→power plant] disaster (31)[of→in] 2011.

A nightmarish treasure of faults like the sentences above may appear too surreal to Europeans to be actually found in English compositions; here in Japan, however, anything goes — among those who don't know where they are going and what they are doing... although 31 mistakes in 3 consecutive sentences are too gorgeous not to be artificial.

Since such elaborately mistake-ridden sentences in English for examinees to correct are among the favorite repertoires of examiners in Japan, students have to be proficient in detecting and correcting errors in such artificially incorrect English. To tell you the blunt truth, however, with this type of detect-and-correct question, practice never makes you perfect: only analytical intelligence based on comprehensive understanding of English does. For that purpose, blindly devouring knowledge is never enough: knowing what you are devouring is the name of the game. In other words, intelligence matters more than diligence. You must not simply memorize what you are being taught: lesson contents need first categorizing according to the nature of the subject and then storing up in your memory according to their respective categories and finally and most importantly reviewing as many times as their priority and your mental capacity demand and warrant. If your memory is short, study long and often; the shorter your memory, the longer and oftener. A subject of top priority needs studying repeatedly and systematically to keep it out of idle oblivion; a matter of lesser priority need only be learnt rather occasionally and randomly.

和訳: 世界中で人気がある日本のアニメーションのキャラクターの一つに、手塚治虫の「鉄腕アトム」があり、英語では「アストロボーイ(Astroboy)」と訳されている。原題を文字通り訳して「鋼鉄の腕を持ったアトム(Iron-armed Atom)」とはせずに、「宇宙少年(Astroboy)」としてあるのが興味深い。後者の「アストロボーイ」には未来的な響きがあり、未来への楽天的な夢を感じさせるが、前者「鋼鉄の腕を持ったアトム」にはまるでその感じがない;内蔵した原子炉を動力源として動く非人間的なロボットを思い浮かべさせるばかりだからである・・・その「内燃型原子炉」というのも、2011年の恐ろしい原発事故後の日本人にとっては、なんだか危険な感じである。

上のやつみたいな悪夢のごとき間違いの宝庫の英作文なんて、ヨーロッパ人の目には非現実的すぎて実際にはあり得ないように思われるかもしれない;が、ここは何たって日本である－自分がこれからどこに向かおうとしているか、今何をしているのか、まるでわかってない人達の世界では、なんでもアリであり、何が起ころうと不思議はないのである・・・とはいえ、三連の文章中に三十一の間違いというのは、あまりに豪勢すぎて作り物なのが見え見えの感はあるが。

こういう手の込んだ間違い満載の英文をわざわざ作っておいて解答者に訂正させるのは、日本の出題者の「おハコ」の一つなのだから、学生としても、こうした人為的間違い英文に含まれる誤りの発見と訂正は得意技にしておく必要がある・・・のだが、有り体に真実を語ってしまうと、この種の「エラーを突き止め訂正せよ」型問題に関しては、闇雲に練習を積み重ねてみても技能はちっとも上達しない:この種の設問にうまく正解できるようになるには、英語に関する幅広い理解に裏打ちされた分析的知性が必要なのである。そのためには、知識を無闇にガツガツ覚え込むだけでは不十分である:いま自分がガツガツ覚え込んでいる知識はいったいどういう性質のものなのかを、きちんと認識することこそが勝負の要諦なのである。別の言葉で言えば、モノを言うのは「勤勉さ」ではなく「賢さ」の方なのだ。教えられた内容を単に暗記するだけではダメ・・・授業の内容はまず第一にその主題の特性に応じてカテゴリー分けし、次いでカテゴリー別の脳内記憶領域に蓄えた上で、最終的には(そして最も大事なこととして)各主題の重要度と諸君自身の脳力に鑑みて「これだけ繰り返さねば覚えられない」・「これぐらい繰り返し覚え込むに値する」と思われるところまで徹底的に繰り返し覚え直す必要があるのだ。記憶力がよくない人は、勉強時間と反復練習の回数を増やすことである;覚えの悪い人ほど、より長くより多くやることである。重要度の高い主題は、サボって忘れたりしないよう、繰り返し、かつ、体系的にまとめて学習する必要がある。一方、重要度の劣る主題であれば、折々行き当たりばったりに近い感じで学べばそれでよい。

- Six analytical categories in systematic studies of English -

In order to be analytically selective in your studies, everything you learn about English must be intelligently divided into the following six(6) categories:

I)English terms (vocabulary);
II)English idioms (collocations);
III)English sentence patterns (SPAT-5);
IV)English constructions;
V)English grammar;
VI)anatomical interpretation of English sentences.

I believe "terms (vocabulary)", "idioms (collocations)" and "sentence patterns (SPAT-5)" need not be clarified here, but most of you will be wondering what "constructions" mean. A "construction" is a group of "KATA(form)" categorized by meaning, not by structural characteristics like the five sentence patterns of English (what this book calls "SPAT-5"), which, according to the actual lessons in English by this author, divides into the following twelve(12) categories:

(1)不定詞(FUTEISHI: INFINITIVE)
(2)動名詞(DOUMEISHI: GERUND)
(3)分詞(BUNSHI: PARTICIPLE)
(4)比較(HIKAKU: COMPARISON)
(5)関係詞(KANKEISHI: RELATIVES)
(6)否定(HITEI: NEGATION)
(7)仮定法(KATEIHOU: SUBJUNCTIVE)
(8)倒置・語順(TOUCHI・GOJUN: INVERSION)
(9)省略(SHOURYAKU: ELLIPSIS)
(10)共通関係(KYOUTSUU-KANKEI: COMMON-RELATION)
(11)挿入(SOUNYUU: PARENTHESIS)
(12)同格(DOUKAKU: APPOSITIVE)

I will not (I CANNOT!) give detailed explanations of these twelve "semantic constructions" of English here and now, and those categories are definitely not fixed and not even authoritative ones; in fact, this author himself would sometimes add one more construction category, (13)名詞構文

－6つのカテゴリーとして分析的に捉える英語の体系的学習－

勉強する際に「あれはそう、これはこう」とテーマごとにその特性を分析して選り分けるためには、英語に関して学ぶ事柄の全てを、以下に示す6つのカテゴリー（範疇）へと理知的に分類して捉える必要がある：

I）英語の「単語：terms (vocabulary＝ボキャブラリー・語彙)」；
II）英語の「熟語：idioms (collocations＝コロケーション・連語関係)」；
III）英語の「文型：sentence patterns (この本で言うところの“SPAT-5”)」；
IV）英語の「構文：constructions」；
V）英語の「文法：grammar」；
VI）英文の「解剖学的解釈：anatomical interpretation」

“単語(ボキャブラリー)”、“イディオム(コロケーション)”と“文型（SPAT-5）”が何を意味するかについてはここで詳しく述べる必要はないと思うが、諸君の多くは「“constructions:構文”って何のこと？」と思っていることだろう。「構文」とは「意味」に基づいてカテゴリー分けされた「カタ（型式）」である・・・「構造」上の特性による区分（本書で言うところの「SPAT-5＝英語の5文型」等）ではない・・・本書の筆者が実際に行なっている英語授業の区分に従えば、以下に示す12のカテゴリーに分かれるのが英語の「構文」である：

（1）不定詞(INFINITIVE)
（2）動名詞(GERUND)
（3）分詞(PARTICIPLE)
（4）比較(COMPARISON)
（5）関係詞(RELATIVES)
（6）否定(NEGATION)
（7）仮定法(SUBJUNCTIVE)
（8）倒置・語順(INVERSION)
（9）省略(ELLIPSIS)
（10）共通関係(COMMON-RELATION)
（11）挿入(PARENTHESIS)
（12）同格(APPOSITIVE)

これら12の「意味別構文」の詳細な説明はここでは行なわない（行なえない！）し、英語の「構文」はこれら12のカテゴリーだけときっちり決まっているわけでもないし、これらの分類にさしたる権威があるわけですらない・・・実際の話、この筆者自身もまた、上記12の構文の他に（13）名詞構文(NOUN CONSTRUCTION)というカテゴリーを加

(MEISHI-KOUBUN: NOUN CONSTRUCTION), in the form of a brief seminar about five days long (three hours each). In short, any pattern of English composition semantically grouped together which requires and is fit for systematic comprehension and memorization can be called “a construction”.

By “grammar” is meant here (rather loosely) any particular rule of English that does not belong to the above-mentioned “terms”, “idioms”, “SPAT-5” and “constructions”.

What “anatomical interpretation of English sentences” means is the practical method and training needed to comprehend the meaning of rather complicated sentences. Take for example the opening headline of this series of paragraphs, “Those who succeed always know what they are doing; those who don't don't know what they are being made to do”. Novice learners may be at a loss what to make of “those who don't don't know” part, wondering if the “don't don't” isn't a sloppy duplication committed by some absent-minded author. Those who are adept at “省略(SHOURYAKU: ELLIPSIS)” construction will instantly interpret it as an abbreviation from “<those who don't [succeed]> don't know”. This is the anatomical interpretation of English, which of course calls for comprehensive knowledge of “terms”, “idioms”, “sentence patterns”, “constructions” and “grammar”. “Anatomy” is only possible after you have perfectly acquainted yourself with both “atoms (terms, idioms and grammar)” and “cosmos (sentence patterns and semantic constructions)”.

- Actual categorization and interpretation -

Well, it's about time we went into details. The artificially faulty English sentences already corrected above and numbered (1) through (31) can each be categorized into the following groups:

questions about:

I)terms (vocabulary)

(11)[literarily → literally]... confusion of “literally = to the letter” with “literarily = in manners suitable for literature”, an awkward mistake persons of authentic literary taste would never make

えて5日間の短期講習(各日3時間)の形で授業をしたことも(時には)あったのである。早い話が、英文を構成する任意のパターンのうち、意味上似通ったグループとしてまとめて捉えて体系的に理解・暗記するのが必要(かつ好適)と思われる一群のものは、何であれ「構文」扱いできるわけである。

この項で言う「文法」とは、上述した「単語」「熟語」「文型(SPAT-5)」「構文」のいずれにも属さない英語の何らかの規則について(かなり大まかな形で)総称した呼び名である。

「英文の解剖学的解釈」とは、かなり入り組んだ構造を持つ文章の意味を理解するのに必要な実践的方法と訓練のことである。この項を構成する一連の段落の最初の見出しを例に取ってみよう・・・“Those who succeed always know what they are doing; those who don't don't know what they are being made to do. 成功する人は常に自分がしていることの意味を知っている;成功しない人は自分がやらされていることの意味を理解していない”・・・英語学習も駆け出しの頃ならば、“those who don't don't know”のくだりをどう解釈してよいものかわからず往生するかもしれない。“don't don't”なんてどこかのボーッとした書き手がついうっかり“don't”を二度書いちゃったやつじゃないの、などと思うかもしれない。が、「省略(ELLIPSIS)」という「構文」に堪能な人なら、この部分は即座に“〈those who don't [succeed]:成功しない人々は〉 don't know:知らない”からのハショリと解釈するだろう・・・これが英語の「解剖学的解釈」というものであり、その解釈のためには当然「単語」・「熟語」・「文型」・「構文」・「文法」の包括的知識が必要になる。“Anatomy:解剖”は、“atoms＝微細な構成要素＝単語・熟語・文法の細目”と“cosmos＝小宇宙＝文型・意味別構文”の双方に完璧に習熟した後に、初めて可能になるものなのである。

－実際のカテゴリー分けと解釈－

さて、そろそろ詳細な検討に移ろうか。上で修正済みの「わざわざ間違いだらけにした英文」の番号(1)から(31)のそれぞれは、以下のようなグループへとカテゴリー分けすることができる:

問題の性質別に分けたカテゴリー:

I)「単語:terms (vocabulary＝語彙)」に関する問題

(11)[literarily→literally]. . . “literally=to the letter:文字通り、一字一句、逐語的に”を“literarily = in manners suitable for literature:文学的に、文芸的表現に似つかわしい形で”と混同したもの。真の文芸的感覚の持ち主ならば決してやらない無様な間違い

(16)[the...to be deleted, or to be replaced with "an"]... the noun "hope" in this context is too vague to require the definite article "the"
(20)[wouldn't simply→simply wouldn't]... the adverb "simply" is to be placed prior to a verb/auxiliary verb for emphatic purposes
(25)[inside nuclear reactor→a nuclear reactor inside / an inner nuclear reactor]... in addition to the omission of "an", the term "inside" is more often used as an adverb (placed after the term it qualifies) than as an attributive adjective (placed before the term it modifies); a more suitable attributive adjective in this context should be "inner"... if you still insist on using "an <inside> nuclear reactor", you'll be declaring "I'm an <outside> speaker of English from abroad"
(28)[Japanese→the Japanese / Japanese people]... the term "Japanese" used without articles means "Japanese language"; add "the" to make it "people in Japan"
(29)[unclear→nuclear]... a typical though not comical typo(=typographical error) in view of the Fukushima nuclear meltdown in 2011 (*actually, there is no such term as "unclear" in English)
(30)[powerplant→power plant]... separating space needed between "power" and "plant"

II)idioms (collocations)
(4)[for all the world→all over the world]... "for all the world" means "never" and is used in a negative context such as "She won't listen to my pleas for all the world"
(12)[as→into/to]... "translate A as B" is a semantic (as opposed to linguistic) expression similar to "interpret/understand/deem/regard/think of/consider A as B", which is unsuitable for this "linguistic translation" context requiring the preposition "into/to" instead of "as"
(17)[in→for]... "in future" means "sometime in the future, not now"; this context requires instead "hope [we now have] for future"
(24)[powered on→powered by / working on]... the preposition "on" means "a basis on which something relies"; "a power source" should be expressed by "by"

(16)[the...削除するか、"an"に入れ替える]. . . この文脈での"hope:希望"という名詞は、具体的希求対象を持たぬ曖昧なものだから、定冠詞"the"を付けるまでもない
(20)[wouldn't simply→simply wouldn't]. . . 副詞"simply"を「強調」のために用いる場合は、「動詞/助動詞」の前に置く
(25)[inside nuclear reactor→a nuclear reactor inside / an inner nuclear reactor]. . . "an"の欠落に加えて、"inside:内側"という語は「副詞(修飾する語句の後に置く形)」で用いる方が「限定形容詞(attributive adjective:修飾する語句の前に置く形)」で用いる場合よりも多い;この文脈で「限定形容詞」として用いるならば、"inside"よりも"inner"の方がより相応しい. . . それでもなお諸君が"an 〈inside〉 nuclear reactor:内蔵型原子炉"に固執するというのなら、諸君は"I'm an 〈outside〉 speaker of English from abroad:私は外国から来た余所者英語話者であります"と宣言しているようなものである
(28)[Japanese→the Japanese / Japanese people]. . . "Japanese"という語を無冠詞で用いると「日本語」の意味になる;"the"を付ければ「日本国の人々」の意味になる
(29)[unclear→nuclear]. . . タイプライター上での"nu"と"un"の打ち間違い(a typographical error・・・俗称はa typo:タイポ)で、よくあるミスだが、2011年の福島でのメルトダウン事故を思えば「nuclear:原子力」ならぬ「unclear=クリアーならざる、不明朗な点がある、クリーンなエナジーとは言いかねる」への転落は、あまり笑えない感じである(注:実際の英単語に"unclear"なる語はない)
(30)[powerplant→power plant]. . . "power"と"plant"の間には区分用のスペース(余白)が必要

II)「熟語:idioms (collocations)」に関する問題
(4)[for all the world→all over the world]. . . "for all the world"は"never:決して〜ない"の意味であり、"She won't listen to my pleas for all the world.:彼女はどうしても私の懇願に耳を貸そうとしない"のような否定の文脈で用いる
(12)[as→into/to]. . . "translate A as B:AをBであるものとして解釈する"は(「言語」ではなく)「意味解釈」を巡る表現であって、"interpret/understand/deem/regard/think of/consider A as B"等の言い回しに近く、ここでの"違う言語へと翻訳する"文脈には似付かわしくない;この脈絡で求められる前置詞は"as"ではなく"into/to"である
(17)[in→for]. . . "in future"の意味するところは"sometime in the future, not now:今ではなく、将来のいつかの時点で";この文脈で求められるのは"hope [we now have] for future:[いま現在の時点で我々が抱いている]未来に対する希望"の表現である
(24)[powered on→powered by / working on]. . . "on"という前置詞は"a basis on which something relies:何かがその上に拠って立つところの土台"を意味する;「動力源」の意味を表わすならば、用いるべき前置詞は"by"である

(31)[of→in]... the year in which something happens is expressed in the form of "in XXXX", not "of XXXX", which is a typical Japanese error, in whom their postpositional particle(助詞) "の" is instinctively associated with the English preposition "of"

III)sentence patterns (SPAT-5)
...NONE...

IV)constructions
(1)[the](RELATIVES)... "先行詞(the antecedent)" of a relative pronoun clause usually requires being modified by the definite article "the"
(5)[translating → translated](PARTICIPLE)... this context requires the passive voice "translated"
(15)[tinged→is tinged](COMMON-RELATION)... while pointing to the same subject "this", the first verbal part "sounds futuristic" does not accompany "be verb", which makes it necessary to newly introduce "is" before the second verbal part "tinged with" which is in the passive voice
(26)[who→which](RELATIVES)... if the antecedent to this relative clause were "鉄腕アトム(Astroboy)", the relative pronoun to be used here should be personal "who"; in fact, the actual antecedent here is the impersonal content "that an inhuman robot is powered by a nuclear reactor inside", which requires the relative pronoun "which" instead of "who"

V)grammar (in general)
Anime-character(2)[s]... since "one of one(=$^1/_1$)" is practically meaningless, the expression "one of A" always requires the plural form of "A"; the mistake of using this expression with the "A" part in the singular is triggered by the sound "one", which naturally suggests "a single one"
(3)[is→are]... as explained above, the "A" part of "one of A" is always plural, never to be used in the singular form, requiring the verb "are" instead of "is"

(31)[of→in]. . . 何かが発生する「年」を表わす表現は“in XXXX”であって“of XXXX”ではない。これは日本人がやらかす典型的な間違い；彼らは「postpositional participle(助詞)」の“の”を英語の「preposition(前置詞)」の“of”と本能的に関連付けて覚えているので、こういう誤りを犯し易い

III)「文型：sentence patterns (SPAT-5)」に関する問題
...該当例、なし...

IV)「構文：constructions」に関する問題
(1)[the](RELATIVES:関係詞). . .「関係代名詞節(a relative pronoun clause)」の「先行詞(the antecedent)」には定冠詞“the”を付けるのが普通
(5)[translating→translated](PARTICIPLE:分詞). . . この文脈で必要なのは「受動態(the passive voice)」の“translated:翻訳される”
(15)[tinged→is tinged](COMMON-RELATION:共通関係). . . 指向する主語は共に“this”ではあるが、最初の述部の“sounds futuristic:未来的に響く”は“be 動詞”を伴わないので、第二の述部として受動態で語られる“tinged with:色彩に染まる”の前には、新たに“is”を入れる必要がある
(26)[who→which](RELATIVES:関係詞). . . もしこの関係代名詞節の先行詞が“鉄腕アトム(Astroboy)”ならば、ここで用いるべき関係代名詞は人称代名詞型の“who:誰”でよい；が、実際には、ここでの先行詞は非人称型の文章内容“that an inhuman robot is powered by a nuclear reactor inside:非人間的なロボットが内蔵型原子炉を動力源として動くということ”であるから、求められる関係代名詞は“which:何”であって“who:誰”ではない

V)「文法：grammar(全般)」に関する問題
Anime-character(2)[s]. . . “one of one(=$^1/_1$):1つあるもののうちの1つ”などという言い回しは現実的に意味を成さないのだから、“one of A:Aのうちの1つ”という表現の“A”は常に「複数形(the plural form)」でなければならない；この表現の“A”部を「単数形(the singular form)」で使う間違いを引き起こすものは、“one:ワン”という語の響きである・・・これは当然“a single one:単一のもの”を思い浮かべさせるものだから、これに釣られて単数形と錯覚しがちなのだ
(3)[is→are]. . . 上で説明した通り、“one of A:Aのうちの一つ”の表現に於ける“A”部は常に複数形であり、単数形では決して用いない以上、求められる動詞も単数の“is”ではなく複数の“are”となる

(8)[was→is]... although "鉄腕アトム/Astroboy" is a classical work of Tezuka (April 7, 1951 - 1968), the time when this author feels "the fact" to be "interesting" is definitely "the present", requiring therefore "is" instead of "was"
(9)[his→its/the]... the author is referring not to "アトム/Astroboy" as a person but to the work itself, which requires the impersonal determinative "its" or the definite article "the"
(10)[is→was]... the act of translation from "鉄腕アトム" to "Astroboy" belongs not to the present but to the past tense, requiring "was" instead of "is"
(13)[an...to be deleted]... this indefinite article "an" is strange and misleading because it seems to suggest this title "Iron-armed Atom" is one of many possible literally translated titles, which is definitely not the case here
(14)[the...to be deleted]... this definite article "the" is totally meaningless because the actually translated title "Astroboy" does not accompany any article with it; the only possible meaning this "the" can have is that of emphasis, which, nevertheless, should be expressed in a more emphatic expression 'that "Astroboy"', making this "the" meaningless anyway
(21)[that → it]... the most usual impersonal pronoun which points to something is "it", instead of "that", for this(=the latter expression "that") is often used in special combination with some other terms such as "which"(eg. "Tastes vary from person to person. That can be distasteful to others which is quite tasty for you."), while that(=the former expression "it") is free from such coordinated association with other terms, except for "that" and "to"(eg. "It is strange that he doesn't know the fact." / "It is painful but not shameful to admit faults.")
(22)[remind→reminds]... a sloppy omission of "s/es" typical of Japanese speakers/writers of English
(23)[a→an]... an unthinkable mistake (only to be made by foreign speakers of English) using "a" instead of "an" before a vowel
(27)[danger → dangerous]... a typically foreign (and novice) mistake confusing a noun with an adjective

(8)[was→is]. . . “鉄腕アトム/Astroboy”は手塚の古典的作品(1951年4月7日～1968年)ではあるが、この文章の書き手が“the fact:その事実”を“interesting:興味深い”と感じている時点は間違いなく「現時点」でのことであるから、動詞は過去形の“was”ではなく現在形の“is”でなければならない

(9)[his→its/the]. . . この文章の書き手が言及しているのは「人物」としての“アトム/Astroboy”ではなく「“鉄腕アトム”という作品そのもの」であるから、ここで必要なのは非人称の限定詞(determinative)である“its:その”か、または定冠詞“the”である

(10)[is→was]. . . “鉄腕アトム”から“Astroboy”への翻訳という行為は「現在」ではなく「過去」の時点で行なわれたものであるから、“is”ではなく“was”でなければならない

(13)[an...削除する]. . . ここで不定冠詞の“an”を使うのは奇妙で、誤解を招く感じ;これではまるで“Iron-armed Atom:鋼鉄の腕を持ったアトム”というタイトルは「幾つも考えられる逐語訳的翻訳タイトルのうちのほんの一例に過ぎない」と言っているように感じられるが、この文脈ではそんなことはまるで言っていないのだから、ヘン

(14)[the...削除する]. . . 実際に翻訳された標題の“Astroboy”は何の冠詞も伴わないのだから、この定冠詞“the”は全く無意味;ここでの“the”に意味があり得るとしたらそれは唯一「強調＝例の、あの、皆さん御存知の」ということになるが、しかし、その場合にはもっと強調的な‘that “Astroboy”’の表現にするべきであるから、どう転んでもこの“the”には何の意味もないことになる

(21)[that→it]. . .「何か」を指し示す非人称の代名詞として最も一般的に用いられるのは“it”であって“that”ではない。その理由は、後者(“that”という表現)は“which”のような他語句との特別な組み合わせで用いられることがしばしばある(例 “Tastes vary from person to person.:好みは人それぞれに異なる That can be distasteful to others which is quite tasty for you.:あなたにはとても好ましいものが、他者にはおぞましい場合もあり得る”)のに対し、前者(“it”という表現)にはそうした「他語句との相関構造で用いるべし」という制約がないからである;但し、“it”が“that”及び“to”と相関構造を成す場合は例外である(例 “It is strange that he doesn't know the fact.:彼がその事実を知らないとは不思議だ” / “It is painful but not shameful to admit faults.:過ちを認めるのは楽ではないが恥でもない”)

(22)[remind→reminds]. . . “s/es”をうっかり抜かした間違いで、日本人が英語を話したり書いたりする場合によくあるミス

(23)[a→an]. . .「母音(vowel)」の前に“an”ではなく“a”を使うという、あり得ない間違い(外国人が英語を話す場合にのみあり得るミス)

(27)[danger→dangerous]. . .「名詞(a noun)」と「形容詞(an adjective)」を取り違えるという、外国人(それも初学者)に典型的な間違い

VI)anatomical interpretation of sentences

(6)[into→in]/(7)[in→into/to]... the object of the action "translate A into/to B" is 'into/to "Astroboy" ', not 'into/to English'; 'in English' is simply inserted in 'translate "鉄腕アトム" into "Astroboy" '... a short-sighted mistake which is quite hard to detect, making it favorite of favorites for hard-core examiners of Waseda University

(18)[but...to be deleted]... the opening conjunction "while" implies contradiction in itself and thus repels the use of "but" at the beginning of the contrasted clause, just as "While she is tall, her husband is short" is never to be written as "While she is tall, but her husband is short"; a too lengthy "while..." part will often invite this type of error, which can hardly be detected by persons of short attention span

(19)[the former→that]... Pay attention to the opening words of the sentence, "While this sounds futuristic"; in this context, that "this" means "the latter one of the two things in question", used in contrast to which is "that"; the expression "the former", though meaning the same thing, must be used coupled with "the latter"... since the use of "that" and "this" in this sense is quite rare, the intentional abuse of it for examinees to correct is too difficult to make sense even as a trick question by an ill-intentioned examiner

- Vocabulary is an endless riddle and struggle -

Well, what do you say to that? While 31 questionable points might have been too much for you to correct, the 31 explanations, at least many of them, should not be too much to understand. But whether you understood them all here and now does not really matter (you certainly will in time if you keep on studying English); what does matter is if you became aware of the division of those thirty-one questions into five different categories (with "sentence pattern SPAT-5" being excluded herein) according to the nature of each and every mistake committed to be corrected.

VI)「文章の解剖学的解釈:anatomical interpretation of sentences」に関する問題

(6)[into→in]/(7)[in→into/to]. . . “translate A into/to B:AをBへと翻訳する”という行為の「目的語(object)」は‘into/to “Astroboy”:アストロボーイへ’であって‘into/to English:英語へ’ではない。‘in English:英語で’の箇所は、単に‘translate “鉄腕アトム” into “Astroboy”:鉄腕アトムをアストロボーイへと翻訳する’の中に挿入されただけの語句である・・・見抜くのが極めて困難な近視眼的間違いであり、本筋の難問を出す早稲田大学の出題者達の一番の大好物である

(18)[but…削除する]. . . 冒頭部に置かれた接続詞の“while”それ自体に「逆接」の含みがあるので、これと逆接的に対照されている側の節の冒頭部に“but”を使うことはできない;これは“While she is tall, her husband is short.:彼女は背が高い一方で、彼女の夫は背が低い”を“While she is tall, but her husband is short.:彼女は背が高い一方で、しかし彼女の夫は背が低い”と書いてはならないのと同じである。“while…”の部分があまりにも長いとこの種の間違いを引き起こしがちで、注意力の及ぶ範囲が短い人にはまず見抜けない

(19)[the former→that]. . . “While 〈this〉 sounds futuristic:〈this〉は未来的な響きがある一方で”の文章の冒頭部の語句群に要注意;この脈絡では、その“this”が“the latter one of the two things in question:その場で問題になっている二つの事柄のうち、後で述べられた方のもの=後者”を意味し、これと対照的に用いられているのが“that:前者”である;“the former:前者”の表現でも意味は同じだが、こちらは“the latter:後者”の表現と対にして用いる必要がある・・・“this:後者”と“that:前者”をこの意味で用いる例は極めて稀なのだから、その表現をわざわざ「誤用」に書き改めた上で解答者に訂正させるような芸当は、悪意を持った出題者の手による引っ掛け問題として見た場合でさえも、あまりに難解すぎて設問として意味を成さない水準である

－「単語の語彙(ボキャブラリー)」は終わりなきナゾナゾと奮闘努力のゲーム－

・・・ということで、いかがだっただろうか？　怪しい箇所が31カ所、というのはいくら何でも訂正しきれなかったかもしれないが、31の解説の方は(少なくともその多くは)難しすぎて理解不能ということはないはずだ。だが、今この時点でそれらの解説の全てが理解できたかどうかなど、実は全くどうでもよいことである(英語の勉強を続けていればいずれ確実にわかるのだから);本当に大事なことは、それら31の問題が、それぞれの訂正用エラーの性質に応じて、5つの異なるカテゴリー(上の問題には“5文型＝SPAT-5”は含まれていなかったが)へと分岐するということを、諸君がきちんと認識してくれたかどうかの方である。

As you must have seen, the "term" category is the fuzziest part of detect-and-correct type of questions. Each English word has its distinctive character that defies generalization, which has to be respectively remembered in the process of vocabulary building, which literally has no goal at all until one (or one's linguistic aspiration) dies. The most learned student (in fact, even the examiners themselves!) could not hope to get full marks in "terminology quiz" without the aid of dictionaries or reference books. It is therefore illogical to aspire for full marks in this type of endless riddle: you have only to try and get as many points as your terminological memory permits. How many "term" points you can get in any given exam largely depends on luck. That is why a really excellent examiner avoids "terminology overdose", which invariably degrades the quality of the exam as a whole too much influenced by how lucky/unlucky each examinee happens to be... although there do exist such universities as will intentionally let luck play a part in making it harder for super-intelligent students to get "reserved seats" at the exclusion of candidates of lesser intelligence, only to be thrown away when they pass exams to higher grade universities... except for such intentionally sloppy ones, examiners too prone to "word quiz" are too low in English literacy to be entitled to be examiners (although Japan is teeming with such "problem makers").

In any case, it is downright foolish to hope for perfect or even good marks in "haphazard terminology quiz". Of course, you have to do your utmost trying to enlarge and enrich your vocabulary, but however great a vocabulary never warrants your success in purely terminological questions... do your best and prepare for the worst. Any point you get in "word quiz" should be considered a "bonus"; high points in exams had best be acquired somewhere else "as planned".

既にもうわかってもらえたはずだが、「単語」のカテゴリーは「誤り発見＆訂正」型問題の中では最もモヤモヤとしてつかみ所のない代物である。一つ一つの英単語にはそれぞれ他とは異なる独自の特性があって、それは十把一絡(じゅっぱひとからげ)の概括的扱いでどうにかなるものではなく、「ボキャビル(vocabulary building＝語彙構築)」過程で個別的に覚え込む必要があって、その奮闘努力には文字通り終わりがなく、人が(あるいはその人の語学への熱意が)死ぬまでずっと続くものなのだ。“単語クイズ”に満点を取ることなど、辞書や参考書の助けを借りなくては、最高の学識を誇る学生といえども(それどころか、出題者自身でさえも！)期待すべくもない無理難題なのである・・・であるから、この種の終わりなきナゾナゾごっこで満点を取る野心を抱くなどという所業は、分別のある人間のすることではない。諸君としては、自らの「語彙の記憶容量」の許す限りの範囲内で出来る限りの高得点獲得を目指しさえすればそれでよいのだ。何かのテストの“単語”カテゴリーで何点取れるか、それを決するのは大部分「運」である。なればこそ、真に優れた出題者は“単語問題の出し過ぎ”は避ける・・・そんなことをすれば、個々の解答者がたまたまどの程度まで「幸運／不運」であったかによって大きく左右されすぎてしまい、試験問題全体の品位が確実に下がってしまうのだから・・・もっとも、中には、わざと「運」が大きな役割を演じるよう仕向ける大学もあることは確かである；飛び抜けて頭の良い学生たちが、知性に劣る他の志願者たちを差し置いて「予約席」を確保してしまった末に、より格上の大学に合格した時点でその「予約券」をポイ捨てにするような事態が生じにくいようにするために、わざわざ「実力に拠らぬ運の演じる余地」を強く残しておくわけである・・・が、こうした「意図的ズサンさ」を計算ずくで演出する出題者を別にすれば、“単語クイズ”に偏りすぎの出題者連中なんてものは、英語教養の水準が低すぎてとてもとても出題者たるべき資格を有する者とは言えない(もっとも日本にはこのテの“問題作りでモンダイ起こす困った連中”がウヨウヨいるわけであるが)。

何にせよとにかく、“出たとこ勝負の単語クイズ”で満点(どころか高得点さえ)望むのは、まったく馬鹿もいいところである。もちろん、自らの語彙の拡充と洗練に最大限の努力を払うのは必要なことだが、たとえいかに偉大なる語彙をもってしても、純然たる語彙問題で成功を収める保証は全くない・・・であるから、最善を尽くした上でなお、最悪の事態もあり得ることを覚悟しておくことである。“単語クイズ”で手にした得点は全て“ボーナス＝思いがけない実入り”とみなすべきである；試験では、“単語以外”のカテゴリーの中で、それも“予定通り”の形で、より多くの得点を稼ぐのが最善のやり方なのである。

- Tangible patterns in questions on idioms and collocations -

Compared with largely haphazard "terminological" questions, "idiom/collocation" category is where the really excellent student can hope to get ahead of their rivals.

Firstly, English idioms, though numerous, are much fewer than English words. While vocabulary is a bottomless pit, there is a practical ceiling on how far you must go in the world of idiomatic expressions; diligent students with moderate intelligence can reach that ceiling while in high school with the help from reasonably well-written books on English idioms for college-bound students.

Secondly, questions on idioms develop around the more or less generalized usage of "prepositions" and are not meant as "trivia on particular terms or expressions". Of course, in the hands of intolerably bad (or intentionally malicious) examiners, there can be such a nonsense quiz as will ask you to fill the blank in "Don't carry (???) to Newcastle", meaning "Don't do what you don't have to". Only luck will decide if you can hit upon "coals"; "oil" or "ships" sounds as fine but doesn't ring the bell; even "coal" won't do because this noun is countable... oh, what a profoundly deep, esoteric and abysmal question it could be! Besides testing the examinee's historical knowledge of the industrial structure of a certain local town on the small island of Britain, it can also test the singular/plural consciousness enough to add "s" at the end of the countable noun "coal", which, though similar to the material and uncountable noun "chalk", still retains its individual countability just like a plate of "slate"! None but the erudite (or lucky!) could ever correctly answer this wondrous riddle... But such lethally stupid questions are quite rare (though not impossible) to find among "idiomatic questions" in Japanese college entrance examinations. If asked as such at all, the expression "Don't carry coals to Newcastle" should be changed into "Don't carry coals (???) Newcastle" requiring the suitable preposition "to" to fill in the blank. To ask to complete "Don't carry (???) to Newcastle" is as foolish as presenting examinees with "Don't carry coals to (???)castle". You could get it right if you only knew "Newcastle United F.C.", but how else?

ーイディオム／コロケーション問題には、それなりの手応えを伴う一定パターンありー

かなりの部分が運任せの“単語”問題に比べて、“イディオム／コロケーション”のカテゴリーは、真に優れた学生が競争相手に抜きん出ることが期待できる分野である。

まず第一に、英熟語の数は(膨大ではあるが)英単語の数より遙かに少ない。英単語の語彙は底なし沼だが、熟語的表現の世界で辿り着くべき頂点には現実的な上限がある。そこそこ頭が働く勤勉な学生が大学受験生用にそこそこよく書かれた英熟語の本の助けを借りて学べば、高校在学中にその頂点に辿り着くことも可能である。

第二に、熟語に関する設問は、「前置詞」に関する(多かれ少なかれ)概括的な用法を巡って展開するものであって、特定の語句や言い回しに関する雑学クイズとして出題されるものではない。まぁ確かに、耐え難いまでにひどい(あるいは意図的に意地悪な)出題者の手にかかれば、“余計なことはするな”を意味する“Don't carry (???) to Newcastle.:ニューキャッスルに(？？？)を持って行くような真似はするな”なる言い回しの余白部分を埋めよ、と要求するようなナンセンスなクイズが出題されることだってあり得るのではあるが。こんなクイズでは、余白に入れるべき“coals:石炭”が思い浮かぶか否かを決するものは「運」のみである；“oil:石油”や“ships:船”だって似たようなものじゃないか、とも感じるが、それでは正解はもらえない；“coal”と書いた場合ですら、この名詞は可算名詞(countable)だから、ダメなのである・・・おぉ、何とまぁ難解で奥深く、知る人ぞ知る底知れぬ深淵の奥底から出てきたような問題も、作ろうと思えば作れてしまうことか！・・・小さなブリテン島の上のとある町の産業構造に関する歴史的知識を解答者が持ち合わせているか否かを試すと同時に、可算名詞である“coal:石炭”(物質名詞で不可算名詞の“chalk:白墨”と似ているものの、板状に整形した“slate:粘板岩”と同じくその個別的可算性は保っている“coal:石炭”)の末尾に“s”を加えられるだけの「単数／複数」意識があるかどうかまで試験できるのだから、まったく恐れ入るではないか。よほど博識な(あるいは幸運な！)人物でない限り、このアタマがくらくらしちゃうほど素晴らしいナゾナゾに、正しく答えることなどできっこあるまい・・・が、殺人的なまでにバカげたこうした設問を日本の大学入試の「熟語問題」中に見出す場面は(あり得ない、とは言わないが)極めて稀である。もしこれを「熟語問題」として出すつもりがあるならば、“Don't carry coals to Newcastle”の言い回しを“Don't carry coals (???) Newcastle”に変えた上で、余白を埋めるべき適当な前置詞“to”を答えさせる形にするのが筋であろう。それを“Don't carry (???) to Newcastle”とするが如き所業は、“Don't carry coals to (???)castle”の形を解答者に示して見せるのと同じくらい阿呆なことである。“Newcastle United F.C.:ニューキャッスル・ユナイテッド・FC(サッカークラブ)”を知ってさえいれば正解できるだろうが、そうでもなければどうやってこの“(New)castle”を正しく知り得るであろうか？

Such silly trivia say "YES" only to those who know, "NO!" to those who don't. Such is the evil of addle-brained esotericism. Universities which have shown themselves hopelessly tainted with it via "haphazard questions" on words or idioms might just as well be avoided by examinees. The choice is yours while you are a mere candidate... you'll have no choice but to be tainted with their intolerably foolish and arrogant esotericism once you get inside their ivory tower, spending too much time and money to walk away from it.

"Idiomatic questions" healthy and reasonable never fail to test your knowledge of "prepositions" and their relationship with particular verbs and nouns, known as "collocations". As such, they can be dealt with as a systematic set of knowledge and can therefore be a truer test of your English literacy than aimlessly random "trivia on words". Would you be a smart aleck, just devour words as pigs do in their sty; if you would really belong in the ranks of the intelligentsia, learn by heart idioms wisely and conquer the world of collocations.

- There is a limited size and assured success in English grammar, in which stand out the two paramount mountains: the handy molds of SPAT-5 and semantic varieties of constructions -

Unlike "words" and "idioms" which have to be respectively remembered and dealt with as more or less individual pieces of knowledge, "grammatical questions" are easier to deal with because they are more questions of logic than tests of sheer memory — you don't have to remember, you have only to use your brains and think. So long as you have established in your brains how to think grammatically, you can assuredly hope for full marks in grammatical questions. Authentically learned masters of English don't even have to think – they can instinctively detect and correct grammatical faults at a glance: unless they can, they can make the same mistakes themselves... a true commander of English detects and avoids possible errors even before they speak or write – that's what it is to command English.

Though not all learners of English are required to be the authentic masters of this language, a certain level of grammatical comprehension is demanded of all college-bound students because it is the very essence of the command

この種の愚かな雑学クイズは、知ってる人にだけ「よし！」と言い、それ以外の人には「ダメ！」と言うだけの代物でしかない・・・これが、腐れ頭の排他的集団の「内奥の真理とやら」の度し難さである。そうした腐れエソテリシズムに自分たちがどうしようもないほど染まり切っているという事実を(単語や熟語に関する"デタラメ問題"を通して)はっきり証明してみせた大学なんぞというものは、受験生の側で避けておくに越したことはない。諸君が「単なる一志願者」である間は、選択権は諸君にある・・・が、ひとたび連中の象牙の塔の内部に踏み入って、あまりに多くの時間とお金を使ってしまい、今更おさらばするわけにも行かなくなってしまった後ではもう、連中の耐え難いまでに馬鹿で傲慢な排他的エラぶり秘密主義の悪弊に、諸君自身も染まってしまうよりほか仕方がなくなることであろう。

健全にして合理的な「熟語問題」ならば必ず、「前置詞」と特定の「動詞」「名詞」との間の("コロケーション＝連語")関係の試験問題になっているはずである。そういう性質の問題であるから、一群の体系的知識として扱うことが可能であり、特定の目的もなくデタラメに出題される「単語トリビア(＝どうでもいい知識を問題にするクイズ)」よりは、英語の読み書き能力をより正しく判定する尺度たり得るものである。知ったかぶりするイケ好かない知識人気取りになりたいならば(豚小屋の中でエサをむさぼるブタの如く)ただひたすら単語をむさぼるように覚えればそれでよい;真の知識人の列に加わりたいと望むなら、熟語を賢く暗記して、コロケーションの世界を制覇することだ。

－英文法世界の大きさは一定、学べば成功もまた確実、その世界の中で際立つ二つの高峰は、便利な鋳型としての「SPAT-5」と、様々な意味別の「構文」たち－

個別的に覚えた上で(程度の差こそあれ)一個一個独立した知識として扱う必要のある"単語"や"熟語"とは異なり、"文法問題"は「単なる記憶力のテスト」というよりむしろ「論理的思考法の問題」だから、扱いは簡単である－「覚える」必要はなく、「頭を使って考える」だけで済むのだから。自らの脳内に「文法的思考法」を確立してしまいさえすれば、文法問題では当然「満点」を取れるものと期待してよい。真の学識を究めた英語の達人の場合、「考える」必要すらない。一目チラと見ただけで文法上の間違いは直感的に突き止めて修正できてしまうのだから・・・もしそうでなければ、彼ら自身もまた同じ間違いを犯しかねないことになる・・・英語を本当に自在に操れる人は、喋ったり書いたりするよりも先に、あり得る間違いの可能性を探知し回避してしまうものなのだ－「英語を駆使する」とはそういうことである。

英語を学ぶ人のみんながみんなこの言語の真性の達人となることを求められているわけではないだろうが、大学入学を志望する学生であれば誰もが、ある一定水準の文法理解力を求められることになる:文法力こそ英語駆使力の精髄そのものだからだ。

of English. Examiners in Japan can and often do make silly, nonsensical trivia as regards "terms" and "idioms", but they can hardly do the same with "grammar". Grammar is a set of established principles of speech and, as such, is much more tangible and manageable than the bottomless pit of English terms or seemingly endless world of idioms and collocations. In order to get high marks in English and pass exams, you have to be adequately proficient in English grammar. You need not be very rich in English terminology, you don't have to be perfectly sure of the world of English collocations with which you become vaguely familiar through learning idioms by heart, but you must be fairly certain of your systematic knowledge of grammar to avoid getting poor marks in English exams and to be really proficient in the use of English.

As have been shown above, even the abnormally rich treasure of faulty English sentences this author elaborately created does not include any errors regarding "five sentence patterns of English (SPAT-5)", for the very simple reason that they are so basic and easy that mistakes related with them are too hard to forge; no self-respecting speaker of English could make such an artificially erroneous sentence as "I gave it him" even in jest. Be advised the perfect understanding and manipulation of SPAT-5 is more requisites than assets in the world of college entrance examination; examiners may test how fast you can run, but will not check to see if you have two legs to run on.

Beyond (but mostly upon) the foundation stones of English sentence patterns (SPAT-5) stand the magnificent edifices of semantic constructions such as INFINITIVE, COMPARISON, RELATIVES or SUBJUNCTIVE. It is in the realms of these constructions that the main battle for the command of English (and entrance to college) is engaged. Unless you are well-armed with knowledge in respective fields of these semantic constructions, the battle is lost, whether in the narrow straits of college entrance exams or in the broader world of actually spoken English.

The world of English grammar is so large that you will be at a loss how to traverse let alone conquer it unless you divide it into three tangible spheres of "sentence patterns", "constructions" and "the rest". What "the rest" contains is still large, but not too large to comprehend after you have subtracted the structural(SPAT-5) and semantic(construction) patterns from the whole picture of English grammar.

日本の出題者は“単語”や“熟語”にまつわる愚かで無意味な雑学的問題を作ってしまう場合があり得る(というか実際しばしばその愚を犯している)が、同様の愚挙を“文法問題”で犯すことはほとんど不可能である。「文法」とは「話し言葉の世界で確固として定まった原則の集合体」であり、その性質上、底なし沼のような「英単語」や一見終わりの見えない「英熟語／連語」の世界よりも、遙かに捉え易く扱いやすいものである。英語で高得点を取って試験に合格するためには、英文法には十分習熟しておく必要がある。英単語の領域ではさほど豊富な学識を誇る必要もないし、英熟語の暗記を通して漠然と馴染んだ英語の連語(コロケーション)の世界についても完璧に把握する必要もないけれど、試験の英語でひどい点数を取らないためにも、真に堪能な英語使いとなるためにも、文法に関する体系的知識は、それなり以上に確実に身に付けておく必要がある。

既に上で示した通り、この筆者がわざわざでっち上げた間違い英文の異様に豊かな宝物殿でさえ、“英語の5大文型(SPAT-5)”にまつわる間違いは含んでいない。理由は非常に単純で、5文型はあまりにも基本的かつ簡単すぎるので、それに絡めての間違いなどは、捏造しようにもどうにもねつ造しきれないのである。まともな自尊心のある英語の話し手なら誰も、“I gave it him.(正しくは当然、I gave it to him.)”みたいなわざとらしい間違い英文なんて(たとえ冗談にでも)作れるものではないのだ。“SPAT-5”を完璧に理解・駆使できる能力は、大学入試の世界では、「持っていれば有利になる」というよりは「持っているのが当たり前」のものである。試験官は、諸君がどの程度速く走れるかを試そうとはしても、走るために必要な二本の足を諸君が備えているか否かなどチェックはしないものだ。

英文の構成パターン(SPAT-5)という礎石を超越したところで(しかしかなりの部分までその礎石の上に)立つ壮麗な邸宅が、「不定詞(INFINITIVE)」「比較(COMPARISON)」「関係詞(RELATIVES)」「仮定法(SUBJUNCTIVE)」といった「意味別構文」である。これらの領域こそ、英語の駆使力の(そして大学合格の)争奪戦の主戦場なのである。こうした意味別構文の個々の分野の知識でしっかり理論武装しておかない限り、戦いは負けである。大学入試の狭い海峡通過レースであれ、より広い世界で現実に話されている英語の修得ゲームであれ、敗残あるのみである。

英文法の世界は広大なので、「文型」／「構文」／「その他」の3つの(感覚的にわかり易い)領域へと区分することなしにこの世界に分け入れば、これを(制覇することはおろか)横断しようにもどうしてよいかわからないだろう。「その他の文法」に含まれるものの数はなお多いものの、英文法の全体像の中から「構造上(SPAT-5)」並びに「意味上(構文)」のパターンを取り去った後に残る「その他(の文法)」なら、広大無辺で理解不能、ということはない。

- "Back to the basics" is a lost cause in linguistics -

Among "the rest" of grammar are contained such basic principles as tense, conjugation, or parts of speech. It is true that you can go nowhere without these basic principles in English, but it is also true that those principles can be learnt anywhere because they are "basic".

Those who get stuck in relatively early stages of English studies — after being introduced to "SPAT-5" and starting to be perplexed at the complexities of "semantic constructions" — simply don't know where they are standing or where and how far they have to go. Not knowing their destination, they will invariably try in vain to "go back to the basics of English"... when their destiny is determined. They will start from writing down and pronouncing the alphabet once again, studiously practice paraphrasing sentences with various subjects, objects or tenses, or sharpen their ability to construe sentences according to the five structural molds (SPAT-5) and... that is all; they can go no further. Beyond the "basic" realm of English, they don't know where or how to go.

The fact is, all those basics can be learnt in a matter of MONTHS, not YEARS. It will take years of practice to get perfectly used to the basics, but those practicing years had best be spent on studying and conquering the paramount summits of "semantic constructions". Remember – basics can be learnt anywhere, at the foot, ridge or top of the mountains. Those who stick to the basic training in the base camp at the foot of the mountains will never start climbing, and will eventually give up their wish to command English. It is not that they are mentally disabled from going any higher. It is simply that they don't know how to categorize the world of English, especially the realm of grammar into three different levels of "sentence patterns", "semantic constructions" and "the rest".

Each semantic construction (INFINITIVE, GERUND, PARTICIPLE, COMPARISON, RELATIVES, NEGATION, SUBJUNCTIVE, etc,etc.) had best be studied in a single stroke, however tough and long the task may seem at first. Since they can never be learnt without arduous and repetitive reviews, it does not matter how tough the first attempt is for novice learners: it will get the less tough and the more lucidly understood the more they run over it.

ー“基本へ戻れ”なんて、語学の世界では負け犬の遠吠えー

文法世界の「その他」の中には、「時制(tense)」「語尾変化(tense)」「品詞(parts of speech)」といった基本的原則の数々も含まれる。こうした英語の基本原則を踏まえずにはどこにも行けないのは確かだが、こうした原則はどこででも学べる(なんたって“基本”なのだから)というのもまた確かなことである。

英語学習の比較的早い段階ー“SPAT-5 の5文型”に触れ、“意味別構文”のややこしさに頭がこんがらがり始めたあたりーで行き詰まってしまう人たちは、自分が今どこに立っているのか、これからどこへ行かねばならぬのか、あとどれぐらい遠くまで行かねばならないのか、とにかくもう何もわからなくなっているのである。自らの行き先を知らないから、彼らは一様に(かつ、無意味に)「英語の基本に立ち返ろう」とするのである・・・が、そんなことをした時点で彼らの運命はもう決まってしまう。彼らはまず「アルファベットの書き取りと音読」からもう一度やり直して、文章の主語・目的語・時制を様々に変えての言い換え練習をせっせとしてみたり、5つの構造上の鋳型(SPAT-5)に照らしての英文解釈能力に磨きをかけたりしてみるのだが・・・それでおしまい;それ以上どこへも行けやしない。英語の「基本的」領域の外の世界に関しては、どこへ行こうという目的地もなければ、どうやって行くかの方法論もない。

実際のところ、そうした基本的事項などというものはすべて「数ヶ月」単位(「数年」単位ではない)で学べてしまうものなのだ。基本に完璧に習熟するには数年単位の練習が必要になるが、そうした練習に費やす年月は、“意味別構文”のそびえ立つ高峰の学習と征服のために費やすのが最善なのである。思い出してほしいー“基本”はどこでも学べるのだ:山麓でも尾根伝いでも山々の頂上でも、基本学習は場を選ばないのである。山の麓のベースキャンプでの基本訓練にばかりしがみつく人々は、決して山登りを始めようとはしないし、英語を使いこなせるようになりたいという望みだってやがては捨て去ってしまうものである。能力的に問題があって高みへ上る力がないから、ではない。ただ単に、英語の世界のカテゴリー分けのしかた、とりわけ「文法」の領域を「文型」「意味別構文」「その他」という3つの異なるレベルへと切り分ける作法を、彼らが知らないから、というだけの話である。

意味別構文(不定詞:INFINITIVE、動名詞:GERUND、分詞:PARTICIPLE、比較:COMPARISON、関係詞:RELATIVES、否定:NEGATION、仮定法:SUBJUNCTIVE、その他諸々)の学習は、それぞれのテーマごとにまとめて一気にやるのが(たとえ最初はどんなにしんどくて時間がかかる作業に思えても)最善のやり方である。こうした意味別構文の修得には、骨の折れる復習の繰り返しが欠かせないわけだから、初学者にとってのその試みが最初の時点でいかにキツかろうが、関係ない:同じ事を復習するそのたびごとに、以前よりラクになり、前にもまして明快に理解できるようになるのだ

While they go over it, they can naturally review "SPAT-5" and "the rest" of grammar over and over again. English "basics" need not (in fact, MUST NOT) be learnt by getting backward: just go forward in your struggle with "semantic constructions", and the conquest of "basics" will be achieved pretty much as a matter of course.

All who succeed in anything, academic or otherwise, know the fact that things apparently hard at first will look easier as they proceed to take on things more progressively difficult. People who achieve seemingly impossible feats, in fact, have a way of overcharging themselves with tasks beyond their current capacity. They simply won't sit practicing "basics" along with other low achievers: they will lose no time in stepping up to "intermediate" level, where they will at once struggle with harder tasks and take their time taming easier things they didn't have much time practicing in the long, tedious lessons of "basics" they promptly turned their backs on. Thus, they will gain a footing in basics while they jump up for something higher. Those who stick to something lower until they are sure they have perfectly gained a footing in basics will never achieve anything really great.

As it happens, Japanese folks are notorious for making too much of "基本(KIHON: basics)" without aspiring for anything higher (or irregular). In fact, most Japanese (learners and teachers alike) simply have no notion of what "上級(JOUKYUU: advanced)" realm of English is made of... no wonder very few of them could ever achieve something in their painfully vain struggle for command of English. They are only swimming in the shallows of English bay, to whom the epic odyssey to the 12(13, fourteen, you name it) semantic seas of constructions is a myth only idle dreamers will ever take seriously.

Learners, never spend too much time playing (or rather, consoling yourselves) with "basics" alone: just step forward and learn basics on the way. The higher you go and the tougher the task gets, the more you can familiarize yourself with really basic matters, which familiarity will confidently encourage you in your struggle with something much tougher to master. Difficulty and confidence go by comparison. In order to tame something you

から、最初のキツさなど問題外なのである。その復習過程で、学習者たちは当然「SPAT-5 の文型」も「その他の英文法」も、何度も何度も繰り返し復習できるわけである。英語の「基本事項」は後戻りして学ぶ必要はない(どころか、後戻り学習なんて絶対にしてはならない!):ただひたすら前進して「意味別構文」との格闘に挑んでさえおれば「基本事項」の征服などは至極当然の結果として達成できてしまうものなのだ。

何事に於いてであれ(学問であれそれ以外であれ)およそ成功者というものはみな、「最初は見るからに難しく思えた物事も、段階的にもっと難しい物事に挑戦して行くにつれて、次第に簡単に見えてくる」という事実を知っている。不可能とも思われる所業を成し遂げる人々は、実際、現時点での自分自身の能力の限界を超えた仕事を自らに無理矢理課すようなやり方をするものである。たいした事もできずに終わるその他諸々の連中に混じってぼんやりと「基本練習」を繰り返すような真似を、彼らは絶対にしない:彼らはすかさず「中級レベル」へと段階を上げては、より一層の難題との格闘を始めると同時に、あっという間におさらばしてしまった長く退屈な「基本レッスン」の中では十分練習時間が取れなかった比較的簡単な物事の数々をもまた、ゆったり時間をかけて手なずけて行くのである。こうして彼らは、より高い何かめがけて跳躍しながら、基本的な事柄に関する地歩をも固めて行く。基本領域での足場を完璧に固めたという確信が持てない限りは低い世界にいつまでも留まり続けようとする人々は、真に偉大な事柄など何一つ達成できはしない。

折り悪しくというべきか、日本の人々は、高みを(あるいは常と異なる特別な何かを)目指しもせずに基本ばかり重んじすぎることで悪名高い。現実問題として、ほとんどの日本人は(学習者も教える側も双方ともに)英語の「上級領域」が何によって形成されているか、皆目見当も付かぬ状態なのである・・・これでは、英語が出来るようになりたくていくら苦しい努力を(虚しく)積み重ねてみても、まともな成果が達成できる者など彼らの中にほとんどいないのは、無理もない話である。彼らはひたすら英語世界の湾内の浅瀬で泳いでいるばかりで、12の(あるいは13、14、各人各様好きに定めてもらって構わないが)「意味別構文」の海へと漕ぎ出す勇ましき冒険の航海などというものは、大方の日本人にとって、つまらん夢物語を思い描く連中以外はまともに取り合わない「神話」に過ぎぬ、ということになる。

学習者諸君よ、ただひたすらに「基本」と戯れる(というよりむしろ「基本練習」の名のもとに惨めな自分を慰めにかかる)行為にあまり多くの時間を費やすのはやめたまえ:ただひたすらに前進し、基本は道々学べばよいのだ。より高い所へ出て、仕事のキツさが増すほどに、本当に基本的な事項への馴染みはその分深まるし、そうした馴染みの深さがまた、遙かに修得困難な物事と格闘する諸君を、確かな自信によって元気付けてくれるのである。困難と自信とは相対的なものだ。最初は修得困難に感じた物事

find it initially difficult to master, just challenge something harder still to tame, and the initial difficulty seems nothing to the new daring challenge, giving you an emotional conquest of the first easier challenge; the conquest may be merely emotional, but the imagined conquest is far better than the feeling of defeat. As ability and effort are the wheels of achievement, so is confidence fuel for success. That's the name of the game in conquering anything really great. The realm where you can really achieve something in your pursuit of the command of English lies beyond "SPAT-5" and "the rest" of grammar – learn them retrospectively while you struggle with much harder "semantic constructions" of English.

- Learn semantic constructions of English, and anatomical interpretation of English sentences will naturally follow -

While you are being taught "basic" things in Japanese classrooms, you will encounter virtually no English sentences complicated enough to require anatomical as opposed to mechanical interpretation. In order to get proficient in anatomical interpretation of English, you naturally have to walk into the thick semantic forests of "constructions".

The sad truth is, most Japanese students are introduced to impossibly small fragmented and seemingly isolated and unrelated portions of the real world of English constructions. What Japanese schools or teachers show you regarding such constructions as INFINITIVE, GERUND, PARTICIPLE, COMPARISON, RELATIVES, NEGATION or SUBJUNCTIVE are all too small and separated to be actually useful; they are fragmented pieces of info rather than systematic knowledge of grammar. As for more highly specialized groups of constructions such as INVERSION, ELLIPSIS, COMMON-RELATION, PARENTHESIS or APPOSITIVE, practically no time or thought is given them in ordinary Japanese schools or books.

The reason for this piteous situation in Japan is simple but hopeless — both teachers and writers of English textbooks (at least most of them) are themselves totally ignorant of these constructions as "a systematic set of knowledge". These constructions exist in the heads of most Japanese teachers or writers as mere fragments of what they feel they know (or even

を「飼い慣らす」ためには、手なずけるのがもっと困難な何かに挑みさえすればそれでよい;そうすれば、最初に感じた困難なんて、新たに思い切って挑戦してみた何かと比べれば、全く取るに足らないものに感じるだろうし、最初の容易な挑戦課題なんて自分はもう征服したのだ、という精神的達成感が得られるだろう;この征服感覚は単なる思い込みに過ぎないかもしれないが、たとえ想像上の達成感であっても、敗残意識よりはずっとマシである。「能力」と「努力」が目的達成のための車の両輪であるように、「自信」は成功の動力源である。それこそが、何であれ真に偉大な事柄をモノにするための勝利の秘訣なのである。英語の駆使能力を身に付けるための営みの中で、諸君が真に大きな成果を得られる領域は、「SPAT−5の5文型」や「その他の英文法」を越えたところに広がっている－そんな事柄は「あぁ、懐かしい、そういう事項って、確かにあったよね」的な感覚で学べばよい・・・遙かに難儀な「英語の意味別構文」の世界との格闘を繰り広げるその中で。

－英語の「意味別構文」を学べば、英文の「解剖学的解釈」も自動的に付いてくる－

日本の教室で「基本事項」を教わっている段階では、(機械的ならぬ)解剖学的解釈を要するほどに複雑な英文に出くわすことはほぼないだろう。英文の解剖学的解釈に習熟するためには、諸君は当然「構文」という意味の世界の木深い森へと分け入る必要がある。

しかし、悲しい事実を指摘すれば、日本の学生たちが紹介されるのはただ、現実の英語構文の世界をどうしようもないほど小さい断片に切り刻んで一見お互い無関係に思える独立した小集団の群れみたいにしてしまった「細切れ構文チラ見せ世界」でしかないのである。「不定詞:INFINITIVE、動名詞:GERUND、分詞:PARTICIPLE、比較:COMPARISON、関係詞:RELATIVES、否定:NEGATION、仮定法:SUBJUNCTIVE」といった構文関連で日本の学校や教師が諸君に見せてくれるものはみな、あまりに細かくてんでんバラバラ状態で提示されるので、実際には役に立たない;体系的な文法知識の体を成していない一口情報のかけらの寄せ集めでしかないのである。さらに一層高度な特殊構文の「倒置・語順:INVERSION、省略:ELLIPSIS、共通関係:COMMON−RELATION、挿入:PARENTHESIS、同格:APPOSITIVE」に関して言えば、日本の普通の学校も本も、そんなものには一切時間もかけず一顧だにしてもいないのが現実なのだ。

日本に於けるこの哀れむべき状況の原因は、単純だが、しかしまた救いようのないものでもある－教える者達も英語の教科書を書く者達も(少なくともその大部分が)彼ら自身これらの構文のことを「一群の体系的知識」としては全く知らないからである。こうした構文については、大方の日本の教師や執筆者の場合、自分が「知っているつもり

“they have seen somewhere”), which they need some reference books to confirm or even understand. No one can give others systematic comprehension of a group of things which they themselves only know in parts, without any idea of the whole picture... tough luck for those who have the misfortune of being taught English by such teachers.

- Be aware where you are going, or get stuck and dead where you are -

The good news is, the author of this book can give you comprehensive understanding and training of 12 semantic constructions of English in the form of WEB lessons composed of ample example sentences and explanations, along with enough numbers of grammatical questions and answers. For more details, check the url below:

http://furu-house.com/sample

If you aspire to achieve something authentic, be my guest. Just ignore my invitation if you can rest satisfied with several years of painfully vain “basic” trainings your schools or teachers force upon you. The choice is yours to make, but please remember – I didn't write this series of principles just in order to invite you to my WEB lessons: ***I created my WEB lessons according to those principles.***

Whether you take my WEB lessons or not, take my word for it that without the distinctive consciousness of what you are studying — terms (vocabulary), idioms (collocations), sentence patterns (SPAT-5), semantic constructions, the rest of grammar, or anatomical interpretation of English sentences – you are sure to get stuck and eventually give up studying and mastering English. Be always aware what you are doing: those who do what they do because they are told to do so can never do anything really great.

の(あるいは「前にどこかで見た覚えがある」だけの)単なる断片的記憶として脳内に存在しているばかりであって、その確認には(どころか「理解」すら)参考書に頼らねばどうにもならない有様なのだ。自分自身でもその全体像を知らず、ただ断片的に知っているだけの一群の事柄を、他者に「体系的に理解させる」ことが出来る人間など、一人もいない･･･そんなセンセイがたから英語を教わる不運に見舞われた人々には、お悔やみ申し上げるしかない。

ー自分が向かおうとしている先を見据えよ、さもなくば今いる場所で行き詰まり、座して死を待つより他はないー

朗報もある:この本の著者には、英語の「12の意味別構文」の包括的理解と練習問題とを、豊富な例文と解説に十分な数の文法問題&解答を添えて、WEB(インターネット)上での授業の形で、諸君に提供する用意があるのだ。より詳しい説明は、以下に記す url(Uniform Resource Locator:インターネット上での「所番地」)で確認してほしい:

http://furu-house.com/sample

本物の何かを身に付けたいと望む諸君は、門を叩いてみてほしい。学校や先生方が何年にも渡って諸君に課してくる苦しくて無意味な「基本的」トレーニングに満足していられる人々は、筆者からのお誘いなど無視すればそれでよい。選ぶのは諸君自身である;が、どうか覚えておいてほしいー筆者がこの項で書いた一連の原則は、自分のWEB授業へと諸君を誘い込むために書いたわけではない:***ここに書いた一連の原則に基づいて創り上げたのが、筆者のWEB授業なのである。***

諸君がこの筆者のWEB授業を受けるか否かはさておいて、次のことは確実に信じてもらいたい:今現在自分が何を学んでいるのかー「単語(ボキャブラリー)」なのか「熟語(コロケーション)」なのか「文型(SPAT-5)」なのか「構文」なのか「文法」なのか「英文の解剖学的解釈」なのかーそれをきちんと識別する意識がなければ、諸君は確実に行き詰まり、やがては英語の学習も修得も、きっと放棄してしまうことだろう。いま自分は何をしているのか、それを常に自覚することだ:誰かに「やれ」と言われたから自分はこれをしてるだけ、という人間は、真の偉業を成し遂げることなど絶対にできっこないのだから。

14. E-to-J translation vs. English interpretation, literal translation vs. paraphrasing: learn their difference through anatomical interpretation

- Anatomical interpretation explained -

As this author has written in the previous section, anatomical interpretation of English is the final product made possible by putting together all the skill in “terms”, “idioms”, “sentence patterns”, “constructions” and “grammar”.

Although it's final, the anatomical task begins (and should begin) in the initial stages of learning English. Although the ultimate stage of English comprehension never needs the intervention of anatomical interpretation — almost instinctively understood without being consciously interpreted or translated – that ultimate stage can only be reached after years of practice after innumerable practice in anatomical interpretation of English.

Let us see the illustrated example of anatomical interpretation in the following sentence:

In the global conflict known as World War II, Germany, Italy and Japan were collectively called the Axis Powers as opposed to the Allied Powers consisting of such eventually victorious nations as Britain, Russia and the United States.

...which, after being anatomized, will look like this:

(In the global conflict {[which is] known as ＜World War II＞}), ＜Germany, Italy and Japan＞ were (collectively) called ＜the Axis Powers＞ (as opposed to ≪the Allied Powers｛consisting of(=which consisted of) such {eventually victorious} nations as <Britain, Russia and the United States>｝≫).

The above is the way a sentence is semantically grasped in the mind's eye of the expert reader/listener of English. Sentences are not comprehended in a single stream of words or sounds, but as a body of mutually related blocks of meaning. To visually illustrate the sentence with conspicuous signs will help learners understand the mutual relationship between composing units of the sentence. With this visual guide in semantic composition of the sentence,

14. 英文和訳と英文解釈の違い、逐語訳と意訳の違い・・・解剖学的解釈を通して学ぶべし

－解剖学的解釈の具体的解説－

先の項で筆者が書いた通り、英語の解剖学的解釈は「単語(terms)」「熟語(idioms)」「文型(sentence patterns=SPAT-5)」「構文(constructions)」「文法(grammar)」の全能力を駆使して初めて得られる最終的産物である。

最終的産物であるとはいえ、解剖学的作業は英語学習の初期段階から既に始まっている(というか、始めるべきである)。英文解釈も究極の段階に達すれば、解剖学的解釈の介在は必要ない－意識して解釈することも翻訳することもなしにほとんど直感的に理解されるものである－が、そうした究極的段階に到達できるのは、英文の解剖学的解釈の実践練習を数限りなく長年続けた人物のみである。

解剖学的解釈の実例について、図解入りの形で、以下の文章を通して見てみよう:

In the global conflict known as World War II, Germany, Italy and Japan were collectively called the Axis Powers as opposed to the Allied Powers consisting of such eventually victorious nations as Britain, Russia and the United States.

和訳: 第二次世界大戦として知られる地球規模の紛争に於いて、ドイツ・イタリア・日本は、総称的に「枢軸国」と(最終的に勝利を収めることになるイギリス・ロシア・アメリカ合衆国等の国々から成る「連合国」と対照する形で)呼ばれていた。

. . . この英文が、"解剖"後には、次のように見えることになる:

(In the global conflict {[which is] known as ＜World War II＞}), ＜Germany, Italy and Japan＞ were (collectively) called ＜the Axis Powers＞ (as opposed to ≪the Allied Powers {consisting of(=which consisted of) such {eventually victorious} nations as 〈Britain, Russia and the United States〉} ≫).

上に示した姿こそ、英語の読解／聴取に熟練した人物が「意味」に着目して捉えた場合の、心の目に映る英文の姿である。文章は「単語」や「音声」の一本調子の流れとして理解されるわけではなく、相互に関連し合う「意味」の塊の集合体として把握されるのだ。分かり易い記号を用いて文章を視覚的に説明することで、学習者は、文章の

learners are liberated from the arduous though mostly meaningless task of translating English into their native language. "Understand as you look or hear" is the common goal of all learners of English, to be sure, but aside from "Howdy English" too simple to require interpretation, sentences well worth reading naturally demand anatomical interpretation of the semantic relationship of their composing units.

Use the signs shown below to semantically clarify the English sentence you meet:

*＜実詞(JISSHI: SUBSTANTIVES)＞

The following substantive units (S:SUBJECT),(O:OBJECT) and (C:COMPLEMENT) are to be grouped together in a pair of angle brackets = "＜山括弧(YAMA-KAKKO) or chevrons or an lt & gt(less-than/greater-than) pair＞"; if more than one unit of substantives are found in the same sentence, the following signs can also be used — a pair of corner brackets or half brackets = "「鉤括弧(KAGI-KAKKO)」"; black lenticular brackets = "【墨付き括弧 (SUMI-TSUKI-KAKKO) 】"; double guillemets = "≪二重山括弧(NIJUU-YAMA-KAKKO)≫"

＜主語(SHUGO: SUBJECT:S)＞

＜動詞の目的語(DOUSHI NO MOKUTEKIGO: VERBAL OBJECT:O)＞

＜前置詞の目的語(ZENCHISHI NO MOKUTEKIGO: PREPOSITIONAL OBJECT)＞

＜補語(HOGO: COMPLEMENT:C)＞

The units contrasted to "SUBSTANTIVES" are "VERBALS":

*動詞／動詞型(DOUSHI/DOUSHI-KEI: VERB/VERBALS:V)

Verbal units include the following expressions:

*熟語(JUKUGO: IDIOMS)

*相関語句(SOUKAN-GOKU: CORRELATIVES)

Idiomatic or correlative expressions are composed of a group of words often in separated positions in the sentence — sometimes too much scattered for beginners to comprehend as an integral semantic unit. So as not to lose sight of these pivotal entities, learners should mark them with something visually outstanding, such as the use of underlines or colorful marker pens.

構成単位相互の関わり合いを理解し易くなる。文章の意味上の構成をこうして視覚的に図示したガイドがあれば、学習者は（大部分は無意味なのに）骨の折れる「英語を自国語へと翻訳する」作業から解放される。「見て／聞いて即座に理解すること」が英語学習者全員の共通の到達目標であることは確かだが、“アイサツ英会話(Howdy English:ハウディ・イングリッシュ)”みたいに単純すぎて解釈の必要もないやつはともかく、十分読むに値するだけの文章なら当然その構成単位どうしの意味上の関係を解剖学的に解釈する必要が生じるものである。

出会った英文の意味を解明するためには、以下に示す記号を活用すればよい：

*＜実詞(SUBSTANTIVES)＞

以下に示す実詞の構成単位の(主語＝S:SUBJECT)・(目的語＝O:OBJECT)・(補語＝C:COMPLEMENT)は“＜山括弧・シェブロン(chevrons)・不等号ペア＞”で一まとめにしておくこと；もし実詞構成単位が同一文章内に2つ以上存在する場合は、以下のような記号も使えばよいー“「鉤括弧・corner(half) brackets」”; “【墨付き括弧・black lenticular brackets】”; “≪二重山括弧・double guillemets(ダブル・ギュメ)≫”：

＜主語(SUBJECT:S)＞

＜動詞の目的語(VERBAL OBJECT:O)＞

＜前置詞の目的語(PREPOSITIONAL OBJECT)＞

＜補語(COMPLEMENT:C)＞

“実詞:SUBSTANTIVES”と対称的な立場にある構成単位は、“動詞型:VERBALS”である：

*動詞／動詞型(VERB/VERBALS:V)

動詞型構成単位の中には次の表現も含まれる：

*熟語(IDIOMS)

*相関語句(CORRELATIVES)

熟語や相関的表現は複数の単語の一群より成るが、それらの単語は文中に離れて存在する場合が多いー時にはあまりにもバラバラに散在しすぎて初学者がそれを単一不可分の意味上の統合体として把握することは困難な場合もある。こういう意味の要になる大事な統一体の姿を見失わないように、学習者は「熟語・相関語句」を視覚的に際立つ記号（例えば下線やマーカーペン）を用いて目立たせておくのがよい。

One very important part of the anatomical illustration is [省略(SHOURYAKU: ELLIPSIS)] — something which does not exist in the sentence but should be complemented, or conversely, something that exists in the sentence but might as well be omitted:

*[省略可能成分(SHOURYAKU-KANOU SEIBUN: OMISSIBLE ELEMENTS)／被省略成文(HI-SHOURYAKU SEIBUN: OMITTED ELEMENTS)]

Since English language makes much of brevity, writers/speakers of English often cut off what should grammatically exist in the sentence. They know what they are saying, and the authentic readers/listeners of English also know what is being said by supplementing the unseen ELLIPSIS, but novice learners of English rarely or never can. It is therefore imperative that beginners should make conscious efforts to imagine what is omitted (if it is not personally impossible) and omit what can be cut off (if not grammatically impossible). Such ELLIPSIS elements should be marked with square brackets = "[大括弧(DAI-KAKKO) or 角括弧(KAKU-KAKKO)]".

Used in close association with SUBSTANTIVES are ADJECTIVE ELEMENTS modifying nouns either from in front of or behind the nouns, which should be marked with curly brackets = "{中括弧(CHU-KAKKO) or 波括弧(NAMI-KAKKO)}".

*{形容詞(KEIYOUSHI: ADJECTIVES: ADJ.)}

A single adjective modifying a noun from ahead (eg. She is a beautiful woman) need not be meticulously marked, but a group of adjective modifiers qualifying a noun from behind (eg. She is a woman {beautiful and intelligent}) or a single adjective which qualifies a noun immediately before it (eg. He is a man {alone}) should be visibly illustrated with {curly brackets} for differentiating purposes.

The most bulky and usually unessential (and often misleading) element of the sentence is the adverb part, which should be excluded from the main, essential parts of the sentence by marking it with round brackets = "(小括弧(SHOU-KAKKO) or 丸括弧(MARU-KAKKO))".

*(副詞(FUKUSHI: ADVERBS: ADV.))

As its name implies, the "adverb" is used in connection with the "verb". This is quite a basic but weighty piece of knowledge — "adverbs" are added on to "verbs" while "adjectives" decorate "nouns".

解剖学的図解の中でも大変重要な部分は[省略(ELLIPSIS)]ー文中には存在しないが補って考えるべきもの、あるいは逆に、文中に存在はするが省いてしまっても差し支えないものーである:

*[省略可能成分(OMISSIBLE ELEMENTS)／被省略成文(OMITTED ELEMENTS)]

英語は簡潔さを重んじる言語なので、英語の書き手／話し手は(文法的に見れば)文中に存在しているのが当然の部分を省いてしまう場面が多い。彼らは自分が何を言っているかわかっているし、本筋の英語の読み手／聞き手であればやはり(見えない省略部を補うことで)何が言われているのか理解するが、英語の初学者には理解不能な場合がほとんどである。それゆえに、初心者の場合、何が省略されているのかを意識的に想像する(ことが彼らにできるならば、そうする)努力を払い、また(文法的に可能ならば)省略できる部分は省いてみる意識的努力も払うことが必要不可欠となる。こうしたELLIPSIS(省略されているもの／省略可能なもの)の要素は“[大括弧または角括弧: square brackets]”で囲っておくこと。

“実詞(SUBSTANTIVES)”と密接な関わりを持って用いられるのが、名詞(NOUNS)をその前あるいは後から修飾する“形容詞(ADJECTIVE)”の要素で、“{中括弧または波括弧: curly brackets}”でくくっておく。

*{形容詞(ADJECTIVES: ADJ.)}

名詞をその直前から修飾する単一の形容詞(例 She is a beautiful woman.:彼女は美しい女性だ)には几帳面に印を付ける必要はないが、名詞をその直後から修飾する形容詞の一群(例 She is a woman {beautiful and intelligent}.:彼女は美しくて聡明な女性である)や、直前の名詞を修飾する単一の形容詞(例 He is a man {alone}.:彼は一匹狼だ)の場合は、他と区別するために“{くびれたカッコ}”に入れて視覚的に図示しておくのがよい。

最もかさばり、大方は意味の中核に関わりを持たず、しばしば人の誤読をも誘う文章内要素は「副詞(adverb)」であるから、文章の主要な精髄部から切り離すために、“(小括弧または丸括弧: round brackets)”で囲っておくべきである。

*(副詞(ADVERBS: ADV.))

“adverb”の呼び名が示す通り、「副詞」は「動詞(verb)」との関わりの中で用いられる。この知識は基本中の基本であるが、とても大事なことであるー“adverbs(副詞)”は“verbs(動詞)に add-on(付加)”する語であるのに対し、“adjectives(形容詞)”は“nouns(名詞)”を飾る語である、と覚えることだ。

- No sweat with no frills -

The first and foremost task of anatomical interpretation starts from separating "SUBSTANTIVE(=nounal)" units along with ADJECTIVES from "VERBAL" units accompanied by ADVERBS, in which the former are often essential, brief and easier to comprehend, while the latter are usually longer and tougher to deal with.

In other words, English sentences can be simply and clearly understood when you tighten them by marking adverbial "flab" and mentally deleting it from your consciousness for initial comprehension... after you have grasped the "essential" components of the sentence (made mostly of substantives and adjectives), you can taste the "flab" at your leisure. Make wise use of round brackets "( )" as "pending" marks for less than essential adverbial elements. Strip a sentence of frills, and the essence is always simple and clear to see.

- Seeing for yourself is one thing; having others see what you see is another; making students write all that they see?... please don't bother -

In mathematics, a formula speaks everything. Good understanding is proved by a flawlessly written formula, while a faulty one disproves your claim that you have understood something. Although English is no mathematics, the above-mentioned anatomical interpretation signs can talk nearly as much as mathematical formulae do. Still, since English is a human speech, there are times when you have to speak in human terms instead of anatomical signs – especially if you happen to study English in Japanese schools: too many Japanese English teachers think too much of translating English into their native Japanese. But, if you really want to excel in English, NEVER write down everything you understood: make wise personal selection of what to write down and what to ignore, regardless of what your teacher says.

Many Japanese teachers of English simply tell students to translate every English sentence they see on textbooks and write down every piece of info graciously given in lessons mostly because they want their students to be too busy to wonder whether they are really doing (or rather, being made to do) the right thing. When hands are busy, brains lie idle. The easiest and sliest

ー飾りさえ取り去れば苦労なしー

解剖学的解釈の最初にして最も大事な作業は、“SUBSTANTIVES:実詞(=nounal:名詞型)”+“ADJECTIVES(形容詞成文)”を、“VERBALS(動詞型)”+“ADVERBS(副詞成文)”から切り離すところから始まる。両者のうち、前者はしばしば意味の中核を担い、簡潔にして意味の把握もより楽に行なえる構成単位であるのに対し、後者は長くて扱いも容易ではないのが普通である。

言い換えれば、英文を単純明快に理解するためには、副詞的“贅肉部”に印を付けてまず最初の内容把握段階ではこれを意識の中から感覚的に削除してしまうことで、文章をこぢんまりとスリム化してしまえばよいのである・・・文章の“主要な”構成要素(実詞・形容詞から成るのが普通)を把握し終えたその後で、“余分”な副詞的構成要素はごゆるりと時間をかけて味わえばそれでよいのだ。丸いカッコ( )を賢く用いて、意味の中核からは遠い副詞的要素には(保留中)の印を付けておくことだ。余分な飾りを文章から取り除いてみれば、後に残る中核部は常に単純で一目瞭然な姿をしているものである。

ー自分が了解するのと、自分が了解したことを他者に示すのとはわけが違う;では、学生には了解内容の全てを書かせるべきかって?・・・どうぞお構いなく、そんな面倒なことしないで結構ですー

数学に於いては数式が万事に於いてモノを言う。正しく理解したならば、完全無欠の形で書かれた数式がそれを証明してくれる;一方、何かを「理解した」と言い張ってみても、欠陥含みの数式を書けば、そんな主張は却下されておしまいである。英語は数学とはまるで違うが、上述した「解剖学的解釈記号の数々」は、数学の数式に匹敵するぐらい雄弁な理解度の証拠たり得るであろう。それでもやはり、英語は人間の話す言語なのだから、解剖学的記号ではなく人間的な言葉を用いて話さねばならぬ場合が多々あるーとりわけあなたがたまたま日本の学校で英語を学ぶ境遇にあるなら、その場面は多いだろう:日本には、母国語である日本語へと英語を翻訳することをあまりにも重んじすぎる英語教師がやたら多すぎるからである。だが、もしあなたが心底から英語に上達することを望むのならば、自分が理解したことの全てを書き出すような真似は絶対にしてはならない:たとえ教師が何を言おうとも、自分としては「これは書き出すべきだが、これは無視して流せばよい」という選別を賢く行なわなければ、真の英語の上達は望めない。

日本の英語教師の多くは、学生たちに、教科書で見た英文は1つ残らず全て翻訳し、授業内で有り難くも教わった情報は一つ残らず全て書き取るように、と命令するが、何のことはない、教師がそんなことを命じる主たる理由は、学生たちが「自分はいま果たして本当に正しいことをしている(あるいは、させられている)のだろうか?」という疑念を抱くこともできぬくらいに彼らをクソ忙しくさせておきたいから、というだけの思惑に過ぎないのである。「手」が忙しく動いている最中には「頭」はぼんやり休んでいるものだ。

way to conceal flaws of fruitless lessons is to deny brains a chance to think by making busy hands, eyes and ears in the constant flow of unilaterally transmitted info in the midst of which students simply have no time to stop and think intelligently. This is the most efficient method of producing a horde of meek, unthinking, manageable citizens that are no good as thinking weeds yet not bad as stable founding stones of a nation and gullible customers for big companies and industries to easily exploit.

In any given lesson enabling students to really grow in intelligence, there is fruitful void of voice making room for brains to think; lessons or teachers that will take you nowhere simply try to make you busy on some pretext or other to give plausible substance to empty lessons. Such teachers as will order you to buy some particular English book and to translate each and every sentence in it on your notebook are one of the worst enemies of yours in your road to intelligence. They just want you to be an unthinking slave. If you can stand being a slave, just do as they tell you; otherwise, think wisely and see through the shallow intentions of such silly bullies of teachers to avoid falling a victim to their whims.

Sad to say, so many Japanese students are imprisoned in schools teeming with teachers wanting students to be meek slaves, not thinking intelligentsia, that this author has to stress once again the need for you to make wise selection between what English sentence you have to consciously translate and what you can just interpret and let go.

Some students might think the same advice should be given to their teachers as well, but this author would not do that because he knows too well that simply inferior teachers have no other way than to drown out the doubts of students with endless voices, orders and homework pressed upon them with authority. If you happen to find yourself under the curse of such adverse teachers, be wise enough not to invite their wrath (which can be quite nasty for being empowered with authority) while being secretly and wisely selective in what tasks to perform and what orders to ignore.

実り少ない授業の欠陥を隠す上で最も安直にして姑息なやり方は、一方的に伝達される情報の絶えざる流れ(その真っ只中に置かれた学生には立ち止まって理知的に考える時間など微塵もないような情報洪水)の中で「手・目・耳」を多忙状態に置くことで、「頭脳」に思考のいとまを与えないことである。「考える葦」としては役立たずだが、国家の揺るぎなき礎石あるいは大企業や産業界をたやすく信じていいカモになる消費者たちとしては悪くはない、そんな従順でロクにモノも考えぬ扱い易い市民の群れを生み出すためには、上述のやり口が最も効率的な方法なのである。

学生がその知性を真に発揮することを可能にしてくれるような授業はみな、どこかで「頭脳」に考える余地を与えるための実り多き「無音」の時間を含むものである。教わってもラチが開かない授業や先生というものは、無益な授業に見せかけだけの中身を添えるためにあれこれと言い訳を作っては諸君を絶えず多忙にしておこうとするばかりである。何か特定の英語の本を買ってその中にある文章を一つ残らずノートに翻訳して書き出せ、などと命じるような類の教師というやつは、諸君が聡明な人間になるための努力過程で遭遇する最悪の敵の一つなのである。連中はただ諸君を「何も考えない奴隷」にしたいだけだ。もし諸君が奴隷の立場に安住できるのならば、そんな教師の命ずるままに動けばよろしかろう;もし奴隷の立場に耐えられないなら、賢慮を働かせて、そのテの愚かなイジメっ子的教師どもの浅はかな思惑などは見透かした上で、連中の気まぐれの犠牲になる道を避けるのがよろしかろう。

言うも悲しいことながら、日本の学生の実に多くが、「考える知識階層」ではなく「従順な奴隷」たることを学生に望む教師だらけの学校という名の「監獄」に閉じ込められているわけであるから、この筆者としてはここで再び力説しておかねばならないー意識して「翻訳」する必要のある英文と、ただ「解釈」したらさっさと流しておしまいにしてよい英文とを、諸君は賢く選別する必要があるのだ、ということを。

こうした助言は、「学生」よりもむしろ「先生がた」にしてやったらどうか、と思う学生諸君も中にはいるかもしれないが、この筆者はそういうことはしない:ひたすらに劣ったセンセイがたは「絶えざる声と命令と宿題の洪水を学生どもに(権威をもって!)押し付けることで連中の疑念を洗い流してやるっ!」というやり口以外には何の手立てもないものだ、という事実を、この筆者はイヤというほどよく知っているからである。もしも諸君が折悪しくそういう逆風教師の呪いの下に身を置く立場をかこっているようならば、彼らの怒りを買うことのないように(なにせ連中は“教師”という“権威のお墨付き”の分だけひどく意地悪なことだってできる存在なのだから)十分賢く立ち回りつつ、諸君として「遂行すべき課題」と「無視すべき命令」とを賢く(しかしあくまで秘かに)選別することである。

- When tempted to anatomically interpret, illustrate a sentence with anatomical signs and try translating it in your head; otherwise, just look and see the meaning without translating -

The act of writing is final: once you write something, whether in your notebook or on the NET, the words you gave out start standing on their own feet and deny correction or deletion afterwards. That is why you have to be very careful in your distinction between what you only think in your head and what you actually express in voice or letters.

What you don't have to write — things too easy for yourself or too much talked about by others — just don't write and remind yourself of their commonness. Being common often means being popular and commercially valuable on the NET, but in the study of English, being common for you translates straight into being unworthy of translation: you can interpret them without translation into your native language, which means you have already mastered them in the same way as native speakers have mastered them. The only time that you have to translate them is when teachers or exams ask you to translate them into Japanese to prove that you have really mastered them. The more proficient you become in English, the less you need to illustrate or interpret, let alone translate a sentence, for it is understood the moment you see or hear it. Your ultimate goal is to reach a point where you need no conscious efforts in interpretation or translation in order to understand English.

- Too much of something is worse than nothing -

Some teachers may still insist upon having students make translations of whatever they see, on the supposed ground that students cannot improve upon their skill in translation without actually writing down Japanese sentences. It may sound reassuring, but the argument is practically powerless. When forced to translate sentence after sentence, students start to stop paying attention to the meaning of each sentence, its relation with other sentences and its relative weight in the whole context; the task of making translations becomes an end in itself and everything else gets lost until the students finish translating them all. Too many Japanese students spend too much time and effort on lessons of English completely in vain, mainly because they are (or their teachers are) totally indiscriminate in their blind passion for translation.

ー解剖学的解釈の意欲をそそられたなら、文章を解剖学的記号で図解した上で、脳内で翻訳してみるがよろしい;それ以外の場合なら、目で見て意味を理解したら翻訳なしで流せばよろしいー

「書く」という行為は最終確定的なものである:何かをひとたび書いたなら、それがノートの上であれネット上であれ、発した言葉は一人歩きを始め、以後、修正も削除も効かなくなる。だからこそ、単に頭の中で考えるだけの事柄と、実際の声や文字にして表明する事柄とを、慎重に区別しなければならないわけである。

諸君として書く必要もない事柄ー諸君にとっては簡単すぎたり、他の誰かが言い尽くしていたりする事柄ーは、書いたりせずにただそれが「ありふれてる」ことを再確認するに留めておけばよい。「ありふれている」ということは、ネット上ではしばしば「人気がある」とか「商業的価値が高い」ことを意味するが、英語学習に於いて諸君にとって「ありふれている」事柄は、「翻訳するに値しない」へと直結する:諸君としては「ありふれている」事柄は自国語への翻訳を経ずとも解釈できるわけであり、これ即ち諸君はその「ありふれている」事柄を、生来の英語国民がそれらを修得済みであるのと同じ形で既にもうマスターしたのだ、ということを意味する。そういう事柄を諸君が翻訳せねばならぬ唯一の場面は、諸君がそれらを「本当にマスターしたのだということを証明するために日本語に翻訳してみせろ」と教師なり試験問題なりに要求された場合のみである。英語に堪能になればなるほど、見たり聞いたりした瞬間に理解できてしまう文章が増えて、図解や解釈(ましていわんや翻訳など)する必要を感じなくなるものだ。英語を理解するのに意識して解釈や翻訳しようと努める必要が全くない状態こそ、諸君が目指す究極の到達目標である。

ー何であれ、やり過ぎは、皆無より悪いー

それでもなおかつ先生がたの一部は、「実際に日本語の文章を書き出す練習をしなければ翻訳技能の向上は図れない」との(彼らの頭の中だけで考えた)根拠に基づいて、「学生には何であれ見たもの全てを翻訳させるべし」とあくまでしつこく言い張るかもしれない。彼らのその言い分には一見説得力がありそうにも思えるが、その論拠は現実的には空しいものである。次から次へと文章を翻訳させられると、学生たちは、個々の文章の意味にも他の文章との関係にも全体の文脈の中に占める相対的重要度にも、注意を払わなくなってくる;「翻訳文を作ること」そのものが自己目的化して、全文の翻訳を終えるまでは、他の一切の事柄はどこかへ吹っ飛んでしまうのだ。あまりにも多くの日本の学生たちが、英語の授業に多大な時間と労力を費やしながらもまるっきり無駄な努力に終わってしまう主たる原因は、彼らが(というか、彼らの先生が)対象を選ばぬひたすら盲目的な情熱を「翻訳作業」に対して傾注しているからである。

The act of writing with a pen on paper takes so much time and physical effort that it will actually spoil linguistic studies. Writing too much never fails to make your handwriting dirty, never leading to better penmanship. Writing down a particular version of translation will prevent you from thinking about any other alternative to the "final manuscript" which it took you so much trouble to write with your own hand. And, when you are finally through writing so many Japanese sentences translated from English, you must heave a heavy sigh of contentment that you have achieved something great... actually to no purpose, unfortunately. Never be such a diligent fool, but aspire to be an intelligent idler, who makes much more of anatomically illustrating and reading aloud the original English sentences than of writing down quick-and-dirty Japanese translations only to your empty satisfaction.

- Writing is one thing, typing is quite another -

The only exception to the principle stated above is when you "type" instead of "writing" your translation. Making your notebook dirty by your handwriting will do you more linguistic harm than good; making your fingers rhythmically busy typing in letter after letter from the keyboard of your computer hardly tortures you physically taking far less time and almost no conscious effort on the part of your fingers and never fails to advance your typing skill, which is a great asset for anyone in a society where computer literacy talks so much.

But then again, indiscriminate translation practice on the keyboard will merely benefit you by making a better typist of you; don't expect it to make you a better translator.

- The authentic translation is an act of creation, not of transplantation -

All good translators are excellent choosers between sentences well worth translating and those which merit only interpretation and no translation. And they rarely write down or type in the translated sentences except when required to do so (for getting marks in exams or for making money as translators). When they detect a sentence worthy of translation, first they make anatomical interpretation of it and grasp the meaning, and then make

「紙の上に筆記用具でものを書く」という行為に要する時間と肉体的努力は大変なものだから、「翻訳筆記作業」は、実は、語学を台無しにするものなのである。あまりに多くの文字を書けば、手書きの文字は必ず汚く崩れてくるから、書きまくることで文字が上手になる、などということも絶対にあり得ない。ある特定の翻訳文を書き記してしまえば、その「手書き最終完成稿」(自らの手をわずらわしてのその筆記には多大なる労力を投じている思い入れある完成品！)に取って代わる別の翻訳可能性を考えることもしなくなるだろう。そうして、英語から翻訳された膨大な数の日本文を最終的にようやく書き終えた時点で、諸君は「偉業を達成した！」という満足の溜息をつくことであろう・・・が、残念ながら、そんなことしても何の効用もないのである。諸君は、そういう「骨折り損のおバカさん」には決してならぬように！・・・「賢くサボる人」を目指したまえ。空しい自己満足のためだけのやっつけ仕事のコキタナイ日本語翻訳文の書き出し作業に血道を上げるより、英語原文に解剖学的図解を施しこれを音読してみる作業のほうを重視するような、より少ない時間と労力で実のある勉強をする人物になりたまえ。

－手書きではなく、タイピングを選ぶというなら話は別－

上述の原則の唯一の例外は、諸君が翻訳文を「手書きする」のではなく「キーボードから打ち込む」場合である。ノートをびっしり手書き文字で埋めてみても、語学の観点からは有害無益である;が、コンピュータのキーボード上から次々文字を打ち込むべく指先を忙しく律動させるのであれば、手書きよりも遙かに短時間で済むし、指先にはほとんど何の意識的努力も必要ないので、ほとんど全く肉体的苦役にはならない上に、諸君のタイピング技能は確実に向上する:これは、コンピュータ関連の教養が大きくモノを言う社会の中にあっては、大変な強みになる。

しかしそれでもやはり、キーボード上で手当たり次第に翻訳に挑んでも「タイピストとしての腕が上がる」だけであって、「翻訳技能の向上」を期待するのは間違いである。

－真の「翻訳」は「創造」の営みであって「移植」ではない－

翻訳が上手な人はみな、翻訳するに十分値する文章と、解釈すればよいだけで翻訳価値皆無の文章との見分けが上手である。そしてまた彼らは(試験で点数を稼いだり翻訳家としてお金を稼いだりといった)必要に迫られない限りは、翻訳された文章を書き出したりタイピングしたりすることは滅多にしない。翻訳に値する文章を発見すると、彼らはまずその解剖学的解釈をして意味を把握し、次いで彼らの「脳内にある意味」

Japanese sentences of the meaning they have in their mind. Note that they do not make a Japanese translation of the original English sentence, but they create a wholly new Japanese sentence suitable for the idea they have in their head inspired by the original English sentence. They are creating rather than translating sentences. This creative type of translating skill will only develop if you stick to two principles; namely, (1)that you must grasp the meaning of English sentences by way of anatomical interpretation, not through Japanese translation and (2)that you will always keep thinking about various ways in which to express the meaning of any given English you happen to meet without holding on to any particular version of Japanese translation as though it were the only authoritative one.

For this purpose, translated sentences in Japanese should be inscribed in your head, not in your notebooks. Once you write down some translation, you are prone to be bound by that particular version of translation, which will hinder you from hitting upon any other (possibly better) translation. Any particular answer written in will stop you from thinking any more. The only purpose of writing an answer is to check to see if you happen to be correct at the very moment that you hit upon the answer, which, naturally, is none of your business afterwards. Don't make your notebooks or textbooks dirty with such personal memoirs, unless it is your main business to cherish nostalgic memories of your past struggle many years later, when you are more likely to have failed in your original desire to master English than if you had made much less of such memorably wasteful efforts.

In summary, interpretation and translation are two different things, in which the former is much more important than the latter. That kind of students who find satisfaction in making heaps of translations are quite likely to fail in their efforts to master English. If you have time enough to write down English-to-Japanese translations, make far better use of it by repeatedly reciting and inscribing in your mind the English sentences you find worth translating. It is the accumulated memories of English in your head, not the mountains of dirty notebooks you painstakingly produced, that will enable you to command English in the end. Never indulge in disoriented diligence, which is the worst suicidal cause of linguistic impasse.

を材料にして「日本語の文章の創造」を行なう。英語原文を材料にして「日本語訳を作る」のではなく、英語原文に触発されて彼らが脳内に抱くこととなった想念を表現するに相応しい「日本語の文章を全く新たに創る」、という点に注目してほしい。彼らは文章を「翻訳」しているのではなく「創造」しているのである。このタイプの「創造的翻訳」技能の発展が見込めるのは、2つの原則をしっかり守った場合のみである；即ち(1)英文の意味の把握は、日本語翻訳を通してではなく解剖学的解釈を通して行なうこと；(2)出会った任意の英文の意味を表わすのに相応しい様々な表現を常に考え続け、何か一つの日本語訳にだけ(あたかもそれが唯一無二の公認版であるかのごとく)すがりつくことはしないこと。

そのためには、日本語に翻訳した文章は、ノートではなく脳内に刻み込むことだ。何かをひとたび書き留めたなら、その翻訳だけに縛られてしまいがちだから、それ以外の(ひょっとしたらもっと良い)翻訳を思い付く可能性を阻害してしまうことになる。何であれ任意の答えを書き込むことで、諸君は、それ以上考えることをしなくなってしまうものである。答えを書き込む目的はただ一つ、その答えを思い付いたまさにその瞬間の諸君がたまたま正しかったか否かを確認するためだけであって、そんなことは当然、ひとたび確認してしまったその後では、諸君にとってどうでもよいことである。そんな個人的思い出を書き込むことで教科書やノートを汚くするのはやめることだ・・・「遠い昔の自分の個人的奮闘の懐かしい記憶を、何年も経ったその後で、愛着をもって眺めること」が諸君の主目的だというのなら話は別であるが、もしそうならば、その遠い未来の諸君はたぶん、「英語を習得すること」という諸君本来の願いには、既に挫折している公算が(そんな「忘れられないほど無益な労力」を遙かに惜しんだ場合に比して)高いだろう。

まとめてみよう:「解釈」と「翻訳」とは別物であって、両者のうちでは前者の重要性が後者を遙かに上回る。山ほど大量の翻訳文を作って満足するタイプの学生は、英語を修得しようと頑張ってみても、失敗する公算が極めて高い。英和翻訳文を書き出す時間があったら、翻訳に値すると感じる英文を繰り返し繰り返し暗誦して自分の脳内に刻み込むことで、その時間をより有効に活用することだ。最後の最後に英語をモノに出来るようにしてくれるのは、諸君の頭の中に暗記した英語の堆積物であって、大変な思いをしながら作成した小汚いノートの山ではないのだ。方向音痴な勤勉さに酔い痴れるような真似は絶対にしてはならない・・・それこそ、語学で行き詰まる最低最悪の自滅的原因となるのだから。

- The delight in getting over the boundary of word-for-word translation by paraphrasing... ought not to be enjoyed too much -

One of the questions many Japanese college-bound students have regarding the ways of translation is “Which is better, ‘直訳(CHOKUYAKU: a literal translation) ’ or ‘意訳(IYAKU: a paraphrase) ’”, to which the answer is simple: “What you find it impossible to translate word for word, you must paraphrase, otherwise, try to make as literal and meaningful a translation as you can out of the original English expression”.

For example, when you see “an enticing woman”, you should write “魅力的な女性(MIRYOKUTEKI NA JOSEI)” instead of “イケてる女(IKETERU ONNNA)”, in order to avoid making an impression that you escaped into the vague expression “イケてる(IKETERU)” just because you happened to be ignorant of the exact meaning of “enticing” meaning “attractive, charming, enchanting”. Remember that teachers and examiners are always doubtful of your ability to exactly understand English and suspicious of your motive for trying to get away with it by equivocation. When you have clearly understood something, make your wording as clear as your head: when you haven't, just equivocate and hope others will misunderstand you for the better.

On the other hand, there are many English expressions which defy word-for-word translation into Japanese. Such ones as “Many thanks” should not of course be literally translated into “いくつもいくつもありがとう(IKUTSU MO IKUTSU MO ARIGATOU)” or rendered as though Chinese into “多謝(TASHA)” but ought to be “ほんと、どうもありがとう(HONTO, DOUMO ARIGATOU)”. Since it is less than formal as a way of expressing gratitude, it must not be rendered too courteously like “幾重にも御礼申し上げます(IKUE NIMO ONREI MOUSHIAGEMASU)”. But this “Many thanks” is nothing difficult, since the term “thanks” is eloquent enough in telling Japanese it is an emphatic version of “Thank you”.

What definitely requires paraphrasing is English expressions for which suitable Japanese do exist but will never come out of literal translating efforts. Take a glimpse at the following English dialogues to detect expressions never to be literally translated and see if you can instantly hit upon their Japanese equivalents:

ー「逐語訳」の限界を「意訳」で乗り越える愉悦・・・を、あまりいい気になって満喫するべからずー

「翻訳」に関し、日本の多くの大学受験生が抱く疑問の一つは「直訳と意訳のどちらがよいか」というものであるが、それへの回答は単純で、「一字一句移し替える形で翻訳するのは不可能だと感じるものは、別表現での言い換えを通してその意味が通じるように訳せ;それ以外の場合は、元になった英語表現を材料に、可能な限り逐語的で意味が通じる翻訳文を作るよう試みよ」ということになる。

例えば、“an enticing woman”という表現を見たら、“イケてる女”などとはせずに“魅力的な女性”と訳すことである。「“attractive, charming, enchanting:魅力的な”を意味する“enticing”の語義をたまたま知らなかったから、“イケてる”という曖昧な表現に逃げ込んだだけだな、コイツは」という印象を与えることがないように、ベタな直訳を心がけるべきなのだ。先生や出題者はいつだって諸君の正確な英語理解能力に疑問を抱き、「正確に理解できない難点を曖昧な言い逃れで何とかしようとしているんじゃないのかコイツは?」と疑っている、という事実を忘れてはならない。何かを明瞭に理解できたその暁には、諸君の頭脳同様、言葉使いも明瞭にしておくことだ・・・明瞭な理解がままならぬ時にだけ、とりあえずボカした言い回しに逃げ込んで、他人がその曖昧さを良い方に「誤解」してくれるのを期待することだ。

さて、その一方で、日本語へと一語一語直訳することが出来ない英語の表現も沢山ある。“Many thanks”みたいな表現ならば当然、これを逐語訳して“いくつもいくつもありがとう”としたり、まるで中国語みたいに“多謝”としたりせずに、“ほんと、どうもありがとう”とするのが妥当である。この“Many thanks”は感謝の言い回しとしてはくだけたものなので、あまりにも丁重に“幾重にも御礼申し上げます”などとしてはならない。が、“thanks”という語が、この“Many thanks”が“Thank you:サンキュー”の強調版であることを日本人に対して雄弁に物語っている以上、この“Many thanks”はちっとも難しい表現ではない。

どうしても意訳が必要になるのは、「その意味を表わすのに相応しい日本語は存在するが、直訳努力の末に出て来るものではない」というタイプの英語の表現である。以下に示す英語の対話をチラと見て、逐語的翻訳は絶対に無理な表現はどれかを言い当て、その意味を表わすに相応の日本語表現が即座に思い浮かぶかどうか、試してみてほしい:

*(FATHER)"Hey, son, you must study as hard as you can while you are a student." – (MOTHER) "Look who's talking!"
*(A FOREIGNER) "I wonder why the Japanese are so laughably inept at speaking English... No offense." – (A JAPANESE) "None taken."
*(MAN A) "I heard Jack had a crush on Betty." – (MAN B) "Speak of the devil..."
*(THE COMMANDER) "There will be no attack from the enemy in this rough weather." – (A WARRIOR) "With all due respect, sir, I believe we must be more careful."
*(WIFE) "Take the highway? Hey, this nav system has no idea how congested it can be at this time of day! Bypath is by far the fastest way, what do you say?" – (HUSBAND) "You are the teacher."
*(WIFE) "It seems we've got lost. The nav map says we are in the middle of nowhere. I believe we have to go back the way we came here. Do you have any better idea?" – (HUSBAND) "Your guess is as good as mine."

The following are the answers to what expressions require paraphrasing instead of literal translations, which sound totally absurd in those contexts:
*"Look who's talking!:あらまぁ、よく言うわねぇ、自分の子供時代は棚上げにして・・・" ng.誰が喋っているのか見てごらんなさい
*"No offense [against you is intended by my comment].:気ぃ悪くしないでね" ng.これは攻撃ではない — "None(=No offense) [was] taken [by me at your comment].:べつに気にしてないさ" ng.何も取られたものはない

*(FATHER) "Hey, son, you must study as hard as you can while you are a student." — (MOTHER) "Look who's talking!"
*(A FOREIGNER) "I wonder why the Japanese are so laughably inept at speaking English... No offense." — (A JAPANESE) "None taken."
*(MAN A) "I heard Jack had a crush on Betty." — (MAN B) "Speak of the devil..."
*(THE COMMANDER) "There will be no attack from the enemy in this rough weather." — (A WARRIOR) "With all due respect, sir, I believe we must be more careful."
*(WIFE) "Take the highway? Hey, this nav system has no idea how congested it can be at this time of day! Bypath is by far the fastest way, what do you say?" — (HUSBAND) "You are the teacher."
*(WIFE) "It seems we've got lost. The nav map says we are in the middle of nowhere. I believe we have to go back the way we came here. Do you have any better idea?" — (HUSBAND) "Your guess is as good as mine."

翻訳:
(父)"いいか、息子よ、学生時代は死に物狂いで勉強しないとダメなんだぞ"ー(母)"おやおや、自分の学生時代は棚上げにして、ずいぶんと大層なこと言ってるわね"
(外国人)"どうして日本人が英語喋るとこう笑っちゃうほどダメダメなんだろ・・・ぁ、ごめん、気悪くしたら、許してね"ー(日本人)"べつに、平気ですよ"
(男A)"ジャックがベティに寅さんボレした(=熱烈に入れ込んだ挙げ句、フラれた)って聞いたぜ"ー(男B)"おっと、噂をすれば何とやら、御当人の登場だ"
(司令官)"この荒天の中では敵襲もあるまい"ー(兵士)"恐れながら申し上げます、閣下、我々にはより慎重な用心が必要であります"
(妻)"「国道に入れ」ですって？　ちょっとぉ、この時間帯の国道がどれぐらい混雑すると思ってるの、このカーナビ全然わかってないわ！　抜け道通るのが断然速いわよ、ねぇあなたどう思う？"ー(夫)"はいはい、あなたの仰せに従いましょ"
(妻)"あたしたちどうやら道に迷っちゃったみたい。カーナビの地図ではどこことも知れぬ原野のど真ん中だし。ここまで来た道を引き返すしかなさそう。他に何かいい考えある？"ー(夫)"俺だってお手上げ、妙案なんて何もないさ"

「逐語訳ではなく意訳が必要な表現はどれか」に対する答えは以下の通りで、直訳してもこの文脈ではまるで間抜けた響きになってしまう:
*"Look who's talking!:あらまぁ、よく言うわねぇ、自分の子供時代は棚上げにして・・・"（×)誰が喋っているのか見てごらんなさい
*"No offense [against you is intended by my comment].:気ぃ悪くしないでね"（×)これは攻撃ではない — "None(=No offense) [was] taken [by me at your comment].:べつに気にしてないさ"（×)何も取られたものはない

*"Speak of the devil [and he will appear]...:おやおや、噂をすれば影、ご当人がおいでなすったよ" ng.悪魔の話をしなさい
*"With all due respect:お言葉を返すようですが" ng.十分な敬意の全てを伴いつつ
*"You are the teacher.:わかったよ、君の言う通りにするよ" ng.あなたは先生です
*"Your guess is as good as mine.:俺に聞かれてもわかるもんか" ng.あなたの推量は私の推量と同じぐらい正しい

What is troublesome with the above-mentioned expressions is that there seems to be nothing out of the ordinary about them, but when literally translated, they will fail you miserably. A sentence like "Jack had a crush on Betty" is impossible to translate until one has consulted a dictionary to confirm the meaning of the idiom "to have a crush on someone" as "to fall desperately in love with someone (often meaning a one-sided love ending up broken-hearted)". Such apparently strange combination of words are all the less troublesome for looking suspicious: none but the novice will fail to detect the idiom inside and to come up with the correct translation with the help of a dictionary. It takes nothing but diligence in consulting a dictionary to deal with such obviously idiomatic expressions, while it takes much more sensitivity to see something strange with seemingly plain expressions like "You are the teacher" and hit upon suitable Japanese expressions which are totally different in form but similar in meaning.

Here is a warning to Japanese learners of English regarding such expressions as "You're the teacher" or "Look who's talking": never take pride in your knowledge of them or try to employ those expressions to prove your superiority to those who happen to be ignorant of them. One of the most laughable (indeed, abominable!) propensities of the Japanese who are actually illiterate in English language is to try to look much smarter than their linguistic ability should warrant by referring to foreign terms and expressions which are supposedly beyond comprehension of other Japanese. Rather than try to increase the store of such "esoteric" expressions, make much more painful yet fruitful efforts to acquaint yourself with the usage of prepositions by way of enriching "normal" stocks of English idioms and collocations; be it also remembered that you can't hope to be wiser by making fools of others.

*“Speak of the devil [and he will appear]…:おやおゃ、噂をすれば影、ご当人がおいでなすったよ” (×)悪魔の話をしなさい
*“With all due respect:お言葉を返すようですが” (×)十分な敬意の全てを伴いつつ
*“You are the teacher.:わかったよ、君の言う通りにするよ” (×)あなたは先生です
*“Your guess is as good as mine.:俺に聞かれてもわかるもんか” (×)あなたの推量は私の推量と同じぐらい正しい

上記の言い回しの困った点は、一見すると何一つ変わったところもなさそうなのに、文字通りに直訳すると惨めな失敗に終わる点である。“Jack had a crush on Betty.:ジャックがベティ相手に crush を演じた”みたいな文章の場合、“to have a crush on someone:誰かに対してcrushする”なる熟語の意味を辞書で引いて“to fall desperately in love with someone (often meaning a one-sided love ending up broken-hearted):誰かをたまらないほど好きになる(最後には失恋に終わる片思いを意味する場合が多い)”と確認するまでは、翻訳のしようがない。こうした「見るからに違和感漂う語句の組み合わせ表現」は、それが怪しく見える分だけ厄介は少ない:初心者でなければ誰でも、その表現の中に熟語が含まれることを見抜き、辞書の助けを得て正しい翻訳に辿り着くことができるだろうから。こうした「明らかに熟語的な表現」に対処するのに必要なのは、辞書引きの勤勉さだけである;一方、“You are the teacher:君は先生”みたいな「一見平明な表現」に違和感を覚え、形は全く違うが意味は似ている日本語の似つかわしい表現を思い浮かべるためには、単なる辞書引き作業よりずっと繊細な感受性が必要になる。

ここで、“You're the teacher.:はいはい、仰せのままに”だの“Look who's talking.:よく言うよ！”だのの言い回しに関して、日本の英語学習者諸君に一言警告申し上げておく:こういう言い回しを自分が知っているからと言って、決してうぬぼれてはならないし、たまたまそれを知らない他の人達に対する自らの優越性の証明のためにこういう言い回しを用いようとしてはならない。本当は英語の読み書きもまるで出来ない日本人が、外国の単語や言い回し(それも、他の日本人には理解できまいと思われるやつ)を引き合いに出すことで、自身の語学力の水準を不当なまでに上回る賢い人物っぽく振る舞おうとするあの度し難い体質は、嘲笑を誘う(どころか、吐き捨てたいほどに汚らわしい！)日本人体質の最たるものだ。そんな“エソテリック＝排他的に難解な”言い回しの品揃えをせっせと増やすようなマネはやめて、もっと遙かに骨が折れるが実りも大きい努力ー英熟語とコロケーション(連語関係)の“ノーマル＝ふつうの”知識を増やすことを通じて前置詞の用例に習熟することーへと向かうべきである・・・そしてまた覚えておくことだ:他人を小馬鹿にすることで自分が賢くなれるわけではないということを。

http://zubaraie.com/denglenglish ←Be sure to check!

Well, that's about it. Stick to literal translation whenever you can. Although paraphrasing looks enticing to those who want to look smart, they'll just make smart asses of themselves by the abuse of it.

さて、と、だいたいこんなところでよいだろう。逐語訳できる場面では常に一字一句文字通りに訳す態度を貫くことだ。傍目にカッコ良く見せたがる体質の人間にとっては「意訳」が魅惑的に映るものだが、意訳の乱用は「かしこブリっこの馬鹿野郎」としての自分を演出するばかりである。

15. Input before output — 英借文:EI“SHAKU”BUN rather than 英作文:EI“SAKU”BUN; English recitation rather than J-to-E translation

- Good output is only possible through considerable amount and quality of input -

The Internet has brought about “information explosion”. Until the middle of the 1990s, the detestable flow of worthless information prevailing in the world through mass media had been lamented upon with a disdainful though manageable phrase of “floods of information”. Now that computer technology has made it possible for everyone with access to the Internet to play the role of “personal media”, the amount of information drowning the Net has lethally increased, while the overall quality of info thus thrust upon mankind has even more murderously degraded to the level of a global farce.

The most abominable thing about numberless (and worthless) “personal” media is the way they “output” whatever they “input” without due process of consideration or accumulation, let alone any added value of their own. Simply speaking, they are mere echoes of someone else and harmful noises to be consciously avoided for intelligent humans to filter out something really important. If the truth were told, such worthless things might as well not exist at all: they are absolutely no good except for the mediocrity's vain self-satisfaction of making their presence felt (possibly to the world!) and for profit-pursuing vultures to take easy advantage of the riffle effect in the echoing mouths of such noisy omnipresent folks in order to promote their sales.

Still, explosive amount of worthless and shameless words do exist and surround humans on the Net... such is the reality of this planet at the beginning of the twenty-first century. In order to survive in this mostly useless info-explosion, you must avoid “direct output of input” both as a reader and a writer. As a reader, you should see through the shallowness of others who just do or say things they see others do or say. Such worthless echoes are quite easy to see and avoid since they all look essentially the same and no different, and consequently, nothing worth. Words worthy to be read have their own weight born in the process of pondering about the original input and assimilating it to form a wholly new output of their own. This added value is what makes you a uniquely worthy writer in eloquent contrast to swarms of worthless echoes and noises.

15. アウトプットよりまずインプットが大事ー英「作」文より英「借」文;和英翻訳より英文暗誦

ー相当量の上質なインプットあってこそ可能になる良いアウトプットー

インターネットは「情報爆発」をもたらした。1980年代半ばまでは、マスメディアを通じて世の中にはびこる価値もない情報の流れは「情報洪水」として軽蔑調(しかしまだしも制御可能な感じ)で呼ばれたものだった。それが今や、コンピュータ技術のおかげで、インターネットに接続可能な人なら誰もが「個人メディア」の役割を演じることが可能になってしまったのだから、ネットに洪水をもたらす情報量は致死的なまでに増大し、そうして人類の上に押し付けられる情報全体の品質の低下は更にまた殺人的、全地球的規模の笑劇と呼べる水準にまで落ちてしまった。

無数の(そして無価値な)「個人」メディアの最も嫌なところは、「インプット:外から取り入れた何か」の全てを、然るべき考慮や蓄積(ましていわんや独自の付加価値)も何も伴わぬままに「アウトプット:外に出す」ことである。要するに、他の誰かの単なる「こだま」に過ぎず、知的人間が真に重要な何かをふるいにかけて取り出す上で意識的に回避せねばならぬ有害な「雑音」でしかないのである。本当のことを言ってしまえば、こんな無価値な存在なんて、存在せぬ方がまだマシなのだ。何の役に立つかと言えば、凡庸な連中が自らの存在を(あわよくば全世界に!)知らしめたいという空疎な自己満足と、そうしてくそやかましい雑音まき散らしながらありとあらゆる場所に存在する大衆の口で繰り返しくりかえしこだまさせることで生じる波及効果を安直に利用して私利私欲のために他者を食い物にする連中が売り上げ増進を図る効用だけ、それ以外にはまったく何の役にも立たないのだから。

それでもなお、無価値で恥知らずな言葉の数々は、ネットの世界に爆発的分量で存在し、人類を取り巻いている・・・それが、21世紀初頭に於けるこの惑星の現実なのである。この(大部分は役立たずの)情報爆発の中で生き残るために、諸君は、読み手としても書き手としても、「インプット内容の即席アウトプット」は避けてかかる必要がある。読者の立場で言えば、他人の行動や発言を見てそっくりそのままの行動・発言を繰り返すだけの連中の浅薄さを見抜くことが必要。そうした価値なきこだまは見抜くのも避けるのも至極簡単である:なにせ、どれもこれもみな本質的に同じ姿でちっとも違いが見えず、当然、何の価値もないのだから。読むべき価値ある言葉なら、最初にインプットされた内容について熟慮しこれを自らの一部として同化した末に自分独自の全く新たなアウトプットを形成する過程で生じる、独特の重みを持っているものである。この付加価値こそが、無数の無価値なこだまや雑音と雄弁な対比を成す形で、独自な価値を持った書き手としての諸君を際立たせてくれるのだ。

The above-mentioned opinion of this author refers mainly to contents (or lack of contents) of the output, but the same thing can also be said about the form of the output: good output (well-written sentences of your own) is only possible after you have absorbed and assimilated considerable amount of good input (example sentences). Easy output given away as an instant, poorly digested imitation of some input is lacking in beauty in shape as well as devoid of unique value or personality.

After all, people of authentic taste will simply ignore linguistically distasteful sentences, however unique or charming their authors may believe themselves to be. Uniqueness or charm can only stand out on the basis of good language. No amount of poorly written English on the Net will make bad English any less distasteful. In this global explosion of less-than-fascinating English, your chance to stand out with well-written English as a beautiful swan in the midst of forever ugly ducklings is all-time-high in the history of this language and will ever be on the rise as noisy echoes ever increase on the Net. You should not only try to read English with freedom; you might as well aspire to speak and write English with finesse enough for others to want to take notice of you.

- EISAKUBUN – English composition by Japanese students must not be made as a translation but as a rendition: create English of your own inspired by the original Japanese sentences -

As regards EISAKUBUN(English composition) by Japanese learners, this author feels he cannot overemphasize the danger of jumping to poor output before being enriched with good input. The author has said in the previous section that a good translation from English into Japanese is not "transplanted literally from the original sentence" but "created out of the mind's image of the translator inspired by the original sentence": the same or even more can be said about Japanese-to-English translation.

You must not try to make English composition the way you will make a model plane, putting together small parts made to resemble the original airplane... you can't hope to fly that way in the skies of English. Instead, you should picture to yourself what the airplane is like, grasping and re-modeling the essence of the original in your mental image, and then finally give shape to your idea of the original in terms of English. You must not simply

筆者が上で述べた意見は、主としてアウトプットの「中身」(というか「中身」のなさというか)に言及したものであるが、同じ事はまたアウトプットの「カタ(型)」についても言える:良いアウトプット(＝上手に書かれた諸君自身の文章)は、良いインプット(例文)を相当量吸収・同化した後で始めて可能になるものだ。何らかのインプットがあった途端に未消化のままこれをモノマネして吐き出す安直なアウトプットは、独自の価値も個性もないばかりか、見た目もまた美しくない。

結局、本物を見分ける目を持った人々は、言葉として見て不快な文章なんて(たとえその作者が自分自身のことをどれほどユニークで魅力的な存在だと思い込んでいても)ひたすら無視して見向きもしないものである。ユニークさや魅力は、良い言葉の土台があって初めて際立つものである。無様に書かれた英語の数々がネット上にいかに溢れ返ろうとも、ダメ英語の不快さがその分薄らぐわけでもない。何の魅力もない英文が地球的規模で爆発的に増大するこの状況下にあって、諸君が良質な英語を書くことで(永遠に醜いままのアヒルの子の真っ只中で美しい白鳥が際立つがごとく)ひときわ抜きん出るチャンスは、英語という言語の歴史始まって以来最高の水準にあり、ネット上でやかましいばかりのこだまが増大の一途をたどると共に、今後も常にそのチャンスは増え続けることであろう。英語が自由に「読める」水準を目指すだけでは物足りない;どうせなら、他の人達が諸君に注目したくなるぐらいに洗練された水準の英語を、自ら「話したり書いたりできる」境地をも同時に目指してみるのがよいであろう。

ー「英作文」は「翻訳」ではなく「翻案」として、日本語原文に触発された諸君独自の英文として創造するべしー

日本人学習者による「英作文」に関しては、筆者としては「良いインプットによる充実を待たずして貧弱なアウトプットに飛び付くことがいかに危険であるか」をいくら強調しても足りない思いである。前項で筆者は「良質な英和翻訳は“原文から一文字一文字移植”する形ではなく、“原文に触発された翻訳者の心内イメージを材料に創出”されるものである」と書いたが、同じこと(どころかそれ以上のこと)が和英翻訳に関しても言えるのである。

英作文を、模型飛行機を作るみたいな感じで作ってはならない。元々の飛行機に似せた形で作られた小さな部品を寄せ集めて組み立てるやり方では、英語世界の空を飛ぶことは出来ないのだ。そうではなくて、「飛行機とはどういうものか」について自分なりの姿を思い描き、原物の本質に関する自らの心的イメージをしっかり捉えてから再度具体的な形に構成し直した上で、その原物に関する諸君の想念に、最終的な「カタチ」を英語の言葉で与えてやるのが、正しいやり方である。日本語原文をそれに対応

transplant the original Japanese to corresponding terms in English. Catch hold of the whole idea of the original Japanese (which someone else has written for you to translate), and try to make that idea known to others in your own words in English, as if the idea sprang up from within yourself.

In trying to perform that kind of "creative" J-to-E translation, which has been wittedly called "英借文(EISHAKUBUN: borrowed expressions from English)" as opposed to "英作文(EISAKUBUN: forged English)", you have need of abundant stores of English terms and expressions, to say nothing of perfect grammatical knowledge. Without such good input, good output is impossible. Bad output might be better than none, to be sure, but why should you rest contented with bad output when good output is guaranteed by a certain amount of systematically accumulated & assimilated input?

- Recite before write -

The practical advice for learners in Japan is, "while a novice, make no attempt at English composition, but simply stick to English recitation". There are so many "terms" and "idioms" in the world of English that you cannot wait until the input is ripe within you regarding these two realms. Unknown words or idiomatic expressions can be found out simply by looking them up in the dictionary; besides, English language is so rich in synonymous expressions that you are sure to come up with some suitable terms or idioms by consulting a good dictionary with reasonable Thesaurus(lists of synonyms) assistance. The realms in which patience (and perfection!) is required until you get sufficiently rich in input are "sentence patterns (SPAT-5)", "semantic constructions" and "grammar". Words and idioms can be rather awkwardly used without much practical hindrance to the meaning or serious harm to your honor, but grammatical errors and structural shortcomings cannot escape unpunished in the severe eyes of self-respecting citizens of the English-speaking world.

The desirable kind of "英借文(borrowed English)" practice should develop around some particular "カタ(KATA: form)" as a focus of creative attention. In other words, it must function as a test to see whether some particular pattern of "SPAT-5", "semantic construction" or "grammar" has been successfully mastered by a student. The following are examples of such dual function questions of "EISHAKUBUN":

する英単語へと単純に移し替えたりしてはならない。(他の誰かが諸君に翻訳させるために書いた)元々の日本文の表わす概念の全体像をつかんだ上で、あたかもその概念が諸君自身の中から沸き上がったものであるかの如く、英語の言葉でその概念を他者に知らしめるべく努めるのである。

その種の「創造的な」和英翻訳－「英作文＝英文の捏造(ねつぞう)」と対照する形で「英借文＝英語からの借り物表現」という機知に富んだ呼ばれ方をしてきた翻訳の作法－を遂行するためには、英語の単語や言い回しのストック(脳内在庫)を豊富にしておく必要があるし、完璧な文法的知識が必要なのも言うまでもない。そうした良質なインプットなしには、良質なアウトプットは望めない。「ダメなアウトプットでも何も言わないよりはマシ」と言えなくもないけれど、体系的に蓄積・吸収された一定量のインプットさえあれば良質なアウトプットが約束されるというのに、貧弱なアウトプットに甘んじるべき理由はあるまい？

－「書く」よりもまず「暗誦」が必要－

日本の学習者に対する現実的な助言は、「初学者の間は、英作文など試みず、英文暗誦のみに徹すべし」ということになる。英語の世界にはあまりにも多くの「単語」や「熟語」があるから、これら2つの領域に関しては、諸君の中での熟成を待っているわけにも行かない。未知の単語や熟語的表現は、辞書を引きさえすれば見つけ出すことが出来る。そのうえまた英語は、類似の言い回しが実に豊富な言語なのだから、それなりのシソーラス(類義語リスト)で諸君を手助けしてくれる良質な辞書におうかがいを立てれば、それ相応の単語や熟語に巡り会えることは確実である。十分豊富なインプットが得られるまで忍耐(＋完璧性！)が求められる領域は、「文型:sentence patterns (SPAT-5)」「構文:semantic constructions」「文法:grammar」である。「単語(words)」と「熟語(idioms)」の場合は、多少ぎこちない使い方をしても、意味の伝達に現実的支障を来たすことはさほどないし、諸君の名誉を著しく傷付けることもないであろうが、文法の間違いや欠陥ある文章構造を英語世界のまともな住人たちの厳しい鑑識眼の目の前にさらけ出してしまえば、おとがめなしでは済まないものである。

「英借文(英語からの借り物表現)」の練習としては、創造的注目の焦点となる何か特定の「カタ(form)」を中心に展開するような設問が望ましい。言葉を換えて言えば、何か特定の「SPAT-5(5文型)」・「意味別構文」・「文法」のパターンを学生がしっかり修得したか否かをテストする役割をも同時に果たすものでなければならない、ということである。以下に示すのは、そうした二重の働きを演じる「英借文」の設問たちの実例である:

SPAT-5-I:"あなた、クサイわよ(ANATA, KUSAIWAYO)" — "汗、そうとう掻いたからなぁ(ASE, SOUTOU KAITA KARANAA)"
"You stink." – "I sweated so much."
SPAT-5-II & COMPARISON & ELLIPSIS: "あれ、僕、遅刻した？(ARE, BOKU, CHIKOKU SHITA?)" — "いいえ、私が5分早かったの(IIE, WATASHI GA GOFUN HAYAKATTA NO)"
"Well, am I late?" – "No, I was five minutes earlier [than the appointed time]."
SPAT-5-III: "イタメシ好き？(ITAMESHI SUKI?)" — "大好物よ(DAI-KOUBUTSU YO)"
"Do you like Italian food?" – "Yes, I love it very much."
SPAT-5-IV & GRAMMAR(TAG-QUESTION): "おっと、ピザ食うとオナラが出るなぁ(OTTO, PIZA KUU TO ONARA GA DERUNAA)" — "ちょっと、いい加減にしてくれる？(CHOTTO, IIKAGEN NI SHITE KURERU?)"
"Oops! Pizza gives me farts." – "Give me a break, will you?"
SPAT-5-V: "君といると緊張するよ(KIMI TO IRUTO KINCHOU SURUYO)" — "あなたと一緒だと、私、恥ずかしいわ(ANATA TO ISSHO DATO WATASHI HAZUKASHIIWA)"
"You make me nervous." – "You make me ashamed."

Fortunately or unfortunately, there are so many English example sentences to learn by heart before conquering the relatively limited spheres (as compared to "words" and "idioms", that is) of "sentence patterns", "semantic constructions" and "grammar" that novice learners will never be in want of good input before they are finally at liberty to turn out their own output. Since such input as they find in English textbooks for them to master something grammatically important are more likely to be good English than bad, systematic accumulation and assimilation of such good input will hardly fail to enable them to produce good output... after several years of intensive memorizing process.

Never make haste. While you are in such an "input" period, don't you ever try to say anything "in your own words": anything said in your own words are most likely to be too bad to make any sense in English. Instead, try to say anything "in someone else's words": you must attempt to memorize and

SPAT-5-I:「あなた、クサイわよ」―「汗、そうとう掻いたからなぁ」

“You stink.” ― “I sweat[ed] so much.”

SPAT-5-II & COMPARISON(比較) & ELLIPSIS(省略):「あれ、僕、遅刻した？」―「いいえ、私が5分早かったの」

“Well, am I late?” ― “No, I was five minutes earlier [than the appointed time].”

SPAT-5-III:「イタメシ好き？」―「大好物よ」

“Do you like Italian food?” ― “Yes, I love it very much.”

SPAT-5-IV & GRAMMAR(付加疑問文:TAG-QUESTION):「おっと、ピザ食うとオナラが出るなぁ」―「ちょっと、いい加減にしてくれる？」

“Oops! Pizza gives me farts.” ― “Give me a break, will you?”

SPAT-5-V:「君といると緊張するよ」―「あなたと一緒だと、私、恥ずかしいわ」

“You make me nervous.” ― “You make me ashamed.”

幸か不幸か、“文型”・“構文”・“文法”といった比較的狭い領域(“単語”や“熟語”に比べれば、の話だが)を制覇するまでに暗記すべき英語例文の数は実に膨大なので、初学者たちが最終的に自由自在に独自のアウトプットを繰り出すことが出来るようになる前の段階で必要になる「良質なインプット」が足りなくて困る、という事態は、決して起こり得ないはずである。文法的に重要な何かを修得させるために英語の教科書に掲載されたインプットであれば、英文としてはどちらかと言えば良質なものである公算が高いのだから、そうした良質なインプットを体系的に蓄積・同化したならば、諸君は必ずや良質なアウトプットを生み出すことが出来るようになるはずである・・・徹底的に覚え込む過程を数年間経た後で、の話ではあるが。

決して焦ってはならない。こうした「インプット期間」に身を置く間は、「諸君自身の言葉で」何か言おうとはしないことである:諸君自身の言葉で何かを言えば、英語としてはまるでデタラメで意味を成さない公算が高いのだから。そんなことはせずに、何を言うにも「誰かさんの言葉を借りて」言うべく試みるのがよい。良質な英文を可能な限り数多く記憶し正確に暗誦できるよう努力しなければならない。軽い気持ちで挑んではな

exactly recite as many good English sentences as possible. Don't you take it too easy, for 100% accuracy in reciting those sentences is required for you to be finally able to produce good output of what you have stored up in your memory as the final result of such intensive input. In the end, you will be able to express your own idea in "someone else's words" which have been so completely assimilated as to be safely called "your own words" — that's the idea of "英借文(EISHAKUBUN)" as opposed to "英作文(EISAKUBUN)", mechanical transplant of Japanese terms into English.

- Incorrect pronunciation disrupts your English -

English is a language meant to be spoken, not to be read in silence, which differentiates it drastically from Japanese language composed mostly of "漢字(KANJI: Chinese characters)". A Chinese character is an ideogram signifying something by its figure, the meaning of which is so clear to the eye (just like icons on the computer screen) that Japanese people are inclined toward silent reading (or rather viewing) of sentences without reading aloud: they tend to depend on visual rather than audible clues to understanding. On the other hand, English is composed of phonograms called "alphabets" meaning nothing but sound in themselves, each of which has to combine with some other in order to convey any meaning (except for such terms as "a = an indefinite article", "I = a singular pronoun in the first person", "o = an exclamation"). Comprehension through silent reading is also possible with English, of course, but memorization and appreciation of English is hardly possible, at least imperfect, without reading aloud.

What is uniquely strange about Japanese language is its lack of attention or respect to spoken sound or traditional usage and meaning of any given term. There are so many Japanese words written in "uniquely strange combination" of Chinese characters that it is practically impossible to correctly read them aloud unless you ask someone who uses them (eg. "大和") for the correct pronunciation (eg. "やまと:YAMATO" or "だいわ:DAIWA"). The same term can be pronounced differently as the case may be, and there is absolutely no general rule of their correct pronunciation: that there is no general rule is the only golden rule of Japanese pronunciation.

らない・・・そうした徹底的インプットの最終成果として諸君の記憶にストックされた物事を「良質なアウトプット」としてようやく創出できるようになるためには、覚え込んだ文章は100％正確な形で暗誦できなければダメなのだから。最後の最後には、諸君の中で既にもう完璧なまでに同化されているがゆえに「自分自身の言葉」と呼んでも差し支えない水準に達している「誰かさんの言葉」を借りて、諸君自身の考えを表現することが出来るようになっていることだろうーそれこそが、（日本語から英語への機械的移植作業としての）「英作文」とは別物としての「英借文」の姿である。

ー不正確な発音は、諸君の英語を台無しにするー

英語は「話す」ための言語であって、「黙読する」ための言語ではない。この点に於いて英語は、大部分「漢字(Chinese characters)」より成る日本語とは劇的に異なる。漢字は「表意文字(an ideogram)」であり、その形象によって何らかの意味を表象するものであって、その表わす意味は（ちょうどコンピュータ画面上のアイコンのように）目で見てはっきりわかるものだから、日本の人々は、文章を音読せずに黙読する（というか、目で見て了解する）状態へと傾きがちである。日本人は、耳で聞いて理解するよりも目で見た何かを手掛かりに理解する傾向が強いのだ。これに対し、英語は「アルファベット(alphabets)」という「表音文字(phonograms)」から構成されている。アルファベットそれ自体は「音声」以外の何の意味も表わさず、何らかの意味を伝えるには他のアルファベットと結び付いてグループを形成する必要がある（例外として、“a:1つの ＝ an indefinite article:不定冠詞”、“I:私 ＝ a singular pronoun in the first person:一人称単数代名詞”、“o:おぉ ＝ an exclamation:感嘆表現”といった語はあるが）。黙読による理解は英語の場合でも当然可能ではあるが、英語の暗記と鑑賞は、音読抜きではほとんど不可能（少なくとも不完全）である。

他の言語とは違う日本語ならではの不思議なところは、任意の単語の発音やその伝統的用法・意味に対して、注意も敬意も払わない言語である、という点である。漢字の「独自で特異な組み合わせ」により表記される日本語の数は実に膨大だから、そうした日本語（例えば“大和”）を使っている相手に対して「正しい読み方（“やまと”なのか、それとも“だいわ”なのか）」を聞いて確かめてみないことには、正確な発音など実際問題として不可能である。同じ単語でも場合に応じて発音の仕方が変わる場合がある上に、その正しい読み方の一般原則など全く何一つ存在しないのだ：「一般原則など存在しない」というのが日本語の発音に関する唯一の鉄則なのである。「伝統的に正し

Since very few Japanese pay homage to "traditionally correct" pronunciations (eg. "CHOUFUKU" for "重複"), "formerly incorrect" ones (eg. "重複" read as "JUUFUKU") will come to claim their place in the practically lawless world of Japanese pronunciation, which makes it more and more difficult for anyone to "correctly read aloud" Japanese sentences. And, remember — Japanese sentences composed mostly of visually comprehensible Chinese characters are quite fit for silent reading without pronouncing anything... as a result, Japanese learners of English, just like in their mother tongue, make too little of English pronunciation for them to be able to correctly speak English, to appreciate English as they read aloud, and to memorize English sentences as phonetic entities stored in their memory in the form of actually spoken language. In logical consequence, the Japanese in general are lethally poor at remembering English sentences, meaning, of course, that they can never hope to master this language, which is made to be spoken, not to be seen.

Let this be a sermon, Japanese fellows, that silently looking at English will take you nowhere — read aloud and memorize as many good English sentences as you can, and the sound of living English reviving from your memory will guide you in the right direction, enabling you to speak in "someone else's words" you have securely made "your own" through years of practice and innumerable recitation. If you still insist on English composition "in your words" even before you are sufficiently rich in mental stores of good example sentences, do me a favor and try reading the English you wrote in "your own words" aloud... sounds good? Congratulations (though I doubt it)! Sounds terrible? Have second thoughts about rushing into bad output before adequate input. You may be allowed to compose Japanese sentences any way you want without regard to general rules of correctness in sound or usage, but English is much more rigid in that regard. Don't forget that the test of good English is in the reading aloud; those who won't even think about reading aloud will never pass any test. Good input of English kept alive in your head by good pronunciation and vivid memory will never fail to make you a good reader/writer/speaker/listener of English.

い」発音(例えば“重複”を“ちょうふく”と読む作法)に敬意を表する日本人の数はごくごく僅かなので、「かつては間違いだった」発音(例えば“重複”を“じゅうふく”と読む作法)もまた、実質的に無法状態の日本語発音の世界の中に独自の地歩を主張するようになってきて、それがまた日本語の文章を「正しく音読」することをますます一層困難にするのである。そしてまた、思い出してほしいー見た目でわかる「漢字」を主たる構成要素として成り立つ日本語の文章は、何一つ発音せずに黙読するのに極めて好都合な言語なのだ・・・その結果、日本人英語学習者は(彼らの母国語の場合と全く同様に)英語の発音をあまりにも軽視し過ぎて、英語を正しく話すことができないし、音読しながら英語を味わうこともできないし、実際に口に乗せて語られる言葉として音声学的実体を持った形で脳内にストックされたものとしての英文暗記もまた不可能なのである。その論理的帰結として、大方の日本人は、英文暗記が致命的に不得意であるから、当然のごとく、「見る」のではなく「話す」べき言語であるこの英語というやつを大方の日本人が修得し得る期待は、ゼロ、ということになる。

日本の諸君よ、「英語をただじっと見ているだけではラチが開かない」ということを肝に銘じておきたまえーなるべく多くの良質な英文を音読して覚え込みたまえ、そうすれば、諸君の記憶の中からよみがえる生きた英語の響きが、諸君を正しい方向へと導いて、長年に渡る修練と数限りない暗誦を通して「自分自身の言葉」として確実に根付いた「誰かさんの言葉」を借りて話すことが出来るようになるであろう。それでもなおかつ、諸君が(良質な例文の十分な心内ストックを構築できてもいないうちに)「自分自身の言葉」による「英作文」に固執するというのなら、どうかお願いだから、その「自分自身の言葉」で諸君が書いた「エイゴ」とやらを、試しに音読してごらんなさい・・・「カッコ良く聞こえる」って？ (疑わしいけど)それはどうもおめでとう！・・・「ヒドい響きだ」って？それなら、考えを改めて、十分なインプットが整う前にひどいアウトプットに突進するのはやめたほうがいい。日本語の文章ならば、正しい読み方だの用法だのの一般原則にはお構いなしに、どうにでも自分の好きなように作ってしまっても許されるだろうが、そういう点に関しては英語は遙かに厳正な言語なのである。「良い英語かどうかは、音読してみればわかる」ということをお忘れなく。音読しようとすら考えもしない人々では、最初から試験にパスする道理もない。良質な英語のインプットを、正しい発音と鮮明な記憶によって脳内で生かし続けておくことが出来たなら、諸君は必ずや、英語の読み手／書き手／話し手／聞き手として、一級品になれるはずである。

16. To consult a portable electric dictionary is too tentative to be meaningful: make wise use of a PC-based electric dictionary along with its consulting log

- There is no arguing against the usefulness of electric as opposed to paper dictionaries -

This, the first to second decade of the twenty-first century, is a turning point in human history where paper is about to be replaced by electric means of record. Regardless of what is being said by people sticking to "traditional" means of record and reference, the overwhelming usefulness of "new" media (and consideration for the dwindling resources of paper pulp on this planet) will soon replace all but "luxuriously elaborate" books such as photo albums of famous stars or privately published memoirs of rich old folks.

In Japan, there still exists (and that in abundance) that kind of people who disagree to the use by the novice of electric dictionaries, but their argument seems to be more sentimental than logical, too personal to be reasonable. It seems that they have never had the experience of using electric versions of dictionaries while studying English as beginners. Their early memories of arduous studies are inseparably associated with the image of themselves turning over the pages of paper dictionaries, the emotional value of which seems to induce them to make much less of the possible merits of electric dictionaries.

- A human touch and a mechanical dream -

Since this author had learnt and mastered English before the advent of such handy gadgets as a pocket electric dictionary or a personal computer, he knows very well what a paper dictionary has and an electric one has not — tactile tangibility.

One can physically touch a paper dictionary, turn over the pages and point a finger at the meaning of a word one wants and give a mental shout "Eureka!" The relative position of a certain term on a certain page, the relative position of that page in the whole dictionary, specks or creases on a particular page, even the smell or touch of the paper, all combine to make the experience of looking up a word in a paper dictionary personally significant and memorable. Any additional time one looks up the same term will add to

16. その場限りのポケット版電子辞書参照だけでは意味がない・・・PC版電子辞書を検索履歴込みで賢く活用せよ

－紙辞書に対する電子辞書の有用性に、反論の余地なし－

今この時期、2000年代から2010年代にかけての十年期は、「電子」による記録方法が「紙」に取って代わろうとしている人類史上の転換点である。「伝統的な」記録・参照の手段に固執する人々が(現時点で)何を言おうとも、「新たな」媒体の圧倒的な有用性は(そしてこの惑星上の紙パルプ資源先細りへの配慮が)、有名スターの写真集だの富裕な老人の個人出版回想録だのといった「贅沢に手の込んだ本」以外の全てに取って代わる時が、もうすぐ来るだろう。

日本にはいまだに(それもかなりの数)「初学者が電子辞書を使うこと」に反対する類の人々が存在するが、彼らの言い分は論理的というよりは感情的、個人的思い入れの部分が多すぎて、理性的論拠とは言い難く思われる。どうやら彼らは、英語初心者として学ぶ最中に電子版の辞書を自ら使った経験などまるでないものと見える。彼らが熱心に勉強していた駆け出しの頃の思い出は、紙の辞書をぱらぱらめくる自らの姿と不可分に結び付いており、その心情的価値の大きさゆえに、彼らは電子辞書の秘めたる利点の大きさを思いっきり過小評価したがるもののようである。

－人間的感触と機械のもたらす夢－

この筆者は、ポケット電子辞書やパーソナルコンピュータといった便利な機材の到来以前の時代に英語を学んで身に付けた人間なので、紙の辞書にはあって電子版にはないものをよーく知っているーそれは「触覚的実体感」の違いである。

紙の辞書は、物理的に「触れる」ことができる;ページをパラパラめくった末にお目当ての単語の意味を指さし確認して心の中で「これだっ！」と叫ぶことができる。とある単語がとあるページの中のどのあたりの位置にあるか、そのとあるページが辞書全体の中でどのあたりに位置しているか、とあるページ上についたシミや折れ目、さらには匂いや紙の質感さえもが、すべて渾然一体となって結び付いた末に、「紙の辞書での単語引き」という体験は、個人的に意義深く思い出に残るものとなる。同じ単語を繰り返し

the strangely nostalgic emotion just like meeting an old familiar friend in an alumni association. One feels one gets used to a certain term by repeatedly attending such “old-pal reunions”.

That kind of feeling, something solid directly appealing to the physical senses and even nostalgia of the dictionary user is strangely lacking in an electric dictionary. Consulting an electric dictionary is less like finding a place by walking through a town than making an inquiry of a policeman about some address on a map. It hardly excites physical (let alone emotional) reaction from the inquirer: it just talks coolly to the intelligent spheres of the brains without any tactile tangibility.

You can find a term much more easily and quickly by typing in its spelling from the keyboard than by physically turning over the paper pages of a good old bulky dictionary. Even if you can't spell it correctly, the powerful search function of the electric dictionary will suggest it and guide you straight to the correct answer. Many electric dictionaries are equipped with audio function to show you the correct pronunciation of a certain word without your having to interpret the intangible phonetic signs (Hepburn's Roman Alphabets). You can jump from one term to its synonyms or antonyms to check their differences with a single click. All these dream-like capabilities are performed at your fingertips!... and are strangely NOT memorable like experiences in a dream due to lack of any physical touch. After you wake up, your dream is gone and so is your memory of it. There is nothing physically left of the dream... except for the bed. An electric dictionary is like a bed in which you can have a dream: a paper dictionary is not a bed but a bunch of dreams (nightmares for some, maybe) physically left over for you to revisit whenever you want to touch and feel it.

- Reference and memorization are two different things -

The above is the reason why many of the users of good old paper dictionaries advocate for the use of them instead of their electric counterparts. To sum it up, an electric dictionary is good when it comes to casually checking the meaning of a word but no good as a constant and permanent guide for students to familiarize themselves with words. This argument may seem reasonable to most Japanese, but not to this author, for he knows better than to confuse consultation with memorization of an English word.

引くそのたびごとに、まるで同窓会の顔ぶれの中で懐かしい旧友に出会った時のような不思議な郷愁の感覚が募る。そうした「旧友再会の場」に繰り返し身を置くことで、とある単語への馴染みは次第に深まって行くものだと感じられるのである。

そうした感じ、辞書使用者の体表感覚に(更には郷愁の念にさえ)直に訴えかけてくるような実体感が、電子辞書には奇妙に欠落している。電子辞書を引くという行為は、街中を歩き回ってある場所を発見するというよりは、お巡りさんに問い合わせて地図上で所番地を確認する作業に近い。所番地がわかったとて、問い合わせをした人が生体的(ましてや心情的)リアクションを示すことはまずない:電子辞書はただ冷ややかに大脳の知的領域に向かって語りかけるだけで、そこに「触覚的実体感」はまるでないのだ。

古き良き時代のかさばる辞書の紙のページを手でパラパラめくるよりも、キーボードから綴りを打ち込んで単語を検索する方がはるかに容易かつ迅速である。たとえ単語の綴りを正確には知らずとも、電子辞書の強力な検索機能が正しい綴りの候補を示してくれて、諸君を正解へとストレートに導いてくれるだろう。電子辞書の多くは音声機能付きだから、わけのわからない音声学の記号(ヘボン式ローマ字)を読み解くまでもなく、とある単語の正しい発音を諸君に教えてくれる。とある単語からその同意語・反意語へとジャンプしてそれぞれの違いを確認することもクリック一つで自由自在。これら全ての夢のような機能が、諸君の指先の動き一つであっという間に遂行されるのだ!・・・それでいて、何の実体的感触も伴わぬがゆえに、夢の中の経験みたいに、不思議と記憶に残らないのである。目が覚めたその後は、夢はどこかへ失せていて、夢の記憶もまた消え去ってしまう。その夢を見た物理的証拠など後には何も残らない・・・寝床がひとつ、ぽつんとあるだけだ。電子辞書は「夢を見させてくれる寝床」のようなもの・・・これに対し、紙の辞書は「寝床」ではなく、手で触れて感じ取りたい時にはいつでも再訪できるようきちんと物理的に残っている「夢のかたまり」(一部の人にとっては「悪夢の山」?)なのである。

―「参照」と「暗記」とはまるで別物―

とまぁ、上に書いたような理由で、古き良き時代の紙の辞書の使い手たちの多くが、電子版のライバルよりも紙辞書の使用を提唱するわけである。かいつまんで言えば、電子辞書は、とある単語の意味を気軽に確認するような時にはよいけれど、学生が単語への馴染みを深めるために座右に置く永続的道案内にはまるで役者が足りない、というわけである。こうした論法は、大方の日本人にとっては筋が通ったもののように見えるかもしれないが、この筆者にとっては筋違いな話である:この筆者は、英単語を「辞書で引く」行為と「暗記する」営みとを混同するような幼稚な取り違えをするほど愚かではないから。

Students do not memorize English words through dictionaries: they do so with much smaller wordbooks, commercially published or personally hand-written. A dictionary is a book for casual reference, not for permanent memory, just as a telephone book is not supposed to be remembered. A wordbook is a list of things to remember, meant to be more a mnemonic aid than a reference book. It does not have to list all possible definitions of a certain term. It tends to contain less information than a dictionary; in a way, the less the better, for it makes it easier to memorize.

It is therefore wrong to argue against the electric dictionary for its lack of tactile tangibility — no serious student really demands it of a dictionary (though personally significant in retrospect years afterwards). A dictionary has only to be a good reference book; it doesn't have to be a good reminder as a wordbook is supposed to be. The tactile tangibility and the nostalgic feel of human touch of good old paper dictionaries are certainly good as a memento of studious olden times, but are too weak as a reason to advocate against the use of much more efficient electric dictionaries.

- From albums to songs, from pages to terms – lack of background is the trend of the day -

The dwindling status of the traditional paper dictionary is not unlike the fate of good old LP records or CDs in the music world. Songs used to be sold in a bundle called "an album" usually consisting of ten to fourteen songs. Today, a song is purchased on the Net as a single commodity, not in albums. Such individual purchase of a particular song is not bad when it comes to consuming popular songs by artists who have only a single good song to offer and nothing else. On the other hand, there are songs which have to be appreciated in the context of a certain album. "Sgt. Pepper's Lonely Hearts Club Band" by the Beatles (1967) is to be appreciated as the opening number of the album of the same title, not to be listened to as an individual piece cut out from the background of "Sgt. Pepper album"; so are "Lucy in the sky with diamonds" and "A day in the life". They could stand alone and stand out brightly, but they shine all the more brilliantly in the ambient atmosphere of the "Pepper".

学生が英単語を暗記するのは「辞書」を通してのことではなく、もっとずっと小さな「単語集」(市販版であれ手書きの自作版であれ)を用いてするのである。「辞書」はさりげなく意味を参照するための本であり、忘れぬように覚え込むためのものではない(「電話帳」が暗記用に作られてはいないのと全く同じことだ)。「単語集」は覚えるべき事柄の一覧表であり、参考書というよりむしろ暗記促進用として作られている。とある単語の語義として考え得る全てを列挙する必要もない。「単語集」に含まれる情報は「辞書」のそれより少ない傾向があるが、ある意味で、情報量は少なければ少ないほどよいのである:少ない分、覚える苦労が減るのだから。

それゆえに、「電子辞書には触覚的実体感がないから」という理由で電子辞書の使用に反対するのは、間違いである。「手で触れて感じられる何か」を辞書に(心底から)望む者など、真剣に学ぶ学生の中には誰一人存在しないのだ(長い年月が経った後で振り返ってみれば、そうした触覚的実体感が個人的に意義深いものであることは確かだが)。「辞書」は単なる「参考用書籍」として優れていればそれでよい・・・「単語集」に求められるような「思い出すためのよすが」として優秀である必要などないのだ。古き良き時代の紙の辞書の持つ触覚的実体感や人間的感触の郷愁感は、勤勉に学んでいた往事の記念物としては素晴らしいかもしれないが、遙かに効率的な電子版の辞書の使用に反対すべき論拠としては、あまりにも弱すぎて話にならない。

ー「アルバム」単位から「曲」単位へ、「ページ」単位から「単語」単位へ・・・「背景」の欠落が現代の潮流ー

伝統的な紙の辞書が衰勢にある現状は、音楽の世界に於ける古き良き時代のLPレコードやCDが辿った運命に似ていなくもない。今日では、音楽は「アルバム単位」ではなくネット上で「1曲ずつ」購入される単品商品となっている。特定の1曲だけの個別購入は、いい曲はたった1曲だけで他には何もないアーティストのポピュラーソングを買う場合には悪くはないだろう。その一方で、特定の「アルバム」の脈絡の中に置いて鑑賞せねばならない楽曲もある。The Beatles(ザ・ビートルズ)の1967年の曲“Sgt. Pepper's Lonely Hearts Club Band:サージェント・ペパーズ・ロンリー・ハーツ・クラブ・バンド”は、同名アルバムのオープニング・ナンバーとして味わうべきであり、“サージェント・ペパー・アルバム”という背景から切り離された個別の作品として聴くべきものではない;同じことは“Lucy in the sky with diamonds:ルーシー・イン・ザ・スカイ・ウィズ・ダイアモンズ”や“A day in the life:ア・デイ・イン・ザ・ライフ”についても言える。これらの楽曲は、単体で聴いても独立した魅力を放ち、他の曲たちの中に置いても異彩を放つかもしれないが、“ペパー”の全体的雰囲気の中で聴いた場合にはなお一層まばゆく輝くのである。

Looking up a word in an electric dictionary is somewhat similar to purchasing a single song on the Net: it is a stand-alone experience totally devoid of context or ambient atmosphere peculiar to listening to a whole album or turning over the pages of a paper dictionary. Some people will lament it, but the trend of the twenty-first century is progressively against albums or paper dictionaries. The lack in them of contextual meaning, therefore, has to be supplemented by individual listeners or learners through some personally meaningful efforts.

- "Relativity" theory of the dictionary – the position of a term relative to surrounding ones gives it a special place in one's memory; let a term stand alone, and it'll always be strangely novel and immemorable -

To come to think of it, our memory (or even likes and dislikes) of a particular song is usually associated with some personal circumstances in which we heard it. The "Sgt. Pepper album" and the psychedelic atmosphere of 1967 are the powerful backgrounds for otherwise flat songs (in this author's personal opinion) like "Fixing a hole" or "Being for the benefit of Mister Kite!". The experience of listening to a song in the context of an album or looking up a term in a thick paper dictionary offers us the background against which the song or the term stands out vividly in our memory.

A term or a song electrically consulted or downloaded is by default devoid of that kind of memorable background. Unless we give such backgrounds to songs or terms which tend to stand alone out of context, they will remain totally alone and immemorable, which will not stay in our mind for long. In fact, lots of songs casually downloaded are thus forgotten and left unnoticed deep inside the HDD(hard disk drive) of your computer. On the other hand, a song incorporated into some personally created "album" and played and enjoyed in the context of that custom program of yours are less likely to be forgotten.

The necessity for such customized play lists — official, personal or automatic — has been increasing greatly ever since songs began to be downloaded one by one instead of being published in an album. Music players (hardware or software) without the ability to offer listeners easy and

1つの単語を電子辞書で引く行為は、1つの曲だけをネット上で購入するのにどことなく似ている:それは単独型の経験であり、アルバム全体を通して聴いたり紙の辞書のページをぱらぱらめくったりする行為に特有の「脈絡」や「全体的雰囲気」にはまったく欠けるものである。嘆かわしく思う人もいるだろうが、21世紀の潮流は「アルバム」や「紙の辞書」には次第に背を向ける形になってきている。であるからには、「1曲単位での楽曲購入」や「電子辞書」には欠落している「脈絡単位の意味」というものは、聴く人／学ぶ人の一人一人が「個人的に意味のある」努力を通して補う必要があるわけである。

ー辞書に関する“相対性”理論・・・周囲の単語との相対的位置関係が、人の記憶の中で、ある単語特有の位置付けをもたらす・・・周囲の単語から切り離されると、単語はいつまでたっても妙に目新しくて記憶に残らないー

よくよく考えてみれば、ある特定の曲に関する我々の記憶は(あるいは好き・嫌いさえも)我々がその曲を聴いた時の個人的状況と結び付いているのが普通である。“サージェント・ペパー・アルバム”と1967年というサイケデリックな雰囲気は、そうした状況がなければ(この筆者個人の意見では)平板な曲たち、例えば “Fixing a hole:フィクシング・ア・ホール”や“Being for the benefit of Mister Kite!:ビーング・フォー・ザ・ベネフィット・オブ・ミスター・カイト!”にとっては強力な背景となっている。ある曲を「アルバム」の脈絡の中で聴いたり、ある単語を「分厚い紙の辞書」で引いたりする経験は、その曲や単語を記憶の中で生き生きと際立たせる「背景」を我々にもたらすのである。

電子的に引いたりダウンロードしたりした単語や曲には、デフォルト(初期状態)では、その種の記憶に残る「背景」がない。脈絡から切り離されて孤立しがちな曲や単語には、そうした「背景」を与えない限り、曲や単語はまったくひとりぼっちで印象の薄いものとなり、我々の記憶に長く留まることもないだろう。実際、ただ何となくダウンロードした多くの曲たちはそうして忘れ去られて、コンピュータのハードディスクの奥底で見向きもされずに放っぽらかしになっているものだ。これに対し、個人的に作り出した何らかの「アルバム」の中の1曲として組み込まれ、自分の手でカスタムメイドした演奏プログラムの脈絡の中で再生して楽しんだ楽曲は、なかなか忘れられないものである。

曲が「アルバムの形で発売」されずに「1曲ずつ個別的にダウンロード」されるようになって以来、こうしたカスタムメイドのプレイリスト(アーティスト公認版、リスナー自作版、音楽プレイヤーの自動作成版)の必要性は、大幅に増大し続けている。音楽プレイヤー(のハードウェアあるいはソフトウェア)のうち、ダウンロードした曲たちを魅力的なプログラムへと手軽に組み入れる機能を聴き手に提供できないプレイヤーは、ひどく劣

fascinating programs of downloaded songs will find themselves at a dire disadvantage. The test of a really excellent music storage is not (at least will not be) how many songs it can hold but how it presents the listener with them according to the mood or circumstances of the moment.

The same goes for the electric dictionary. Quickly showing the definition of a term on demand is good enough today, but in not so distant future, it will leave so much to be desired: pre-programmed and personally customizable repertoire of words, idioms or grammatical information will be featured as the strong selling point of an electric dictionary. Unfortunately for English learners of today, however, electric dictionaries with such strong programming features are not in existence in the real world, nor is it clear whether it exists in the to-do list of dictionary makers.

What does not exist has to be created on your own... but how?

- How to make the best of an electric dictionary -

The first thing you need is an electric dictionary which can copy the terms and definitions you have consulted and paste them onto a single file (in the form of "plain text", not in some specialized formats incompatible with anything else). In other words, you are going to make "a personal wordbook" of the words you looked up in the electric dictionary. From this standpoint, most portable electric dictionaries are out of the question, for lack of capability to make such consulting logs (and that in "plain text format" which can be processed on any computer). The simple (and practically the single) solution to the problem is: just forget your pocket electric dictionary, and consult a dictionary software on your personal computer along with some editor (or word-processor) to process a log file.

Since consulting logs produced by most electric dictionaries only show you "terms" and no "definitions", the process of creating your own "wordbook" is rather rough and arduous. It is anything but automatic and hardly systematic (wildly random, in fact) but quite fruitfully personal in the end. Once you know its enormous merits, there is no returning to a paper dictionary. Follow the steps shown below to benefit from the use of a computer-based (as opposed to a portable) electric dictionary:

勢に立たされることになるだろう。音楽保存用装置が本当に優れているか否かの試金石は、「どれだけ多くの曲を保存できるか」ではなく「その時々のムードや状況に応じて、それらの曲たちを聴き手にどのような形で提供するか」なのである(現状はともかく、今後はそういうことになるはずである)。

同じことが、電子辞書に関しても言える。現時点では、指定された単語の語義を素早く表示するだけでも十分良いと言えるが、近い将来はそれだけでは大いに物足りないことになるだろう。単語・熟語・文法に関する情報のレパートリーを、予め組み込んだり個人的にカスタマイズできる形で織り込んであることが、電子辞書の強力な売り物となるだろう・・・しかしながら、今日の英語学習者にとっては残念なことに、そうした強力なプログラム機能付きの電子辞書は現実世界には存在しないし、辞書を作る側の人々の「作るべきものリスト」の中に存在するのかどうかすらも定かではない。

存在しないものならば、諸君自身の手で作り出すしかない・・・が、どうやって?・・・答えは以下の通りである:

－電子辞書を最大限に活用する方法－

最初に必要なのは、辞書上で参照した単語とその語義をコピー(複写)して単一ファイルへと(他と互換性のない独自フォーマットではなく、“プレインテキスト”形式で)ペースト(貼り付け)できる電子辞書である。言い換えれば、その電子辞書で引いた言葉たちを素材に、諸君独自の「個人的単語集」を作るわけである。この観点から見ると、「携帯版」電子辞書のほとんどは論外となる:上述したような辞書引き履歴を(それもどのコンピュータ上でも加工できる“プレインテキスト形式”で)作成する機能を持たないからである。この問題の解決策は単純(かつ、実質的にただ一つ)である:ポケット版電子辞書のことは忘れて、パーソナル・コンピュータ上で電子辞書を引き、ログ(使用履歴)ファイル加工用のエディタ(またはワードプロセッサー)ソフトと一緒に使うことだ。

ほとんどの電子辞書が作る検索履歴のログファイルは、「単語」だけで「語義」までは明記してくれないから、諸君独自の「単語集」作りの段取りは、少々荒削りで手のかかるものとなる。自動的に作れるなんて夢にも思ってはならないし、体系的な単語集からも程遠い(どころかメチャクチャ乱雑である)が、最後には諸君個人にとって極めて実り多いものが出来上がるだろう。ひとたび諸君がその巨大な利点を知ったなら、もう「紙の辞書」に戻ることは出来なくなる。以下に記す段階を踏んで、(携帯型ではない)コンピュータ上の辞書ソフト使用者としての利便性を享受してくれたまえ:

(1)Start an editor (or a word-processor) on your computer and make a new file in any given name (eg. "engwb001.txt", which stands for English Wordbook No.1 with the extension "txt");
(2)Whenever you meet a term which you believe you should pay special attention to, copy the term and the definition (or even the whole definitions!) that you believe to be important, and paste them onto your personal electric wordbook (in the case above, "engwb001.txt");
(3)In order to jump between terms by way of search function of the editor/word-processor, don't forget to insert some separating sign at the top of each term you have just pasted which NEVER appears in the definitions of any terms (eg. "%%", "^^", "_ _ ", etc,etc.). Avoid using "--" or "■" or "●" or such marks, for some word-processors (such as Microsoft Word) will do the kind job of automatically converting them (at their default settings) into "—" or serial numbers (1, 2, 3, 4, ... n), making them totally useless as separating signs;
(4)Don't be too much selective in what to copy/paste and what to ignore. If you come across a term with which you are not completely familiar, just look it up and enter it onto your personal wordbook. Even if a single wordbook includes the same term/definition more than once, just leave them as they are and never try to delete them to make the wordbook look neat and clean: it is counter-productive. Such redundant entries are the proof of how important you believed those terms/definitions were at the moment of the consultation. Such seemingly awkward redundancy will make meaningful "backgrounds" to that particular term. When later you open up your wordbook and find the term "awkward" entered over and over again and are faced with the same old definition often enough, chances are, you'll never have to look up (let alone copy and paste) the term "awkward" again. That's the beauty of building up your vocabulary by the ugly means of electrically repeating the same thing to the level of being awkward (or even crazy!), which is never possible by the traditional means of physically writing it down on a sheet of paper;
(5)Avoid entering "pronouns(代名詞:DAIMEISHI)", "conjunctions(接続詞:SETSUZOKUSHI)" and "prepositions(前置詞:ZENCHISHI)" — they are the stuff for "grammar", not for "vocabulary building";

(1)コンピュータ上でエディタ(またはワープロ)ソフトを起動し、任意のファイル名(例“engwb001.txt ... English Wordbook No.1/拡張子はtxt”)で新規ファイルを1つ作成する;
(2)特に注目すべきだと思われる単語に出会ったらいつでも、その「単語」と「重要だと思われる語義」をコピーする(全部重要だと思ったなら語義全体をコピーしたって構わない!)・・・それを諸君の「私的単語集」(上例で言えば“engwb001.txt”)にベタッとペースト(貼り付け)する;
(3)エディタ(あるいはワープロ)の検索機能を用いて単語間をジャンプできるようにするためには、ペーストしたばかりの各「単語」の冒頭部に何らかの区切り記号を挿入することをお忘れなく・・・その記号はどの単語の語義にも決して登場しないものでなければならない(例 “%%”、“^^”、“_ _”、その他諸々)・・・但し、“--”あるいは“■”あるいは“●”等々の記号は避けること・・・(マイクロソフトの“ワード”等の)一部のワープロソフトでは、上記の記号を“—”だの連番(1, 2, 3, 4, ・・・n)だのの別文字へと(出荷段階で設定されているオプションのままだと)書き換えてしまうというご親切な仕事をしてくれた挙げ句、区切り記号としては全く役立たずにしてしまうからである;
(4)コピー/ペーストすべきか無視して流すべきかの選別については、あまり細かく考える必要はない。「完璧にお馴染み」とは言えない語句に出会ったなら、とにかく辞書で引いて諸君の「私的単語集」へと書き加えるのがよい。1つの単語集に全く同一の「単語/語義」が何度となく重複して登場する場合でも、そのままにしておくのがよい。単語集の見栄えを良くするために重複する単語や語義を削除しよう、などという気は絶対に起こさないこと・・・非建設的で逆効果だから。そうした「見出しの重複」は、(辞書を引いたその瞬間に於いて)その「単語/語義」を諸君がどれほど重要だと思っていたかを示す証拠となる。そういう一見「ぶざま」な冗長性が、その単語に「意義深い“背景”」をもたらしてくれるのだ。後日、諸君が自作の「単語集」を開いてみた時に、“awkward”なる単語が何度も何度も重ねて登録されているのを発見して、毎度お馴染みのその語義(=ブザマな)に幾度となく直面させられる経験をしたならば、たぶん、諸君はもう二度とどんな辞書でも“awkward”なる単語を引く必要は(コピー&ペーストする必然性も、当然)なくなっていることだろう・・・これこそが、「ブザマ」(あるいは「イカレてる」!)と呼べるほどの水準で何度も何度も同じ事柄を電子的に繰り返す「カッコわるい」やり方で諸君の語彙を増強する「カッコいい」ボキャビル(vocabulary building=語彙増強)方法なのである・・・こんな冗長なやり方なんて、紙の上に物理的に手書きする伝統的な手法では、決して出来るものではない;
(5)“pronouns(代名詞)”・“conjunctions(接続詞)”・“prepositions(前置詞)”を見出し語として登録するのはやめておくこと—こうした品詞は「ボキャビル(語彙増強)」の対象ではなく、「グラマー(文法)」のネタなのだから;

(6)Don't try to make "a single complete version" of wordbook. Just make as many wordbooks as the number of your lessons at school or the chapters of a book you are reading. Remember – a wordbook is a list of words and definitions to remember, which is useless if it disinclines you to remember (or even read!) due to its daunting length;

(7)NEVER print out your electric wordbook on paper. Grow out of your dependence on tactile tangibility for comprehension. The authentic test of the intelligentsia of the 21st century is whether or not to be able to understand in an abstract manner without recourse to physical aid like writing by hand or reading on paper. Anything you see on a computer screen, just comprehend then and there, or be left behind and frowned upon by those whose understanding needs no tactile intervention.

This author refrains from recommending any particular computer-based dictionary and editor (or word-processor) software, for fear of sounding nostalgically out of date when you read this years later. Just search on the Net for anything with reasonably adequate copy/paste capability, or ask someone around you who has taken the right step in this electric enlightenment.

Many of "wondrous technologies" proudly advocated by evangelists are good for nothing in the world of linguistics, but the method shown above of "creating your own personal wordbooks via computer-based software" is so really powerful that you are sure to be left hopelessly behind by those who believe and prove it by actually improving upon their vocabulary that way. Take my word for it that you should go electric... or go elaborately awry.

(6)“単一完璧版”の「単語集」を作ろうとしないこと。学校の授業の数だけ、あるいはいま読んでいる本の章ごとに、別々の単語集をたくさん作ればそれでよい。忘れるな－「単語集」は覚えるべき単語や語義のリストであるから、尻込みするほど長すぎて「覚えよう」(どころか「読もう」)という気分になれないものを作ってしまえば、「単語集」としては役立たずになる、ということを;

(7)「電子版」の単語集をわざわざ「紙に印刷」するようなマネは絶対にしてはならない。何かを理解するのに「触覚的実体感」に依存する体質は、いい加減、卒業したまえ。21世紀型知識人とそうでない旧人類を分ける真の試金石は、自分の手で文字を書いてみたり紙に印刷された本を読んでみたりといった物理的な手助けに頼ることなく、抽象的な形のまま理解できるか出来ないか、である。コンピュータ画面上で見たものは何であれ、その場で、そのままの形で、把握してしまうこと・・・それが出来ない諸君は、手で触れてわかろうとする段階を間に挟まずとも理解出来る人々からは取り残され、(けっ、ノロくさいやつめ!)と眉をしかめられてしまう羽目に陥ることであろう。

この筆者としては、何年も経ってから読み返した時に郷愁を誘うまでに時代遅れに聞こえる文章など残したくないので、コンピュータ版の辞書・エディタ(あるいはワードプロセッサー)のソフトウェアとしては具体的に何が良いかをここで推奨することは差し控えておくことにする。コピー/ペーストがまともに機能するやつをネット上で探すか、上述のやり方で電子的に賢くなる方向性へと正しい一歩を既に踏み出している諸君の身の回りの誰かさんに質問してみれば、それでよかろう。

福音伝道者気取りの誰かさんが誇らしげに提唱する「素晴らしいテクノロジー」とやらは、語学の世界では全く役立たずである場合が多いものだが、上で紹介した「コンピュータ上で動くソフトウェアを通じて諸君の個人的単語集を作る」やり方は、実際、とてつもなく大きな威力を発揮する・・・であるから、筆者を信じて実際そのやり方で自らのボキャブラリーを向上させることを通じてその方法論の正しさを実証してみせた人々を前にすれば、それをせずにいる諸君は、絶望的なまでの置いてけぼりを食らうことになるだろう。悪いことは言わないから、諸君も「電子化」したまえ・・・さもなくば、ひどく骨の折れる努力を払った末にブザマな不首尾に終わるのがオチなのだから。

17. On entering a junior high school, acquire touch-typing skill: learn to type English without seeing the keyboard

- Typing in Japan yesterday and today -

Before the 1990s, few people were able to type here in Japan. Most Japanese had no other way to write than handwriting. They imagined typing to be a special skill peculiar to professional typists or writers, alien to normal people who had their own hands to write with. Towards the end of the twentieth century, however, typing skill came to become “a must” even in Japan due to the explosive spread of personal computers and the rapidly growing network of WWW(World Wide Web or the Internet).

The general typing skill (or method) of Japanese people today, however, leaves too much to be desired to be deemed as a sort of computer literacy. So many Japanese are engaged mostly in KEITAI(cell-phone) mail and rarely write on computer keyboards that their typing can hardly grow out of “chopstick dancing” – too much stress on forefingers while others remain idle. As for most Japanese youngsters busily writing mail on KEITAI, their act is even too strange to be called “typing”... it should more appropriately be called “pecking”, using only the thumb to tap on ten-keys on the cell-phone to weave short sentences. While in the rest of the world, the thumb on the right hand does nothing but hitting the space key, it does everything in the KEITAI pecking. It is uniquely Japanese, to be sure, but like many other Japanese originals, it is too uniquely Japanese to survive in the global society. Thumb-pecking-tap-dance belongs more to parlor tricks than to typing skill.

By any standard, Japanese people in general are anything but good typists.

- The fundamental reason why most Japanese type and write so poorly -

Word-processing through thumb-pecking seems too arduous to be realistic in the eyes of foreigners, but even with nine fingers (minus the left thumb), weaving Japanese sentences on the computer is a hard task, hardly rhythmical with too many stops for typists to pleasantly ride on the stream of writing.

17. 中学入学と同時に英文タッチタイピングスキル(キーボードを見ずに文字を打ち込む技能)を身に付けよ

－日本でのタイピング事情の昔と今－

1990年代以前には、ここ日本にはタイピング技能を持つ人々はほとんど存在しなかった。大部分の日本人の筆記手段は「手書き」のみであった。彼らのイメージでは、「タイピング」は職業タイピストやプロの作家だけのもので、ちゃんと手がある普通の人々には無縁のもの、といった感じであった・・・が、20世紀も終わりに近付くと、そんな日本でさえも、パーソナルコンピュータの爆発的普及とWWW(World Wide Web、あるいはインターネット)のネットワークの急速な発展とともに、タイピング技能は次第に「必需品」となって行く。

しかしながら、いま現在の日本人全般のタイピング技能(というか、方法)にはあまりにも問題が多すぎて、「コンピュータ技能」の一種とみなすには難がある。実に多くの日本人は、携帯電話でのメールのやり取りが主であって、コンピュータのキーボード上では滅多に文章を書かないから、彼らのタイピング技能は「お箸踊り(チョップスティック・ダンシング)」の域をほとんど出ない－両手の人差し指にばかり過大な負担をかけつつ他の指は何もせずただ遊んでる状態なのである。携帯メールをせっせと書きまくっている日本の若者の大部分に関して言えば、その挙動はあまりにも奇妙すぎて「タイピング」とは呼べない代物となっている・・・携帯電話のテンキー(数字の1～10が並んだパッド)上を親指だけを使ってコツンコツン叩きながら短文つむぎ出すそのやり方は、「タイピング」というよりむしろ「ペッキング(キツツキ入力)」と呼ぶのがふさわしいだろう。日本以外の世界では、右手の親指は「スペースキー(余白)」を打つ仕事しかしないが、「携帯ペッキング打鍵法」では万事を親指一本がこなすのである・・・これは確かに日本独自のユニークなものではあるが、その他多くの「和風オリジナル」同様、そのあまりに独自すぎて日本でしか通じぬユニークさゆえに、地球社会の中での生存は不可能な鬼っ子と化している。「親指キツツキ式タップダンス」はどちらかと言えば「隠し芸」であって、「タイピング技能」という感じではないのである。

総じて、日本人は、御世辞にも「タイピング上手」とは呼べないわけである。

－大方の日本人のタイピング・筆記の水準がかくも低い本源的理由－

「親指一本キツツキ打ちスタイル」でのワープロ作業は、あまりにシンドすぎて外国人の目には現実離れして見えるであろう・・・が、たとえ9本指(左手の親指は除く)を総動員したとしても、コンピュータ上で日本語の文章をつむぎ出す仕事は重労働であり、一時停止を強いられる場面があまりにも多すぎて、タイピストが心地良く筆記の流れに乗ってリズミカルに打鍵することなどほとんど不可能な作業なのである。

What, then, makes you stop in typing Japanese? Yes, of course, you know — "かな漢字変換(KANA-KANJI HENKAN: the conversion of KANA into Chinese character)", archenemy of rhythm, speed and accuracy in electrically processed Japanese.

For example, if you want to type "漢字", you have to go through two steps:
(STEP-1) Type in from keyboards "k" "a" "n" "j" "i" — "かんじ" — in KANA(Japanese syllabic writing system). If not in Roman alphabet conversion style, it is "T" "Y" "D" "@"... confusing already? Be prepared it can be much more so hereafter;
(STEP-2) From the many candidates of "kanji" shown on the computer screen ("感じ", "幹事", "監事", "完治", "官寺", "患児", etc,etc.) find and decide on "漢字" to correctly complete the conversion.

When every time you want to type in any given KANJI, you are forced to stop, find and decide on the right candidate of the "漢字", how can you rhythmically type Japanese? Typing in Japanese is such a stressful task so much full of GO/STOP, GO/STOP that writing speed is compromised for accuracy or, worse still, vice versa. If you hate to stop and check conversion errors (like "かんじ" converted into "幹事" and not "漢字") in the process of writing fluently, your sentences will be full of such absurd Japanese as "内臓メモリー(NAIZOU MEMORY: built-in memory = 内蔵メモリー incorrectly converted into internal organ memory)", "深いな経験(FUKAI NA KEIKEN: a disgusting experience = 不快な経験 suggestively converted into a profound experience)" or "指摘会話(SHITEKI KAIWA: a personal conversation = 私的会話 critically converted into pointing out conversation)".

Such structural hindrance inherent in Japanese writing system never fails to thwart the Japanese in their typing speed and accuracy. But the saddest truth of all is this: the Japanese themselves, most of them, do not know the sad truth of their writing handicap because of their inability to compose and type English. Those who have no mirror to reflect themselves in have no true notion of themselves in the eyes of others. Japanese self-image drawn in the void of objective perspective is often too larger than life to be taken seriously or even humorously.

では、日本語をタイプする際に一時停止を強いる物事とは何か？・・・そう、諸君も当然御存知であろう：日本語を電子的に処理する際に「リズム」「スピード」「正確性」の不倶戴天(ふぐたいてん)の敵となるあの「かな漢字変換」である。

例えば、"漢字"とタイプしたい時、諸君は次の2段階を踏まねばならない：
(第1段階)キーボードから"k" "a" "n" "j" "i"(かんじ)を(仮名で)打ち込む。「ローマ字変換」でない場合は"T" "Y" "D" "@"と打ち込む・・・既にもう頭がこんがらがってきただろうか？・・・が、この先もっとややこしくなるのだから、覚悟してもらいたい；
(第2段階)"kanji"(かんじ)の候補としてコンピュータ画面上に表示される幾多の候補たち("感じ"、"幹事"、"監事"、"完治"、"官寺"、"患児"、その他諸々)の中から、"漢字"を見つけ出してこれを確定し、以て正しい変換作業を完遂する。

どんな漢字をタイプするにもその都度「タイピング停止／正しい漢字候補の発見／変換確定」を強いられるとあれば、日本語のタイピングをリズミカルにこなすことなど、どうして出来るだろうか？・・・無理な話である。日本語でのタイピングとは、かくも多くの「ゴー／ストップ」だらけのストレスのたまる作業なのだから、正確に打とうと思えばその分筆記スピードは減速を余儀なくされるし、へたすればその逆の事態となる：つまり、速打ちに走れば間違い変換の漢字が増えるのだ。すらすらと流れるように書く筆記過程の中で、いちいち立ち止まっては("かんじ"が"漢字"ではなく"幹事"に化けるような)変換間違いの確認作業を嫌えば、諸君の文章は「内臓メモリー(built-in memory = "内蔵メモリー"が間違って"体内器官の記憶"に化けたもの)」だの「深いな経験(a disgusting experience = "不快な経験"が"深遠なる経験"などと思わせぶりに変換されたもの」だの「指摘会話(a personal conversation = "私的会話"が"何かをあげつらいまくる会話"へと批判的に変換されたもの」だのの誤変換日本語満載の馬鹿っぽいものと化すだろう。

日本語という言語の筆記体系に構造的に付きまとうこうした障害は、日本人がタイピングを行なう際に、必ずやその「速度」と「正確性」の阻害要因となるのである。が、何よりも悲しい真実は何かと言えば、日本人の筆記に関するこの悲しき真実を、日本人自身、その大部分が(英語を作ってタイプする能力を持たぬがゆえに)自覚できていない、ということである。自らの姿を映す鏡を持たぬ人々は、他人の目に映る自分の真の姿をまるで知らずにいる。客観的観点も何もない状態で一人勝手に思い描いた日本人の自画像はあまりに過大評価され過ぎていて真面目に取り合ってやるに値せぬばかりか、笑って流してやることすらもはばかられる水準である場合が多いのである。

Avoid becoming such a self-crowned clown by acquiring some reliable standpoint to enable you to see yourself objectively. Typing in English will be a desirable starting point. You should start as early as possible, although this author will refrain from saying “the sooner the better”: too soon will be too much in something. The time is well ripe for starting to type English when you have graduated from primary school (where you should have acquired an adequate vocabulary of KANJI) and are about to start learning English in earnest.

- Japanese students should learn typing through English, not through their native Japanese -

Since this is the 21st century, you will invariably try to master typing through some computer-based tutoring system, not by the traditional method of typing in whatever sentences you find on paper textbooks. To tell you the truth, however, there is no fundamental difference between computerized and paper-based practices in typing, once you have mastered the positions of the keys and what keys to hit by which fingers of yours.

The advantage of computerized lessons over paper typing practice is not having to prepare physical forms of textbooks, and being able to check the accuracy level of your typing by comparing the original sentences with what you actually typed in. In the hand of capable programmers, computerized typing lessons can be a great fun in addition to being instructive. Inept programmers will try to make it all fun, and end in a bunch of shit neither interesting nor instructive. In order to avoid such shitty typing tutoring programs crowding (and clouding) the Japanese market, you simply have to obey two rules: (1)avoid Japanese-oriented programs and choose English-based ones... never forget that the interruption of KANA-KANJI conversion is the archenemy of typing!; (2)avoid programs proudly featuring “LOTS OF FUN”... more often than not, what is fun to the programmer is none (or dung!) to the learner.

In short, choose “English-oriented software designed to make a good typist of you”, and NEVER “Japanese fun-oriented software designed to make money by making a fool of you”. Unless you turn your back on Japanese as a novice, you can't hope to be a great typist. It is not necessary to totally

そんな「自分のことを王様だと思い込んでいる道化師」に成り下がらぬためにも、自分自身を客観視できるような頼れる視座を持つ必要がある。英語のタイピングは、その理想的な出発点となることだろう。始めるなら早いほうがよい・・・もっとも「早ければ早いほどよい」とまではこの筆者は言わないが(早すぎれば残念な結果に終わる物事も世の中にはあるのである)。英文タイプを始める機が十分熟したと言えるのは、小学校を卒業して(となればもう漢字の語彙は十分身に付けているはずの段階で)英語学習を本格的に始める頃合いである。

ー日本の学生は、母国語である日本語を通してではなく、英語でタイピングを学ぶべしー

今は21世紀だから、諸君がタイピングをマスターしようとする際にはまずもって、昔ながらの「紙の教科書にある文章をことごとくタイプ打ちするやり方」ではなく、「コンピュータ上で動く個人指導システム」を通して学ぶことになるであろう。しかし、実のことを言えば、タイピング練習では(キーの位置を覚え、どのキーをどの指で打つかを身に付けてしまった後はもう)コンピュータ化しようが紙本ベースであろうが、本質的な違いはない。

コンピュータ化されたタイピングレッスンが、紙版タイピング練習よりも有利なのは、教科書を物理的に用意しなくても済む点と、原文と実際打ち込んだ文字とを比較することで諸君のタイピングの正確度をチェックできる点とである。有能なプログラム作成者の手にかかれば、コンピュータ上のタイピングレッスンは、教育的に役立つ上に、とても楽しいものにもなり得る。が、ヘボなプログラマーの場合、タイピング練習ソフトをひたすら楽しいものにしようとして、結果的には面白くもなく教育効果もない駄目ソフトをまき散らしておしまい、ということになる。今の日本の市場を賑わせ(かつ、曇らせ)ているその種のゴミカス同然のタイピングプログラムを避けるためには、次の2つの原則を守りさえすればそれでよい:(1)日本語指向のプログラムは避けて、英語ベースのプログラムを選ぶべし・・・かな漢字変換による中断がタイピングの大敵であることを決して忘れるべからず！;(2)「すごく楽しい」ことを誇らしげに売り物にするプログラムは避けるべし・・・プログラム作成者にとっては楽しいかもしれないが、大方そんなものは、学習者にとっては何ということもないもの(どころかクソそのもの！)である。

早い話が、「諸君を優秀なタイピストにするために作られた英語指向のソフトウェア」を選び、「娯楽指向で金儲けするために作られた諸君を小馬鹿にしたような日本製ソフト」は絶対に選ぶべからず、ということになる。初学者の頃に日本語に背を向けておかないと、諸君は決して優れたタイピストになることなど望めない。タイピングレッスンの

exclude Japanese language from typing lessons, but any attempt at KANA/KANJI transfer in typing tutoring programs will do more harm than good. From this author's personal experience, most of the typing lesson programs made in Japan are totally out of the question due to the obvious lack of command of English on the part of the programmers: they belong more to the genre of "gaming" than to "education" software... and not much fun, either.

- Don't think: just type! -

Some of you may be afraid to step into the world of typing composed solely of English sentences, wondering if you can really understand their meaning while typing. Well, this author will tell you this secret, which is unknown to all but the exceptional Japanese who can type, read, write and understand English with perfect freedom (meaning "the truth about typing virtually unknown in Japan") – that an English typing lesson is possible (even desirable) by those who can't make head or tail of English sentences.

The goal of typing is not to understand as you type but to type without thinking or understanding. Typing by experts is a totally spontaneous act: they may be thinking, but their fingers are not. Between what they see and what they type, there should never be an interruption by any conscious thought; thinking will only spoil speed and even accuracy in typing. DON'T THINK, JUST HIT THE KEY is the way to go.

In this regard, English natives will find themselves at a disadvantage because they can (and WILL) understand what they are typing. Japanese folks who can see alphabets but don't know what to make of them will naturally gain in speed and accuracy in English typing because their brains are free from unnecessary thinking process. They can make desirable "automatic typing machines" of themselves!

After years of practice both in typing and English itself, Japanese typists will naturally come to think about and understand the meaning of texts while they are typing. Bliss of innocence will not last forever, but enjoy it while you can. While your "beginner's luck" is still active, learn to type without thinking, let your fingers spontaneously type in whatever you see the moment you see

中から「日本語を100%排除」する必要はないが、タイピング指導プログラムに「仮名漢字変換」を持ち込もうとする試みなど、百害あって一利なしである。この筆者個人の経験から言えば、日本で作られるタイピング練習プログラムの大部分は(そのプログラム作成者に英語力が明らかに欠落しているのが原因で)全く論外な代物であり、「教育」というより「ゲーム」ソフトのジャンルに属する・・・しかも、あんまり楽しくもないのである。

－考えるな、ひたすら打て！－

英文のみで構成されたタイピングの世界へと足を踏み入れるのに怖じ気づく諸君もいるかもしれない。タイプしている最中に文章の意味が本当に理解できるだろうか、と不安な諸君もいるであろう・・・ということで、筆者はここで諸君に一つの秘密を教えてあげよう:これは、英語を完璧に自由自在にタイプし読み書き理解できる能力を持った類稀なる日本人以外は誰も知らない秘密(つまり「日本ではほとんど誰一人知らないタイピングに関する真実」)である・・・即ち、英語のタイピングレッスンは、英文の意味がさっぱりわからない人でも可能(どころかむしろそういう人こそ理想的)なのである。

タイピングの目標は「タイプしながら理解する」ことではなく、「思考・理解を一切伴わずにタイプする」ことである。熟練タイピストのタイピングは、全く無意識のうちに行なわれる自律的な営みである:タイピスト本人は頭の中で何か考えているかもしれないが、指先の方は何も考えていない。「見る」と「タイプする」の間には、意識的思考が一切介在しないのが望ましいのだ。「思考」はタイピングの「速度」更には「正確性」までも阻害するだけなのである。「考えるな、ただひたすら打鍵せよ」・・・それがタイピングのあるべき道なのだ。

この観点からみて、英語を母国語とする人々は、自分がタイピングしている文章の意味を理解できてしまう(そして理解しようと意識的に努めてしまう)から、不利な条件下にあると言える。「アルファベットは見てわかるけれどそれが何を意味するかはわからない」という日本人ならば、無駄な思考過程に大脳がわずらわされることもないのだから、英文タイピングの速度と正確性はしごく自然に向上するであろう。そういう日本人こそが、自らを理想的な「全自動タイピングマシーン」と化すことができるのである！

タイピング並びに英語の練習を長年積み重ねた後では、日本人タイピストでも当然のごとく、自分がタイプしている文章の意味を考え、理解するようになるだろう・・・「無知なるがゆえの至福」も永遠には続かないわけだが、享受できる間にその至福は享受すべきである。「初心者ならではの幸運」の効き目がある間に、考えずにタイプすることを覚え、見た瞬間に指先が勝手に見たものことごとくを打ち込むようにし、「タイプする

it, make typing as instinctive as speaking or walking... and your typing and command of English will be greatly improved upon; along with it, your status in the world connected by the Net, where excellently typed English of yours never fails to stand out among self-complacent gibberish.

- What to keep in mind in trying to master typing skill -

Pursued in the correct way, typing skill can be mastered in less than a couple of months: you won't need half a year at the longest. After that, speed and accuracy will progressively increase until they hit the roof (probably in some years, not in decades). To minimize the time and effort and maximize the accomplishment, keep in mind the following principles and keep moving in the right path (don't waste your energy in questionable methods or software):

(1)The first skill to acquire is to type without seeing the keyboard or the positions of your fingers. Your eyes should be fixed on the computer screen (or paper texts for typing) without running up and down nervously. This "touch-typing" skill will greatly reduce the physical pressure on your eyes, neck and shoulders while working on computers.

(2)Primary attention should be paid to acquiring the skill to type at high speed with constant rhythm and never to stop here and there for confirmation and correction. In this regard, Japanese sentences full of GO/STOP converting process of KANA/KANJI are totally out of the question in typing lessons. Forget all about Japanese while you are a novice typist... unless you are just typing in "ひらがな" and no "漢字" at all.

(3)Typing accuracy should be given a back seat and should NEVER be practiced in long tiresome sentences but in short snappy ones like newspaper headlines or famous adages. Accuracy should be tested and acquired in sentences in which one feels inclined to be accurate, not where one can be reasonably sloppy.

(4)Sentences to be used for typing practice should be customizable: in addition to built-in texts prepared by the programmer, learners should be given the freedom to use any sentences they want to type in the program. The boring disadvantage of using the same sentences for typing practice over and

こと」を「喋ること」や「歩くこと」と同じくらい本能的なものと化す･･･それが出来れば、諸君のタイピング技能も英語力も大いに向上するであろうし、それと共に、ネットで結ばれた世界の中での諸君の立場もまた向上するはずだ･･･ひとりよがりのちんぷんかんぷんな書き散らしばかりの世界の中で、見事にタイピングされた諸君の英語は、必ずや際立つはずなのだから。

ータイピング技能の修得を目指す際に留意すべき事柄ー

正しいやり方で追究すれば、タイピング技能の修得は2～3ヶ月以内に可能となる:どんなに長くとも半年もあれば十分である。その後は、打鍵速度も正確性も段階的に向上して行った末に、いずれ「天井を打つ」ことになるだろう(恐らくは数年以内のことであり、数十年単位の話ではない)。時間と労力を最小限に抑えつつ最大限の成果を手にするには、以下の原則を心に留めて正しい道を(疑わしい方法論やソフトウェアのせいで諸君の活力を浪費せぬように)たゆまず歩むことである:

(1)まず第一に修得すべき技能は、キーボードも自分の指先の位置も見ずにタイプする技術である。眼はコンピュータの画面上(またはタイプすべき紙のテキスト上)に固定し、上下にうろうろ不安げに視線をさまよわせることのないようにすること。この「タッチタイピング」の技能を身に付ければ、コンピュータ作業時の眼･首･肩への物理的負担は劇的に減少することになるだろう。

(2)練習の最大の主眼点は、高速度で一定のリズムに乗せてタイプし、そこかしこで確認･修正のために立ち止まるようなマネは決してしない技術を身に付けることである。この観点に於いて、「仮名漢字変換」の過程ごとに生じる「ゴー／ストップ」だらけの日本文は、タイピングレッスン用としては全くの論外ということになる。タイピストとして駆け出しのうちは、日本語のことはきれいさっぱり忘れることだ･･･もっとも、「ひらがな」をタイプするだけで「漢字」は一切なし、というのなら話は別であるが。

(3)タイピング時の「正確さ」は(「速さ」に比して)二の次の扱いにし、その練習には長くて退屈な文章は避けて、短くてイキのいいやつ(例えば新聞の見出しや著名な格言みたいなもの)を選ぶべきである。「正確性」の試験並びに修得用の文章には、正しくタイプしたい気分にさせてくれる文章を選ぶのが当然であり、いい加減な打ち方になっても無理はないような文章を選ぶのは間違いである。

(4)タイピング練習に用いる文章は、個人的なカスタマイズ(独自仕様)の余地があるものが望ましい。プログラマーが事前に用意してプログラム本体の中に組み込んである文章に加えて、プログラムの中でタイプしたい任意の文章を選ぶ自由を学習者に与えるのが理想的なのだ。タイピング練習用に全く同じ文章を何度も何度も繰り返し使

over again should be turned to great advantage by making use of personally selected sentences which one wants to learn by heart (not merely learn to type), such as favorite lyrics of popular artists, example sentences quoted from wordbooks, or even the whole sentences copied from English textbooks which one must memorize to prepare for the exam. Tech-minded folks should use programming terms or even a whole functional program as example sentences to type in and to naturally memorize through fingers.

- Gospel of typing for Japanese learners of English -

Typing will really replace handwriting once you have mastered "touch-typing" (a politically-correct paraphrase of the traditional appellation of "blind touch" in view of the feelings of those physically handicapped in their eyes). Once you enter a phase of English study where you can write and store anything you see or think by typing on keyboards, you'll be blessed with the following benefits.

(benefit 1)

You can type tens of times faster than you write without falling into illegibly dirty handwriting. Indeed, "quick and legible" is the primary reason why English natives usually type and rarely write their documents. Hand-written English can be a great ordeal for the reader (illegible!) as well as a unique identifier of the writer (characteristic!) just like a fingerprint.

(benefit 2)

When you become proficient enough both in typing and English, your typing skill will give you an enormous advantage in practicing "英作文 (EISAKUBUN: English composition)". The speed at which you manually write is so much slower than the speed at which you speak that the act of writing English will never help you become fluent in English speech or thinking. On the other hand, you can type English nearly as fast as you speak or think of it, making it possible to ride on the flow of the sentence of your own making, while detecting and correcting errors on the computer screen. What you write down on a sheet of paper tends to become "final" in your consciousness, making it difficult to re-examine and correct its contents after you have finished writing it. What you type in on a computer is always "in the

用する不利は、(単にタイピングを学ぶのみならず)丸ごと覚え込んでしまいたいと思える文章を個人的に選んで使用することで、大いなる利点へと転じてしまうべきなのである。例えば、ポップアーティストのお気に入りの歌詞や、単語集から引用した例文、更には試験に備えて暗記せねばならぬ英語の教科書から丸ごとコピーした文章などを、タイプすると同時に覚え込むようにしてしまうのだ。技術系に関心のある人たちは、プログラミング用語、更には実際に機能するプログラムの全文をタイピング用の例文として用いて、指先を通して自然に暗記してしまえばよい。

－日本人の英語学習者にタイピングがもたらす福音－

ひたたび「タッチ・タイピング」(昔は「ブラインド・タッチ」という呼び名だったが、目の不自由な人々の感情をおもんばかって"政治的に正しく"言い換えたもの)を身に付けてしまった後では、本当にもう手書きなどまるでしなくなってタイピングのみで通してしまうようになるものである。英語学習も、見たり考えたりした事柄は何であれキーボードからタイプして書いたり保存したりするような段階に達すると、諸君は次のような様々な特典に恵まれることになる:

(特典1)

手で書く場合の数十倍の速さでタイプしながら、キッタなくて読めたものじゃない手書き文字みたいに崩れることもない。実際の話、この「スラスラ速く書けるうえにハッキリ読める」というのが、英語人種が普段タイプ打ちを選んで滅多に手書き文書など作らない一番の理由なのである。手書きの英文というやつは、読み手にとっては大変な試練(読めないっ!)になり得るし、「指紋」と全く同様に筆者を見分ける唯一無二の身分証明の手段ともなり得る(それほどに強烈な個性がにじみ出る!)ものなのだ。

(特典2)

タイピングも英語もともに熟練の域に達すると、「英作文」の練習時に大変有利になる。手で書く速さは口で話す速さより遙かにずっと遅いものだから、英語を手書きしても、英語を話したり頭の中で考えたりする際の流暢さに磨きをかける練習には全くならない。これに対し、タイピングならば、英語を話したり考えたりする場合の速度にほぼ匹敵する速さで打鍵できるので、コンピュータ画面上で間違いを発見したり訂正したりしながら、自作の文章の流れにきちんと乗ることができる。紙の上に何か手で書くと、それは諸君の意識の中では「最終決定稿」的に捉えられがちで、折角それを書き上げた後でその内容を再吟味したり修正したりするのも困難になる。コンピュータ上で打ち込む内容はどれもみな常に「制作途中」で修正や変更の余地があるものだから、その

making" and open to correction or alteration, giving you much more perfection and possibility for improvement. Those who compose English only on paper (or on their tongues or even in their heads alone) are much less likely to improve upon their writing than if they made a point of typing their sentences on computers.

(warning about writing/typing for memorization)

If you are a novice learner of English, you should make much more of reading aloud and memorizing than typing English. If you have time enough for typing a ready-made sentence, make better use of the time by repeatedly reading it aloud. Although you can type much faster than you can write, never try typing the whole English sentences from your textbooks – it is simply meaningless except as a typing practice. If you try typing sentences at all, try it with the sentences you have learnt by heart and stored in your memory to check and see if you have memorized them all to the letter.

Japanese learners of English have a way of writing down English words (or even idioms or sentences!) over and over again on paper trying to inscribe them on their memory... to absolutely no avail. They are totally illogical in that they ignore the structural difference between phonograms (English words) and ideograms (漢字:KANJI = Chinese characters).

In essence, a Chinese character is a "picture" whose "figure" stands for a certain meaning: you can know its meaning by seeing it, but you must practice "drawing the picture" with your own hand to be able to write the KANJI yourself. Practice in writing KANJI is more a lesson in art than in linguistics. If you doubt me, think about the status of "書道(SHODOU:Japanese calligraphy)" in the eyes of English speaking people — isn't it a kind of visual art like painting or photography?

Unlike KANJI, English words are no pictures: you don't have to practice "drawing" them, you just have to memorize the combination of the alphabets composing them, for which purpose "writing them down" is absolutely unnecessary. If you are uncertain of the spelling, just try typing a term about ten times or so, and your fingers will remember it for you. Typing "薔薇(BARA: a rose)" dozens of times from keyboards will never enable you to write this KANJI on paper with your own hand, but typing "rose, rose, rose" will be more than enough for you to correctly remember and spell this English term ever afterwards.

完成度も改善可能性も、手書き原稿の場合よりずっと高いものとなる。英語を紙の上でしか(あるいは口に乗せてしか、さらには自分の頭の中でしか)作らない人達は、コンピュータ上で文章をタイプする習慣を身に付けた場合に比較して、作文技能の向上可能性がずっと低くなってしまうのである。

(覚え込むために手書き/タイピングする、という行為に対する注意書き)

英語学習の初学者の場合は、英文をタイプするのよりも、音読して覚え込むことの方をもっとずっと重視するのが正しい。出来合いの文章をタイプする時間があるならば、その文章を繰り返し音読することで同じ時間を有効活用するべきだ。タイピングの速度は手書き速度よりずっと速いとはいえ、教科書の英文すべてをタイプしてやろうなどとは決して思わぬ方がよいーそんなことをしても、タイピング練習として以外はまるで無意味である。それでも何でもとにかく試しに文章をタイプしてやろうというのであれば、既にもう暗記して脳内の記憶領域に溜め込んである文章で試すとよい:すべてを一字一句正確に暗記したかどうか、タイプして打ち出して確認すればよいのである。

日本人の英語学習者には、ややもすれば、英単語を(更には英熟語や英語の文章そのものさえ!)紙の上に何度も何度も書き出してはそれを記憶に焼き付けようとするようなところがある・・・そんなことをしても全く何の効果もないというのに。そういうことをする日本人は、表音文字(英単語)と表意文字(漢字)の構造的違いを無視している点に於いて、全く非論理的な思い違いをしているのである。

本質的に、漢字は「絵」であり、その「形」がある種の意味を表わしている。その意味は目で見ればわかるが、その漢字を自分の手でも書けるようになるためには「絵描き」の練習を積まねばならない。漢字の書き取り練習は、「語学」というより「絵画」の授業に近いのである・・・「そんな馬鹿な!」と思う人は、英語人種の目で見た場合の「書道(Japanese calligraphy)」の位置付けについて考えてみるがよいー「絵画」や「写真」と同様、「視覚芸術(visual art)」の一種であろう?

漢字とは違って、英単語は全然「絵」ではない。その「描き方」を練習する必要など一切なく、その英単語を構成するアルファベットの組み合わせを覚えればそれでよいのであって、そのために「書き取り」する必要など全くないのである。綴り字に確信が持てないなら、試しに10回ほど、その英単語をタイプしてみれば、諸君の代わりに指が綴りを覚えてくれるだろう。「薔薇(ばら:a rose)」を幾度も幾度もキーボードから打ち込んでみたところで、諸君がこの漢字を紙の上に手書きできるようになることなど絶対にあり得ないが、「rose, rose, rose」と3度ほどタイプしてみればもうそれだけで、諸君はその後末永くこの英単語を正しく覚えて綴ることができるようになるものである。

(benefit 3)

If you type English sentences on computers, you will enjoy the helpful benefit of having your sentences checked by computer programs for correcting spelling or grammatical errors. As of today, such computerized grammatical correction programs are far from perfect... but something is better than nothing. On the other hand, a spelling checker program in English is nearly 100% accurate and reliable; at least much more so than human scrutiny. Their benefits for novice learners are so enormous that making no use of them is simply illogical: the logical choice is only open to those who type instead of writing.

(benefit 4)

Finally, it is also those who type only that can make their sentences available on the Net. By making your sentences available and processable for your teacher, you can have them checked, corrected and evaluated by scrutinizing eyes of the examiner. Those who still insist on a hand-written answer sheet will have to resort to the archaic means of FAX(facsimile) – visually copying and transmitting "a document" in the form of "a picture"... which is an unbearable burden both for the sender and the receiver. This author simply cannot bring himself to accept such hardly legible "pictorial" documents; checking them for errors and referring to and correcting them by making wholly new electrical documents for myself is simply out of the question. If you hate to be excluded from any activity on the Net, you just have to learn to type.

- ローマ字(Roman alphabets) or かな(KANA), that is the question?... No, there's no question at all: the answer is just ROMAN, no KANA -

One more advice meant solely for Japanese learners of typing. As the input/conversion method, you MUST choose "ローマ字変換:ROUMAJI HENKAN = Roman alphabet conversion" and NEVER choose "かな変換:KANA HENKAN = KANA conversion"! There is no question about it: 「かな変換は絶対に選ぶな！:Just say NO! to KANA conversion」. Even those who have already chosen "KANA" would be well-advised to convert to "ROUMAJI"... if they want English literacy at all, that is. If you can rest

(特典3)

英文をコンピュータ上でタイプすれば、自作の文章の綴り字や文法上の間違いを訂正するためのコンピュータ・プログラムでチェックできるという、大助かりの恩典に浴することができる。今日の段階では、文法上の間違いを訂正してくれるコンピュータ・プログラムの完成度は、完璧からは程遠い・・・が、ちょっとしたものでも何もないよりはましである。一方、英語のスペル間違い確認プログラムの方は、ほぼ100%正確で頼りになるものだ・・・少なくとも人間の眼で入念にチェックした場合よりも圧倒的に正確で信頼度が高い。こうしたプログラムは初学者にとって巨大な恩典をもたらすものだから、それを使わずにいるなんてまったく非論理的なことである・・・論理的選択が出来るのは、手書きではなくタイプする人々だけである。

(特典4)

最後に、これもまたタイピングする人のみに許された恩典として、自作の文章をネット上に公開することができる。自作の文章を教師に差し出して手を加えてもらうことで、その内容確認と訂正、更には試験官の厳しい目で見た評点をも仰ぐことができる。今なお「紙の解答用紙に手書きの答えを書き出すこと」に執着する人々の場合、FAX(複写機＝「文書」を「絵柄」の形で視覚的にコピーして転送する装置)という古くさい手段に訴えるより他はない・・・これは、送り手側にも受け手側にも、共に耐え難いまでの負担である。この筆者の場合、そんな判読も困難な「絵みたいな」文書など、受け取る気分にもまるでならないし、そんなお絵描きFAXを訂正のために吟味した末に筆者自身の手で全く新たな電子文書を作ってその間違いに言及したり訂正してあげたりするなんて、まったく論外の話、絶対にしてやるつもりはない。ネット上で展開するいかなる営みからも排除されてしまうのが嫌な諸君は、タイピングを学ぶより他はないのだ。

－「ローマ字」か「かな」か、それが問題・・・か？・・・否、まるで問題にすらならぬ:答えは一つ「ローマ字」あるのみ、「かな」など論外である－

タイピングを学ぼうという日本人のみに向けた助言をもう一つ加えよう。「入力／変換」の手段としては、必ず「ローマ字変換」を選び、「かな変換」は絶対に選ばないこと！　議論の余地など全くない:「"かな"変換は絶対に選ぶな！」である。既に「かな変換」を選んでしまった人達も、悪いことは言わないから「ローマ字変換」に転向するべきだ・・・いやしくも英語での識字能力を身に付ける気持ちが少しでもあるならば、の話であるが。諸君が全くの英語文盲状態に甘んじて何の不満もないというのなら、どう

satisfied with the status of TOTAL ENGLISH ILLITERATE, just go ahead and keep on typing KANA keys. Otherwise, just KILL OFF KANA keys and GO ROMAN. If you happen to have chosen the wrong way, don't take it personally; just take it logically and convert to Roman conversion... better late than never.

There is absolutely no sense in forcing your brains and fingers to remember two totally different arrangements of keys and to switch between them. While an English/Japanese bilingual is a dream come true for many Japanese, "かな変換日本語(Japanese terms via KANA conversion)／アルファベット打ち英単語(English terms via alphabets) bilingualism" is a nightmarish redundancy.

The greatest (indeed the only) point in favor of KANA conversion is the relatively fewer steps needed to type in any given sound in Japanese. For example, when you want to type in "かな変換", it takes ten(10) steps (k-a-n-a-h-e-n-k-a-n) via Roman alphabet conversion, while it takes only six(6) steps (T-U-^-Y-T-Y) through KANA conversion. 40% reduction appears to be a great advantage?... Well, haven't you forgotten about something? Typing in Japanese is a structurally stressful act full of GO/STOP every time you must convert KANA into KANJI. Since KANA-KANJI conversion must spoil your speed anyway, why bother to gain negligible speed by burdening your brains and fingers by double standards of "かな文字(KANA characters)" and "アルファベット(alphabets)"?

Such being the case, practically all companies in Japan reasonably international are (and should be) equipped with computers working on "ローマ字変換:Roman alphabet conversion", not on "かな変換:KANA conversion". In order to avoid being a black sheep in the middle of Roman folks, start learning typing by way of Roman alphabet conversion and JUST SAY NO TO KANA CONVERSION. If you still prefer Japanese to logic, or the haphazard choice of yours to the sensible choice of others, so be it... at your own risk.

Anyway, Roman or KANA, make a good typist of you, and the road to English mastery will be incredibly smoother, broader and brighter.

ぞ御自由に「かなキー」でのタイピングを続けるがよろしかろう。さもなくば、「かなキーは殺してローマ字でゴー」である。たまたま諸君が既にもう間違った道を選んでしまっていた場合でも、感情的に取らないように。個人攻撃と曲解して筆者を恨みに思うのはやめて、ただひたすら論理的に事を解釈した上で、「ローマ字」変換に転ずるのがよい･･･過ちを正すのに、遅くとも、何もせぬよりはまだよいのだから。

2つの全く異なるキー配列を頭脳と指先に無理矢理覚え込ませてはそれら2つの別世界の間を切り替えながらタイプするなんて、全く何の意味もないことである。「英語も日本語も話せる」バイリンガル(二カ国語使用可能者)は多くの日本人の夢かもしれないが、「かな漢字変換での日本語打ちもできる／アルファベット打ちで英単語も書ける」両刀遣いなんて、悪夢のような二度手間というものだ。

「かな」変換の最大の(というか実のところ唯一の)利点は、任意の日本語の音をタイプする際に必要になる段階が比較的少ない、というだけのことである。例えば、"かな変換"とタイプしたい場合、「ローマ字変換」だと"k-a-n-a-h-e-n-k-a-n"と10ステップを要するのに対し、「かな変換」なら"T-U-^-Y-T-Y"と6ステップで済む。40%の削減は大いなる利点･･･に見えるだろうか？･･･おやおや、何かお忘れじゃありませんか、諸君？･･･日本語でのタイピングなんてものは、仮名漢字変換作業のたびごとに繰り返される「ゴー／ストップ」だらけの構造的にストレスのたまる営みなのだということ、忘れてもらっては困る。どのみち「かな漢字変換」が諸君の打鍵速度を台無しにするというのに、わずかばかりの速度向上を図るために、わざわざ「かな文字／アルファベット」の二重規格で自らの頭脳と指先に負担をかけて、一体何の意味があるというのだ？

とまぁ、そういう次第で、まがりなりにも「国際的」な日本の企業であればほぼ全て、そこに備え付けのコンピュータは「かな変換」ではなく「ローマ字変換」で動いている(し、そうあるのが当然なのである)。ローマ字打ちの人々に混じってポツンと浮いた仲間外れの黒羊になるのを避けるためには、タイピング学習の出だしで「ローマ字」方式を選び、「"かな"変換なんて問答無用でお断わり！」の態度を貫くことである･･･こうまで言ってもなお「論理」より「日本語」が好き(というよりも「たまたま自分が選んでしまった何か」の方を「他者が行なう妥当な選択」よりも偏愛する)諸君がいるようならば、まぁ、好きにするがよろしい･･･その結果生じるいかなる不利益も諸君自身の危険負担で受け入れる覚悟をもって、御自由に(どうなっても筆者は一切関知しないからそのつもりで)。

まぁ何にせよ(「ローマ字打ち」であれ「かな文字打ち」であれ)とにかくタイピング上手になることである。そうすれば、英語修得への道のりは、信じられないほど平坦で幅広く輝ける道となって、諸君の眼前に広がるはずである。

18. English ought to be spoken, not written: minimum memos, maximum memory & no notebook (4m2n) is the way for 'em to English mastery

- Those who make efforts for show will make no real progress -

With English or anything else, those who make the greatest efforts are least likely to succeed. Paradoxical as it may sound, this is true: efforts are energy wasted and hindrance to anything really great. Efforts are consciously painful, and will come to mean much more than it should due to the weight of the pain and the time spent enduring it. In the end, efforts will become an end in itself and are proudly shown off... when success will naturally fly away. Too many Japanese are wasting too much of everything, time, energy, money or patience both of themselves and of others just in order to give unwarranted value to their meaningless efforts.

Those who really succeed make no efforts at all: they just do what they are sure they must do and will benefit them in the end. They do it with all their might, which may seem to others to be really painful efforts, but they actually feel no pain: they are just feeling the weight of success to come. The weight of a pair of dumbbells are a tangible guarantee for future muscles in the consciousness of body-builders, while being simply painfully heavy to idle viewers. Pain is no pain when you can take pleasure in it, nor is an effort any effort but simply fun when you are sure you are doing something meaningful, not just enduring something painful.

Just look at yourself studying English — is it fun, or pain for you? If painful, should you feel you are making conscious efforts with perseverance, chances are that something is wrong, terribly wrong with what you are doing in the name of studying English. It is not effort but energy coupled with pleasurable enthusiasm that is needed in mastering English. Painful consciousness inherent in efforts will spoil pleasure and enthusiasm to result in a flop, which is painfully evident from the countless examples of Japanese failures in English.

18. 英語は書かずに話すべし:メモ書き最小・暗記極大&ノート皆無・・・それが英語修得の王道

ーこれ見よがしの努力をする者に真の進歩なしー

英語に関してであれ他の何に関してであれ、最も多くの努力を払う人々は最も成功から遠い人々である。逆説的に聞こえるだろうが、これは真実である:「努力」とは「精力の浪費」であり、真に偉大ないかなる物事をも阻む代物なのである。「努力」というものは「わざとらしく苦しいもの」であり、その苦痛の重みとそれに耐えながら費やされた時間の長さの分だけ、分不相応に重い意味を持つようになるものである。そうして遂には、「努力」それ自体が自己目的化し、誇らしげに見せびらかされるに至る・・・事ここに至れば、「成功」は当然のごとくどこかへ飛び去ってしまうのだ。今現在、あまりにも多くの日本人が、自らの無意味な努力に過分の価値を与えようとして、ありとあらゆるもの(時間・精力・金銭・忍耐力)の過度の浪費を(自他ともに)強いている。

真の成功者はまったく「努力」などしない:自分がやらねばならぬと信じること、最後には自分のためになるはずのことを、ただひたすら行なうのみである。彼らはそれを全力で行なうので、他者の目には実に「苦痛に満ちた努力」に見えるかもしれないが、彼らは実際には「苦痛」などまるで感じない:彼らはただ「来たるべき成功の重み」を感じ取っているだけである。両手に握るダンベル(鉄亜鈴)の重さは、ぼんやり眺めるだけの人々の目には「ひたすら苦痛な重圧」に過ぎないだろうが、ボディビルダーの意識の中では「未来の筋肉を実感させる約束の重み」なのである。「苦痛」は、そこに「快楽」を見出せる者にとってはもはや「苦痛」ではないし、「努力」もまた自分が確実に意味ある何かを行なっている実感がある者(単に苦しい何かに耐えているだけではないのだと信じられる者)にとっては「努力」でも何でもなくただひたすらに「楽しいこと」に過ぎないのだ。

ちょっとここで思い浮かべて見たまえ、諸君、自らが英語を学んでいる姿をーそれは諸君にとって「楽しい」だろうか、「苦しい」だろうか? もし苦しいとしたら、「耐え忍びながら努力」している意識が諸君にもしあるとしたら・・・たぶん「英語学習」の名のもとに諸君が行なっている営みには、どこかおかしい、ひどく間違っている点があるのだろう。英語の習得に必要なのは「努力」ではなく、心地良い情熱と抱き合わせの「活力」である。「努力」に付きものの「自分は苦しい事を行なっているという意識」は、「快楽」や「情熱」を損ない、結局は大失敗に終わってしまう・・・それは、数限りない日本の英語落第者の実例を見れば痛々しいまでに明らかなことである。

- Write and learn is the Japanese way: recite, memorize and replicate is the way of English -

The most common and foolish mistake Japanese English learners make is trying to master English the way they mastered their native Japanese: learning by writing down words, idioms, sentences and translations, to little or no avail. The fault to be found with this method – vainly trying to master phonograms by making them visually tangible as ideograms are supposed to be – has already been pointed out in this book. Still, so many Japanese stick to writing and learning English to pre-destined failure for one simple reason – they positively hate to read English aloud... for several reasons:
(1)they don't know how to intone;
(2)they don't know how to accentuate;
(3)they can't be sure if they are pronouncing correctly;
(4)they get stuck at every word they are not completely familiar with.
... These are minor hurdles you can get over simply by diligence and practice, while the next one is really troublesome:
(5)They are presented with too many English sentences (or too boring ones) for them to feel inclined to read aloud, let alone learn by heart.
... This is the most seriously damaging reason why most Japanese students positively hate to read aloud and memorize English sentences, thereby making themselves virtually illiterate in English.

Schools and teachers should choose only such texts as their students can and will try to read aloud and memorize. They have to be not too long, grammatically meaningful and preferably fun to read... Fun element aside, selection of grammatically meaningful short sentences is one of the most important tasks on the part of teachers, schools and textbooks to enable students, especially beginners, to acquire the good habit of memorizing as they read aloud English sentences... The sad truth is, too many Japanese schools, teachers, or even textbooks are neglectful (even unaware!) of their duty to be selective about what to present students with.

ー「書いて学ぶ」は和式のやり方:「暗誦・暗記・複製」こそが英語流のやり方ー

日本人の英語学習者が最も一般的に犯す愚かな過ちは、自国語の日本語を身に付けたのと同じやり方で英語を習得しようとすることである・・・「単語」「熟語」「文章」「翻訳文」を紙に書き出してみても、結局はほとんど何の役にも立たない、というテイタラク・・・このやり口ー表音文字(英語)を、表意文字(漢字)の場合のお約束の「目で見てわかるようにする」やり方で修得しようと無益にあがくやり方ーのどこが悪いかについては、既にもう指摘した通りである。それでもなお多くの日本人が英語を「書いて学ぶ」やり方に固執しては予め定められた運命通りに失敗する理由は一つー実に単純なことだー日本人は「英語を音読するのがとにかくキライ!」なのである・・・その理由は一つではなく幾つもある:

(1) 日本人はイントネーション(抑揚)の付け方を知らない;

(2) 日本人はアクセント(強勢)の置き方を知らない;

(3) 日本人は自分が正しく発音できているかどうか確信が持てない;

(4) 日本人は確実に見知ったわけではない未知の単語に出くわすたびに立ち往生する。

・・・これらは、勤勉に練習を積むだけで乗り越えられる取るに足らない障害物に過ぎないが、次の事情は本当に困ったものである:

(5) 日本人が宛がわれる英文は、あまりにも分量が多すぎたりあまりに退屈すぎる内容だったりするので、「音読」してやろう(ましてや「暗記」してやろう)という気分になどなれたものではない。

・・・日本の学生のほとんどが英文を積極的に音読したり暗記したりしたがらない(がゆえに英語の読み書きが実際まるで出来ない状態に陥る)最も深刻なまでに有害な理由がこれである。

学校や教師は、学生たちが音読・暗記可能な(そして、彼らに音読・暗記の意欲を起こさせるような)テキストのみを選別すべきなのである。テキストは長すぎてはならないし、文法的に意味あるものでなければならず、できれば読んで楽しいものであるべきだ・・・まぁ「読んで楽しい」という要素はさておくとして、「文法的に意味のある短い文章」というのは、学生(とりわけ初学者)たちに「英文を音読すると同時に暗記する」という良い習慣を身に付けさせる上で最も重要な、教師・学校・教科書側の仕事なのである・・・が、悲しいことに、学生に提供すべき課題の選別義務に関しては、あまりに多くの日本の学校・教師は(更には教科書さえもが)軽んじている(どころかまるで自覚してすらいない!)のが現実なのである。

It follows from this that you, students, have to be very, very selective in what to read aloud and remember and what to just browse through and forget. If what your school gives you are all unworthy of memorization, you will have to seek and find for yourself some worthy textbooks full of meaningfully memorable sentences, which you must read aloud and remember, while dealing half-heartedly with immemorable stuff your school thrusts upon you.

Do not kid yourself into believing that you can neglect whatever you find uninteresting: your feelings notwithstanding, what is meant to be memorized (such as example sentences in your "grammar" textbooks or tasteless English you find in "reader") must be memorized, no matter how terrible you personally find them. What you can rightly and lightly browse for tentative interpretation and not for permanent memorization is stuff like a whole book of some novelist your teacher orders you to buy and read (and even translate!) as homework during summer vacation, or casually quoted newspaper articles meant to introduce you to "生きた英語(IKITA EIGO: English ALIVE!)".

Don't take this advice too lightly: to wisely select (by school or teacher or for yourself) English sentences for you to read aloud and learn by heart is the first step in your road to English mastery: without good selection, you'll simply go nowhere.

- Speak well, or you can't hear, read or write English at all -

Since English language is meant to be spoken, not to be seen and visually understood like Japanese, "sound" plays a much greater role in English than in Japanese. All Japanese know that, and falling "out of tune" is their greatest fear in speaking English, which eventually leads to their not speaking (and mastering) English at all.

In this author's younger days, it was quite hard for Japanese learners of English to confirm whether they were in tune or out of sync in speaking English. There was no Internet, no multi-channel TVs full of English broadcasting, no multi-media English tutoring programs to give you audio guidance. Still, this author was quite sure of the correctness of his English

以上のことから、諸君ら学生は「音読して覚えるべきものは何か？／ただ読み流した末に忘れてしまってよいのはどれか？」といったことに関しては、本当に慎重に自ら選別する必要がある、ということになる。もし学校が諸君に与えてくるものがことごとくみな暗記に値しないものばかりだったなら、諸君としては、学校が諸君に押し付けてくるその記憶に残らぬ代物たちを(気乗りのしない態度で適当に)あしらう一方で、音読して暗記すべき意義深く記憶に残る文章を満載した価値ある教科書を、自分自身で探し求めて見つけ出さねばならないことになる。

断わっておくが、自分が「面白くない」と感じるものなら何でも無視してよいと思い込むような馬鹿な真似をしてはならない。諸君の個人的感覚にはお構いなしに、「暗記用」として用意されているもの(例えば「文法」の教科書の中の例文や、「読本」の中の無味乾燥な英文など)は、諸君がそれを個人的にいかにヒドい代物だと感じようが、とにかく暗記せねばならない。長らく覚えておくまでもなく軽く読み流しては一時的に解釈してそれでおしまいにして当然なものとは、夏休みの宿題として「買って読め(更には、翻訳せよ！)」と教師が諸君に命令してくるどこかの小説家の本まるごと一冊だの、諸君に「生きた英語」を紹介するために何気なくどこかから引っ張って来た新聞記事だのといった代物のことである。

以上の助言、決して軽く流してはならない:(学校であれ教師であれ諸君自身であれ)声に出して読んで心に刻みつけるべき英文を賢く選択することは、英語修得のための第一歩なのである:この選択が良くないと、諸君はどこへも行けやしないのだ。

－上手に話さないかぎり、ちっとも聞き取れない・読めない・書けないのが、英語－

英語は「声に出して話す」べき言語であり、日本語のように「目で見て視覚的に理解する」べき言語ではないので、英語では日本語よりも遙かに「音」が重要な役割を演じる。日本人なら誰でもそのことを知っており、「調子っぱずれ」に陥るのが、日本人が英語を話す時の最大の不安要因となっていて、そのせいでやがて日本人は英語をまったく話さなくなる(そして身に付けられなくなる)のである。

筆者の若い頃には、日本人学習者が英語を話す時に「自分が英語をきちんと喋っているのかあるいはズレているのか」を確認することは極めて困難であった・・・当時は、インターネットもなければ、英語放送満載の多チャンネルTVもなく、音声ガイド付きのマルチメディア英語個人指導プログラムも存在しなかったのだから・・・それでもなおかつこの筆者には、自分の英語の喋り方は絶対に正しいハズ、という確信があった・・・

speech... Do you know why? The reason is quite simple and logical: he made it a rule to cast spotlights in sound on semantic partitions in a sentence and never to stop absurdly in the middle of a stream of meaning. Since no sound in English can possibly go against meaning, to rhythmically connect meaningfully separated blocks of terms will never fail to sound good as English. As for anatomical interpretation of English via visually conspicuous signs (< >「 」{ }( )[ ]), this author has already shown you how. This is the most reliable guidance for you to follow in speaking English. Speak English well, and you will automatically understand its meaning well as well.

- Spend less time and energy in preparation and more in recitation; least in notation and most in memorization -

Most Japanese students (try to) make grandiose notebooks independent of English textbooks, the creation of which is mistakenly considered to be the study of English. If you are one of them, you are bound to end up in the miserable line of English illiterates in Japan.

NEVER make notes outside your English textbooks: it is an act of linguistic suicide. Notation must be made in the form of footnotes/headnotes in between the lines of your textbooks. Since such small space can hold only so much information, you can't write in too much info. You must make wise selection here, too: what info to write down and what others to store up in your memory, and what else to simply ignore.

At preparation stage, check unknown words, look them up in the dictionary, confirm their meaning, and mark the words with some tentative signs — W. or w.(standing for "word"), !(exclamation), ?(question), #(sharp), *(asterisk), etc,etc. — but don't write in their meanings. At reviewing stage, check to see if you can remember their meanings correctly. If you can't, admit your defeat with a good grace, consult the dictionary again and write the meanings in between the lines. Even if you can, don't wipe out the tentative signs of your uncertainty: they will serve you well in preparing for the exam as your possibly weak points.

何故だかおわかりか？　理由は極めて単純かつ論理的にみてしごく当たり前のことである:筆者は、文章内の意味上の区切りに「サウンドによるスポットライト」を当てること、意味の流れのど真ん中で馬鹿みたいに立ち止まるような真似は絶対にしないことを心がけていたからだ。英語の「音」が「意味」に逆らうことなど絶対にあり得ない以上、意味の上から区切った単語の塊をリズムよく連結して行けば、英語として良い響きにならないハズがないのである。英語の「解剖学的解釈」を(<　>「　」{　}(　)[　]等の)視覚的に目立つ記号を通して行なうやり方については、筆者はもう既に述べてある。これこそが、英語を話す際に諸君が従うべき最も頼れる指針なのである。英語は「上手に話す」ことだ･･･喋り方が上手なら、自動的に、その意味もまたしっかり理解できるはずである。

－「予習」にかける時間と精力は少なめに、「暗誦」にはより大目に･･･「筆記」の時間と労力は最小限に、「暗記」は最大限に－

日本の学生の大部分は、英語の教科書とは別に独立した大袈裟なノートを作る(というか、作ろうとする)ものであり、そうしたノートを作ることこそ「英語の勉強」だと勘違いしている。諸君がもしそうした連中の一人なら、諸君も日本の英語無学者の惨めな列に加わっておしまい、の運命である。

英語の教科書の外にノートを作るような真似は絶対にしてはならない！･･･語学に於いては、それは自殺行為なのだ。書き込みをするならば、教科書の行間に「脚注／頭注」の形で行なわなければならない。そんな小さな空間では、収まる情報もたかが知れているのだから、あまり多くの情報を書き込むことはできない。ここでもまた諸君には賢い選別が求められるわけである。書き込むべき情報を選別し、それ以外の情報のうちのあるものは自身の脳内記憶庫に保管することにし、それ以外は軽く流しておしまいにする、そうした選択を諸君自身の手で行なわねばならないのだ。

予習段階では、未知の単語をチェックして、辞書で引いて、その意味を確認した上で、その単語には何らかの仮の記号－例えば“word”を意味する W.や w.、”！(感嘆符)“、”？(疑問符)”、“＃(シャープ)”、“＊(アスタリスク)”等々－でその未知の単語に印を付けておく･･･しかし、その単語の意味は書き込まないこと。復習段階になったら、印を付けておいたかつての「未知の単語」の意味が正しく思い出せるかどうか確認すること。もし思い出せない場合は、潔く自らの敗北を認め、辞書で再度調べて、その意味を行間に書き出すべし。たとえ単語の意味が思い出せた場合でも、不確実性の証しの「仮記号たち」は消さずに残しておくこと(自分の弱点となり得る箇所として、試験勉強の際にうまく役立ってくれるはずだから)。

Don't try to write down grammatical info (which you happened to find in some reference book or from the teacher's mouth) in between the lines: you simply can't, due to the limited time and space. Instead, just mark the terms or expressions which demand grammatical consideration with signs (GR./gr.) for “grammar”. What about the grammatical information itself?... Store it up in your memory the moment you find it!... Impossible?... Well, then, just write in (beside the “gr.” mark) the page of the reference book where you can find detailed explanation... What if the info casually comes off the teacher's mouth?... Just summarize it or think about some snappy title or keyword to remember it by.

In any case, don't let the act of writing in play a major role in your studies: give top priority to the reading, thinking and memorizing process. The more you write, the less you read and think: and the least reader and thinker is most likely to fail in mastering English.

As for idioms you found in sentences, mark them with IDIOM signs (ID. or id.) and just write in their meanings you found in the dictionary as footnotes/headnotes in between the lines of your textbook: you don't have to hide the meanings of idioms for later examination – the test of an idiom does not lie in correctly remembering the meaning, but in perfectly reciting the whole example sentence it is used in. Try to store up the idiom in your head in the context of the sentence, not just to memorize the short definition.

Finally, give anatomical interpretation signs only to those sentences which you find worth anatomizing: just ignore all else and leave them untouched. In actual lessons in the classroom, be all eyes and ears to check to see if what you anatomized at preparation stage has really been correctly interpreted. Pay attention to your teacher's explanation, for, besides what you already marked at preparation stage, there may be some other sentences which are worthy of anatomical interpretation in the opinion of the teacher: that particular opinion of the teacher may count much in the exam later on!

Now you can see that you don't have to spend too much time or energy in preparing for an English lesson — so long as you are wisely selective in what to write down on paper, what to inscribe in your memory, and what else to simply go through and let go. The real battle for mastery begins when the

行間には「文法に関する情報」(何かの参考書でたまたま見つけたものであれ教師の口から聞いたものであれ)を書き込もうとはしないこと・・・時間も空間も限られている以上、そんなことは出来っこないのだから。その代わり、「文法的に考慮を要する単語や表現」には、"grammar"を意味する記号(GR.あるいは gr.)だけササッと振っておけばよい。肝心の文法情報そのものはどうするかって?・・・見つけると同時に諸君の記憶の中に保管してしまうのだ!・・・無理だって?・・・まぁ、その時には(gr.印の横に)詳細な情報のある参考書のページ番号だけ書き込んでおけばそれでよい・・・・その情報が教師の口からポロッと漏れただけの場合はどうするか?・・・内容を短くかいつまんでまとめるか、その文法事項を思い出すための何かキレの良い標題なりキーワードなりを考え出せばよい。

いずれにせよとにかく、「書く」という行為が学習の主役にならないようにし、「読む」「考える」「記憶する」という過程にこそ高い優先順位を与えることが大事である。「書く」場面が増えれば増えるほど、「読む」ことや「考える」ことは減って行く。読み、考える場面が少ない学習者の場合、英語修得の可能性は極めて低くなる。

文章内に「熟語」を発見した場合、それには(ID.あるいは id.といった)"IDIOM"の印を付けて、辞書で見つけたその意味は教科書の行間に「脚注/頭注」の形でササッと書き込んでおけばよい。後々テストする目的で熟語の意味は隠しておく、などという真似はしなくてよろしい－熟語がモノに出来たか否かのテストは、「意味が正しく思い出せたかどうか」ではなく「その熟語が用いられた例文を丸ごと完璧に暗誦できたかどうか」なのだから。熟語はその文章の脈絡の中で脳裏にしまい込むようにし、短い語義をただ暗記するだけにはしないことである。

最後に、解剖学的解釈に値すると諸君が感じる文章に対してのみ、解剖学的解釈のための記号類を割り振るべし。それ以外の文章は軽く無視して手つかずのまま残しておけばよい。教室で実際に授業を受ける際には、目も耳も全開にしてよーく説明を聞いて、予習段階で自分が施した解剖学的解釈が、本当に正しい解釈だったか否かを確認すること。教師の解説には注意を払うべし:諸君自身が予習段階で印を付けた部分以外にも、(「その教師の意見」によれば)解剖学的解釈に値するような他の文章も存在するかもしれないから(後々の試験で「その教師の意見」が大きな意味を持つかもしれないではないか!)。

さぁ、これで諸君もわかったろう:英語の授業は、その予習段階では、「紙に書き出すべき事柄」「記憶に刻み込むべき事柄」「ただ通り過ぎたらそれっきりで流すべきその他の事柄」を諸君が賢く選別してくれさえすれば、それ以外にはあまり多くの時間や精力を費やす必要などないのである。英語修得のための真の戦いが始まるのは、授業

lesson is over: give all you've got to reciting and memorizing what you should. If you can correctly remember all those sentences you found worth noting and remembering, all the relevant information related with them will naturally come up to your mind along with the sentences – in sound ringing in your ears, not in letters written on sheets of paper!

All knowledge of English — words, idioms, sentence patterns, semantic constructions, grammatical info — ought to be fortified in your memory with some particular sentences in the spoken form, so that whenever you try to confirm a certain piece of knowledge, it will come up coupled with some sentence, not as an abstract academic information itemized in a rule book. Preparation and reviewing stages of your English lessons are the opportunities to enrich yourself with such combination of example sentences with related info and knowledge. Make as many couples as possible, and make them perpetually memorable by reading them aloud over and over again.

- English illiterate Japanese invariably make too much of pronunciation with no regard to rhythm or intonation -

Next to the correct choice of what English to read aloud and memorize comes the question of how to correctly read aloud. Here will the Japanese invariably get stuck due to their queer notion of what English should sound like. They never fail to imitate “GAIJIN SOUND” and fail to sound like English.

Most Japanese notion of anything foreign tends to go strangely awry and come back to haunt them in hands-on experience. To take a rather WESTERN example, virtually all Japanese citizens have no actual experience of shooting a handgun, thanks to the ban on guns which makes this country the safest in the world. Thanks to this vacuum, Japanese ideas of wars, combats, weapons (and peace) are all out of sync with the world outside. Wars and combats might as well not be experienced personally, but there are some Japanese who want to experience shooting real guns, which leads them to foreign countries where casual tourists are allowed to shoot this “dream weapon” of theirs. Most Japanese tourists, naturally, are lousy shots due to

が終わったその後だ:暗誦して覚え込むべき事柄を、全力を傾注して暗誦・暗記するのが本当の戦いなのである。注目・記憶に値すると諸君が判断した文章をすべて正しく思い出すことが出来たなら、それらの文例と結び付いた関連情報の全てもまた、文章ともども自然な形で諸君の脳裏に(それも、紙に書かれた単なる文字の羅列としてではなく、耳に鳴り響く音声の形で!)浮かんでくることだろう。

英語の知識のすべて－単語(words)、熟語(idioms)、文型(sentence patterns)、構文(semantic constructions)、文法情報(grammatical info)－は、諸君の記憶の中で(音読された形の)何らかの文章によって補強しておくべきなのである:何らかの知識を確認したい場合に「ルールブックに箇条書きされた抽象的な学術情報として」ではなく「特定の文章と結び付いた形で」飛び出してくるようにするために、例文との抱き合わせ記憶が望ましいのである。英語の授業の予習/復習段階は、そうした「例文」と「関連情報・知識」との抱き合わせ例を増やす好機である。出来るだけ多くのカップルを作り、何度も何度も音読することで、いつまでもずっと覚えていられるようにすることだ。

－英語の読み書きが不自由な日本人はみな一様に「発音」にとらわれすぎて、「リズム(律動)」も「イントネーション(抑揚)」もほっぽらかしである－

「音読して暗記すべき英文」の正しい選択が行なえたなら、次に来るべき問題は「いかにして正しく音読するか」の方法である。この段階で、「英語の音声はかくあるべし」という彼ら独自の奇妙な思い込みのせいで、日本人はみな一様にドツボにはまる。彼らは決まって「外人サウンド」のモノマネをして、どうにも英語らしく聞こえぬヘンテコ音声に陥るのである。

何であれ外国の物事全般に関する日本人の概念は、大方、奇妙におかしな方向にねじ曲がっていて、自らそれを実体験する段になると、そのねじくれ方が我が身に跳ね返ってひどい目にあうのが日本人というものである。少々「ウエスタン」な方面の実例を紹介すると、日本国市民はほぼ全員(この国を世界一安全な国家たらしめている銃器禁止令のおかげで)「拳銃を撃った経験」がない。この真空状態のせいで、「戦争」「格闘戦」「武器」(そして「平和」)に関する日本人の概念は、どれもみな外の世界とはズレている。「戦争」だの「格闘戦」なんてものは個人的に体験しないに越したことはないが、日本人の中には「本物の銃を撃つ体験」をしてみたがる人々がいて、その思いから彼らは(通りすがりの観光客でも、彼らにとっての「夢の武器」の射撃を許可されるような)諸外国へと足を運ぶわけである。実体験がないのだから、当然、日本人観光客の大部分は射撃が下手くそである。が、中でも最悪なのは、もの言わぬモデルガンを

their lack of experience. But the worst of all are those Japanese shooters who have been accustomed to imitate the real shooter's reaction to the violent recoil of a handgun with a silent model gun in their hand. Their image of Dirty Harry shooting a legendary 44 magnum is never complete without the powerful reaction of the bullet swinging his right arm upward the moment it goes off! So, with a fake plastic revolver firmly held in their hand, Japanese gun nuts imagine themselves shooting a real gun and dealing with the gigantic recoil of shooting by swinging their arm sky-high... Those who have been accustomed to this kind of preconceived notion and reaction of "what shooting guns should be" are less likely to shoot correctly than those Japanese shooters who have never dreamt of themselves shooting a real gun. Japanese would-be shooters will instinctively add their imaginary version of "a real gun's recoil" to the natural physical recoil of the gun they are actually shooting... how could they aim and shoot correctly when their guns' muzzles will jump up not only physically but also mentally? They will invariably end up shooting considerably above the target!

The same preposterous mistake is habitually repeated by the Japanese sticking to their imaginary versions of "what GAIJIN SOUND should be". This author has no intention of pointing them out here in detail. Suffice it to say that the Japanese are gazing too nervously at trees to see the whole forest.

One great source of this Japanese farce is the undue weight they put on particular pronunciation in a particular word. The minor difference in sound between "l" and "r" does not matter so much as the innocent Japanese believe; "red" or "led", "His face was red with shame by being misled by preconception" will never be misunderstood as "His face was LED with shame by being MISS RED by preconception". English speaking people will understand the meaning of particular words according to the context they are used in, and will never be misled by mere sound. Although it is shameful to say "SHIT here" when you want someone to "SIT here", no sane person will take your word for it (or for the sound) and sit down before you to bring down their pants to shit there.

握り締めては「本物の拳銃」の強烈な反動への「現実の射撃手」の反応をモノマネするクセが身体にしみついてしまっている日本人射撃手たちである。「伝説の44マグナム」をブッぱなす「ダーティ・ハリー」のイメージは(彼らの脳裏では)発射の瞬間にその右腕を上方へと跳ね上げる「44マグナム弾の強力な反動」抜きには成り立たない。というわけで、その手にプラスチック製のオモチャのリボルバーを固く握り締めながら、日本の拳銃マニアさんたちは、射撃時の巨大なリコイルショックをうまく処理しながら実銃ブッぱなしている自分自身の姿を、自らその腕を「空高く舞い上げて見せる！」ことで、イメージしているわけである・・・「拳銃射撃はどうあるべきか」に関して習慣的に形成されてしまったこの種の先入観＋反応つきの人々の場合、自分が本物の銃を撃つことになるなどとは夢にも思わなかった日本人射撃手の場合よりも、正しい射撃が出来る可能性は低い。「なんちゃってシューター」の日本人というものは、現実にブッ放した銃の自然な物理法則に基づく反動に加えて、「本物の銃のリコイル」として彼らが思い描いていた「想像上の反動」までをも本能的に上乗せしてしまうものなのだから・・・銃口が「物理的」に加えて「心理的」にもハネ上がってしまう彼らが、正しく狙って正確に的を射抜くことなど、どうして出来るだろうか？・・・彼らの行き着く結末は、「狙ったターゲットよりかなり上を射っておしまい」というのが常である。

これと同様の本末転倒な間違いが、「外人サウンドはどうあるべきか」に関する想像上の解釈に固執する日本人の間では、常習的に繰り返されている。筆者は、その実例をここで詳細に指摘するつもりはない。「日本人はあまりにもオドオドと“木々”を見つめてばかりいて“森全体”の姿が見えていない」と言えばそれで事足りるであろう。

日本人の演じるこのお笑い芝居の最大の根本原因は、特定の単語の中の特定の発音に対してあまりにも過大な重みを置きすぎることである。「l(エル)」と「r(アール)」の些細な発音の違いなど、何にも知らない日本人が思い込んでいるほどには、ちっとも重要でもなんでもないのである。「red:赤」と読もうが「led:導いた」に聞こえようが、どう転んだところで、「His face was red with shame by being misled by preconception.:思い込みのせいであらぬ方向へと走ってしまったことで、彼の顔面は恥ずかしさで真っ赤っかだった」という文章を「His face was LED with shame by being MISS RED by preconception.:先入観により MISS RED(赤色女史)となってしまったことで、彼の顔面は恥辱によりLED(light-emitting diode:発光ダイオード)と化した」などと誤解されることなんてあり得ない。英語人種は、特定の単語の意味を理解する際に、その語が用いられている「文脈」に応じて解釈し、単なる「音」に導かれて誤解に陥るような真似は絶対にしないのだ。誰かさんを相手に「SIT here.:ここにすわって」と言うつもりで「SHIT here.:ここでウンコして」と口走るのは確かにこっぱずかしいことではあるが、さりとて(マトモな人なら)誰も、諸君の言葉を額面通り(というか「発音」通り)に受け取った末に、諸君の眼前でしゃがみ込んでパンツを下ろして排便するような真似はしないであろう。

Refined pronunciation is certainly good news, but too much consciousness of it will do you more harm than good. There are two other things beginners should pay much more attention to than pronunciation. The first has been already referred to: semantic blocks in a sentence, the distinction of which is essentially important but rather hard for beginners. The second is also important in making you understood in English, but is easier in a way for the Japanese: accentuation in each term in the sentence.

- Don't stick to perfect pronunciation; correct accent and intonation will make you understood in English -

Novice learners may not even know the distinction between pronunciation and accentuation. Take the term “parallel” for example. The favorite (or most dreaded) distinction of the Japanese people between “l” and “r” is found in this term: if you say it like “paLaReRu”, you are making a mistake in pronunciation; if you say it like “paraLLEEEL”, you are putting a wrong accent on “le”. You must accentuate “pa” in “parallel”: this knowledge is much more important than the phonetic distinction between “l” and “r”. Most Japanese people can hardly expect to sound right (just like GAIJIN) in their pronunciation of English words, while they can make themselves decently understood by making correct accents in each term.

Forget about pronunciation and just remember to accentuate correctly. When looking up a word in a dictionary, you should first pay attention to the primary accent of the word. Remember: accents can only be put on a vowel, never on a consonant. If you haven't got a dictionary near at hand, make alphabetical anatomization of the term and find out the position of “a, i, u, e, o” (and sometimes “y”); then, try putting theatrical accent on each “a, i, u, e, o (and y)” one by one, and see how it sounds: the least queer sounding position should be the vowel to put the primary accent on... Sounds too rough and unreliable to your ears? OK, then, if you are an authentic Japanese, here is one incredibly reliable method of correctly detecting the primary accent in any given English term — you have only to go against the accent the Japanese put in pronouncing “外来語(GAIRAIGO: Japanese terms derived from abroad)” in order to accentuate it right.

洗練された発音は確かに素晴らしいが、発音を意識しすぎるのは有害無益というものだ。初心者にとっては「発音」よりもっとずっと注意を払うべきことが他に2つある。1つめについては既にもう言及した:「文章内に於ける意味上のまとまり」である・・・この「意味ブロック」を弁別することは本質的に重要なことだが、初心者にとってはかなり難しいことでもある。一方、2つめの方は、英語を話した時にきちんと通じるようにする上では「意味ブロック」同様重要なことだが、ある意味、日本人にとっての難易度は低い:「文章内の個々の単語のアクセント(強勢)」がそれである。

ー完璧な「発音」に固執せずとも、正しい「強勢(アクセント)」と「抑揚(イントネーション)」で英語は通じるー

初学者の場合は「pronunciation(発音)」と「accentuation(アクセント=強勢)」の違いすらもわからないかもしれない。「parallel(パラレル=平行)」という単語を例に説明しよう。この単語は「l(エル)」と「r(アール)」という日本人の大好きな(あるいは最も恐れる)違いを含む:これを「paLaReRu」のように言ったら「pronunciation:発音」上の間違いを犯していることになる。これを「paraLLEEEL」のように言ったら「le」の部分に間違った「accent:強勢=アクセント」を置いていることになる。「parallel」という語では「pa」の部分を強く発音せねばならない:この知識は「“l”と“r”の響きの違い」よりもっとずっと重要である。大方の日本人の場合、英単語の発音を(外人並みに)正しくキメることなどほとんど期待すべくもないが、そんな彼らでも、個々の単語に正しい強勢(アクセント)を置けば英語が通じるようになるのである。

発音なんて忘れて、ただひたすらに正しい強勢を心がけることだ。どんな単語を辞書で引く時でも、最初に注意を払うべきはその語の「第一強勢(the primary accent)」の位置である。アクセントが置かれ得る位置は「母音(a vowel)」上のみであり、「子音(a consonant)」の上には決して強勢を置かないということを覚えておくことだ。もし辞書が手近にない場合、単語をアルファベットごとに解剖して「a(ア)、i(イ)、u(ウ)、e(エ)、o(オ)・・・時として、y(ィ)」の位置を確認してから、個々の「a、i、u、e、o、(+y)」の一つ一つに(芝居の舞台で台詞を読み上げるみたいに大袈裟な感じで!)アクセントを置いてみて、どんな響きになるかを確認してみればよい:一番「ヘンじゃない響き」の位置が「第一強勢を置くべき母音」になるはずだ・・・諸君の耳には乱暴すぎて当てにならない響きの話だって?・・・よろしい、それなら(諸君がもし正真正銘の日本人ならば)任意の英単語中の第一強勢を正しく言い当てるための「信じられないほど頼りになる方法」を一つ教えてあげようー外来語(外国語由来の日本語)を日本人が発音する際の日本人のアクセントの逆を行けばよいのだ:ただそれだけで、その外来語に正しい強勢を置いて発音できるようになる。

http://zubaraie.com/denglenglish┴ ←Be sure to check!

For some reason, the Japanese people have a way of changing the position of the primary accent in any English term they introduce to their language as GAIRAIGO. If you are a Japanese, try saying "display" or "endeavor" both in your language and in English to see what this author means. When the Japanese pronounce a foreign term as GAIRAIGO, they will either kill the accent altogether (eg. "engineer", "guitarist", "pioneer", "pianist") or shift the primary accent to some wrong position (eg. "accessory", "curriculum", "musician", "success"). To pronounce "display" in the Japanese way as if it were "this play" or "this prey" is too crazy to make any sense in English consciousness, but such is the way of the Japanese: maybe it is in the nature of Japanese to go against the authentic English accent. Whatever the reason, this phenomenon is something you Japanese students of English should put to good use: when in doubt about accent in any given term, go against the Japanese way, and you will probably accentuate it right. Trust me: anti-Japanese accents rarely fail to sound right in English.

- In the end, copy the whole book in your brains, and nothing will stand in the way of your road to intelligence -

As you can see, all the above-mentioned knowledge should not and cannot be written down on "a perfect guide to English" notebook of your own making, but simply has to be inscribed upon your memory (with a little help from footnotes/headnotes in between the lines of your textbooks). Less than intelligent Japanese are in the nasty habit of being unduly satisfied with making a note of something: really intelligent people will never be satisfied until they have succeeded in memorizing and recollecting something in their own brains.

理由はわからないが、日本の人々にはどうも、外来語として日本語に取り込んだ英単語はどれもこれもその第一強勢の位置を変えてしまう習癖があるようだ。諸君が日本人なら、「display:ディスプレイ＝展示・表示装置」や「endeavor:エンデバー＝(かつてのアメリカの)スペースシャトルの名で、“努力”の意」という単語を、諸君の母国語と英語とで発音し分けてみれば、筆者が何を言いたいかわかってもらえるだろう。外国の単語を日本人が外来語として発音する場合、彼らはその語の強勢を完全に殺すか(“engineer:エンジニア・技師”、“guitarist:ギタリスト”、“pioneer:パイオニア・先駆者”、“pianist:ピアニスト”等)あるいは第一強勢の位置をどこか違った場所に移すか(“accessory:＜ア＞クセサリー”、“curriculum:＜カ＞リキュラム”、“musician:＜ミュ＞ージシャン”、“success:＜サ＞クセス”等)のいずれかの行動を取る。「display:ディスプレイ」という語を、まるでそれが「this play:この芝居・このプレイ」か「this prey:このエジキ・犠牲者」であるかのごとく(日本人ふうに)発音するなんて、英語の感覚ではまるっきりイカれていて意味不明の感じだが、それが和風のやり口なのである・・・ひょっとしたら、「真性英語アクセントには逆行すべし」というのが日本語の本能なのかもしれない・・・理由が何であれ、とにかくこの現象は、諸君ら日本人の英語学習者としては大いに有効活用すべきものである:「任意の単語の強勢の位置に迷った場合、和風アクセントの逆を行けば、ほぼ間違いなく正しい強勢で読むことができる」のだから・・・大丈夫、信じてもらっていい:「非日本的アクセントなら、英語らしい響きにならないことは滅多にない」のである。

ー最後には、自分の脳内に本を一冊丸ごとコピーすればよい・・・そうすれば、知性への道に立ちはだかる障害物など何もなくなるー

おわかりいただけたろうが、上述の知識はどれもみな、諸君自作の「英語ガイドブック完璧版」めいたノートの中に筆記で書き出すべきものではなく(というか、書き出そうとしても書き出せるものではなく)、諸君の記憶の中にただひたすら(教科書の行間の「脚注／頭注」のちょっとした助けを借りて)刻み込まねばならない知識なのである。ちっとも知性的でない日本人の場合、「何かをノートに書き留める」という行為だけで、「おいおい！？」って言いたくなるほど過度の自己満足にひたってしまう困った癖がある。真に知的な人々の場合、自らの脳内に何かを記憶しその記憶をまた後で引き出すことにきちんと成功できるまでは、決して満足しないものである。

In this age of information explosion and mega storage in the form of electrical devices, people are getting less and less selective of what is really worth noting and memorizing, more and more dependant on mechanical memory for later retrieval, thereby making themselves progressively unintelligent or even anti-intelligence. To go against this trend of "mechanical deintellectualization", the value of the study of English (for that matter, French, Spanish, Italian, whatsoever) and world history (not just the local chronicles of your small country) are priceless. It takes selective intellect and constant memorization, recollection, reviewing and rewriting to be a good linguist and reasonable historian. The task is arduous, but is well worth the effort, I mean, pleasurably enthusiastic journey. Be diligent and intelligent enough to be able to speak about what you really believe is worth mentioning – with people from all over the world – in English, which happens to be the de facto standard language of today, in which you can expect to make yourself understood to the largest number of people all over the world.

And, in studying and commanding English, get to know better your own language, own country, own people and your own mind. English will be a good mirror to reflect yourself in. The more and deeper you look in, the more beautiful and intelligent you can be as a self-respecting citizen of the twenty-first century.

「情報爆発」と「電子装置の形を取る巨大記憶装置」に取り巻かれた今の時代にあって、人々の「選別能力」は次第に落ちてきている:注目や記憶に本当に値する物事を選りすぐることもせずに、機械的記憶装置にとりあえず記憶しておいて後でまた引き出せばそれでいい、という態度に陥りがちなのだ・・・そういう惰性的な非選別性によって、人々は次第に「知的でなくなる」のみならず、「知的な人・物に対し反感を抱く」ようになって行くのである。この「機械がもたらす反知性化」という潮流に逆行するためには、「英語」(この伝で言えばフランス語・スペイン語・イタリア語・何語であっても構わない)と「世界史」(諸君の小さな国の地元版年代記に留まらぬ人類全体の大きな歴史)の学習の持つ価値は、計り知れないほど大きい。「語学」が得意で「そこそこの歴史観」を持った人物になるためには、選別的知性と、絶えざる暗記作業と、折りに触れて思い出したり復習したり脳内記憶の改訂を図ったりする作業が必要になる。骨の折れる仕事だが、そうした努力(=心地良く情熱的な長い旅)に十分値する作業でもある。勤勉に励んで知的になりたまえ－真に言及に値すると信じる物事について(世界中の人々と)語り合うことができる水準の勤勉な知性を持ちたまえ・・・そのためには「英語」が話せるようになりたまえ:今の世の事実上の標準言語は(たまたま)この英語なのだから、英語で話せば、世界中の最大多数の人々に話を聞いてもらえる期待が持てるわけだから。

そうして、英語を学び使いこなす過程で、自分の母国語を、自分の祖国を、自分の国の人々を、そして自分自身の心の中を、もっとよく知ることだ。「英語」は諸君自身を映し出す「良き鏡」となるだろう。この「鑑」をより多くより深く覗き込むほどに、諸君は、より美しく知的な21世紀の立派な市民となることだろう。

Greeting and invitation from *author* Jaugo Noto
筆者・之人冗悟(のと・じゃうご)よりの御挨拶&御招待

Thank you very much for taking (even *READING!*) this book.

本書を手に取って(更には読んで！)いただき、感謝します。

If you found it useful, you could find it much more so by visiting **the WEB site presented by this author**:
「役に立つ本だなぁ」と感じた方は、**筆者提供の WEB サイト**に更にもっと役立つ何かを発見できますよ：

<WEB forum regarding "reversENGLISH">
本書（でんぐリングリッシュ）専用 WEB フォーラム
http://zubaraie.com/denglenglish

<WEB lesson on English constructions>
英語構文インターネット・レッスン
http://furu-house.com/sample

http://zubaraie.com ←合同会社ズバライエ(ZUBARAIE LLC.)ホームページ

— about **the author** of this book (本書の著者について) —

Jaugo Noto **is a professional educator in linguistics, who makes it his business to enable students to see, do, or be what he's been through and what he can see through, in ways other humans have never imagined or even thought possible. His field of business activity ranges from modern English to ancient Japanese, developing not so much on paper or in the flesh as on the WEB currently.**

之人冗悟(のと・じゃうご)は語学教育の専門家。彼本人の実践・予見の体験を、学生にも認識・実践・体得させること(それも、他者が想像もせず、不可能とさえ思っていた方法で可能ならしめること)を仕事とする彼の活動の幅は、現代英語から古典時代の日本語まで多岐に渡る。現在、紙本執筆や生身の授業よりインターネット上での事業展開が主力。

— about **ZUBARAIE** LLC. (Limited Liability Company) (合同会社ズバライエについて) —

ZUBARAIE LLC. was established in Tokyo, Japan, on July 13th (Friday), 2012, as a legal vehicle for Jaugo Noto to perform such services as education, translation, publication and other activities to help enlighten people.

合同会社ズバライエ(ごうどうがいしゃZubaraie)は、2012年7月13日(金曜日)(おまけに仏滅)、日本国の東京にて、之人冗悟(のと・じゃうご)が教育・翻訳・出版その他の啓蒙(けいもう)活動を遂行(すいこう)するための法的枠組として設立された。

「でんぐリングリッシュ:英和対訳版(reversENGLISH)」

ISBN 978-4-9906908-0-9

1st edition published from ZUBARAIE LLC. 2013/01/25

= *also from the same* ***author*** **之人冗悟(*Jaugo Noto*)** =

***B**eneath **U**mbrella of **Z**ubaraie* *LLC.*

★本書★『**でんぐリングリッシュ：**英・和 対訳版』ISBN 978-4-9906908-0-9

日本の初学者&再挑戦者に贈る、英語を真にモノにするための心得（英文／和訳見開き対訳本）。

・・・本書一冊では効果半減：『英文解剖編』との併用により、真の英文解釈力の開眼を図るべし。

☆！併読推奨！☆『**でんぐリングリッシュ：**英文 解剖編』ISBN 978-4-9906908-1-6

同書の全英文を、解剖学的解釈の詳細な構造図で「**可視化**」した古今未曾有の英文読解指南書。

英語がこの形で「見える」ようになることこそ、全学習者の理想形・・・よーく見て、マネ(真似)ぶべし。

『**古文・和歌**マスタリング・ウェポン』ISBN 978-4-9906908-2-3

大学入試で出題される古文と和歌の知識を完全網羅。暗記必須事項は抱腹絶倒の語呂合わせで、

重要事項の全ての暗記＋確認は巻末穴埋めテストで、調べ物は詳細な索引で、完全サポート。

『**古文単語千五百**マスタリング・ウェポン』ISBN 978-4-9906908-3-0

充実の語義解説で大学入試古文にも和歌・古文書解釈にも不自由を感じぬ完璧な古語力を養成。

入試得点力に直結する受験生の福音書にして、日本語・日本文化への目からウロコの知識の宝庫。

『**ふさうがたり(Fusau Tales)扶桑語り**：古文・英文・現代和文対釈』ISBN 978-4-9906908-4-7

『古文単語千五百』の**全見出語1500**（＋**平安助動詞37**＆**平安助詞77**全用法）で書かれた22編の

擬古文歌物語で『古文・和歌マスタリングウェポン』の説く古典読解法の実践を図る英和古対釈本。

www.ingramcontent.com/pod-product-compliance
Lightning Source LLC
Chambersburg PA
CBHW051647040426
42446CB00009B/1012

* 9 7 8 4 9 9 0 6 9 0 8 0 9 *